THE BUILDER OF SOULS

THE LIFE AND TEACHINGS OF SERIGNE SALIOU MBACKÉ

(1915-2007)

Sallalâhu Allah Muhammadin

All rights reserved. No part of this book may be reproduced or utilized in any form or by any means, electronic or mechanical, including photocopying, recording, or by any information storage or retrieval system, without permission in writing from the publisher, except as provided by U.S.A. copyright law.

Printed in the United States of America
Djannatul Mahwa Publishing Copyright © April 12, 2022

TABLE OF CONTENTS

DEDICATION	16
ACKNOWLEDGEMENT	18
SATISFACTION OF THE KHALIF OF SERIGNE SALIOU MBACKE	20
PREFACE	22
DEFINING THE LIFE	26
INTRODUCTION	30
RESEARCH METHODOLOGY	33
FIRST: COMPILING THE SOURCES	33
SECOND: CRITICISM AND ANALYSIS	33
THIRD: NARRATION AND COMPOSITION	34
OBJECTIVITY	35
PART ONE: THE MAN AND HIS ENVIRONMENT	38
CHAPTER I - A HISTORICAL OVERVIEW	40
THE ENTRY OF ISLAM IN AFRICA	40
THE PENETRATION OF ISLAM IN SENEGAL	42
SCIENTIFIC AND CULTURAL DEVELOPMENT	43
THE EFFORTS OF THE FIRST MUSLIM SCHOLARS IN WEST AFRICA	44
THE ROLE OF MARABOUT FAMILIES IN THE DIFFUSION OF ISLAM	48
THE MAJOR ISLAMIC CENTERS	49
CHAPTER II - THE FAMILY ENVIRONMENT	52
THE DIVINE ELECTION	52
PATERNAL LINEAGE	53
MATERNAL LINEAGE	56
THE FAMILY TREE OF MBAKOL	58
THE PACT OF ALLEGIANCE OF THE DIAKHATES TO KHADIM RASSOUL	59
THE MATRIMONIAL TIES BETWEEN SHEIKHUL KHADIM AND THE DIAKHATÉ FAMILY	61
THE CHARACTERISTICS OF SOKHNA FATY DIAKHATÉ	62
THE INSTALLATION IN THIÉYÈNE	63
CHAPTER III - HIS CHILDHOOD AND RELIGIOUS EDUCATION	66
HIS BIRTH	66
THE BLESSED CONSECRATION	67
A NAME FULL OF MEANING	68
HIS EARLY CHILDHOOD	71
HIS INTELLIGENCE SINCE CHILDHOOD	72
THE PERIOD OF TEACHING AND EDUCATION	73
ANECDOTES FROM THE TEACHING PERIOD	75
HIS FREQUENT VISITS TO HIS FATHER	76
MEMORIZATION OF THE HOLY QURAN	80

PART TWO: THE MAN AND HIS JOURNEY	**82**
CHAPTER IV - HIS INTELLECTUAL TRAINING	**84**
His Studies with Sheikh Makhtar Dieng	84
The Stay at Serigne Habiboullah Mbacké's House	85
At Serigne Mor Sasoum	87
At Serigne Makhtar Sow	89
His Studies With Sheikh Muhammad Dème In Diourbel	90
The Testimony of Sheikh Muhammad Dème on Serigne Saliou	92
Languages Spoken by the Sheikh	93
Intellectual Curiosity and Erudition of Serigne Saliou	94
His Interest in Arabic Literature and Civilization	95
His Letter to Serigne Fallou (2ND Khalife of the Mourides)	96
His Interest in the Four Schools of Jurisprudence (Fiqh)	96
His Interest in Philosophy and Theology	97
His Knowledge of Sufi Epistemology	97
His Interest in The Islamic World and Reformist Movements	99
His Interest in Modern Currents of Thought and Geopolitics	102
His Interest in Knowledge and New Discoveries	104
His Interest in Ethnology and Anthropology	105
His Appreciation of Different Civilizations	105
His Interest in Geography and Geopolitics	107
His Interest in Scholarship	108
Peregrinations and Travels	109
His Travels Through Senegal	109
His Talibes and Dahiras	111
His Spiritual Evolution	112
The Sufi Environment	112
The Reality of *Tasawwuf* According to the Sufi Corporation	113
Tasawwuf in the Life of Our Sheikh	117
Tasawwuf is Practical	118
His Awrad (Litanies), Adhkar (Evocations) and Ahzab (Collection of Ayahs)	119
The Practice of the Ma'khouz Wird	120
The Wird Shadhili	121
Prayers and Supplementary Works	121
Tasbih Prayer	123
The Night Watch	124
Serigne Saliou and the Quran	125
His Attachment to the Qasaids of Khadimou Rassoul	128
His Days	131
His Program of The Day	132
His Night Program	132
His States of Jamal and Jalal	133
CHAPTER V - HIS VIRTUOUS CHARACTER	**136**
The Place of Virtues in Sufism	136
The Prophetic Heritage	138

THE VIRTUOUS CHARACTER TRAITS OF THE HEIRS	140
THE IMPORTANCE OF REPENTANCE (TAWBA) FOR SERIGNE SALIOU	141
THE SENSE OF REPENTANCE IN SERIGNE SALIOU'S WORK	142
THE ASCETICISM OF SERIGNE SALIOU	146
HIS SOBRIETY	150
LONG-LASTING DEVOTION	151
HIS ATTACHMENT TO THANKSGIVING (SHUKR)	153
HIS SCRUPULOUS ATTITUDE	155
HIS MODESTY	156
TO LOVE FOR THE FACE OF ALLAH AND TO HATE FOR THE FACE OF ALLAH	158
THE SOFTNESS OF HIS HEART AND HIS SENSITIVITY	159
HIS MERCY TO ALL	160
SERIGNE SALIOU AND DIVINE WISDOM	162
HIS LOVE AND MERCY FOR CHILDREN	163
IN THE STATIONS OF MAJESTY (JALAL) AND BEAUTY (JAMAL)	167
PURE SERVITUDE (UBIDIYA KHALISA)	169
RESPECT FOR HUMAN DIGNITY	171
PART THREE: THE MAN AND HIS MISSION	**176**
CHAPTER VI - THE PORTRAIT OF THE MOURIDE SADIKH	**178**
THE IMPORTANCE OF THE SPIRITUAL WILL IN THE JOURNEY TO ALLAH	178
THE REALITY OF THE SPIRITUAL WILL	179
SERIGNE SALIOU, AN EXAMPLE OF THE TRUE MOURIDE	181
THE CHARACTERISTICS OF THE TRUE ASPIRANT (MOURIDE SADIKH)	182
SINCERITY IN THE LOVE OF SHEIKHUL KHADIM	183
THE DISCUSSIONS OF SERIGNE SALIOU	185
RESPECT FOR THE STATUS OF SHEIKHUL KHADIM	187
HIS HIGH ASPIRATION IN ALLAH	188
HELPFULNESS TOWARDS HIS BROTHERS	192
AVAILABILITY FOR THE BENEFIT OF MOURIDES	193
HADIYA (PIOUS GIFT)	194
A MODEL IN SPENDING FOR THE SAKE OF ALLAH	195
FOLLOWING THE MODEL OF HIS ILLUSTRIOUS FATHER	198
HIS LOVE FOR HIS FATHER'S COMPANIONS	199
CHAPTER VII - SERIGNE SALIOU AND DIVINE SERVICE (KHIDMA)	**200**
SERIGNE SALIOU AND KHIDMA	200
THE CONCEPT OF KHIDMA	203
SERVICE IN THE EDUCATIONAL FIELD	205
THE SERVICE (KHIDMA) IN ITS SPIRITUAL AND INTELLECTUAL DIMENSION	206
SERVICE (KHIDMA) IN ITS SOCIETAL DIMENSION	207
THE PHILOSOPHY OF DRYLAND DEVELOPMENT	208
LAND SERVICING IN MOURIDISM	211
THE DAARAS FOUNDATION FOR EDUCATION AND AGRICULTURE	213
THE GOTTE FOUNDATION	214
NEKHANE'S FOUNDATION	216
THE FOUNDATION OF THE DIOBASS DAARAS	217

THE FIRST GENERATION OF HIS DISCIPLES	217
THE DIAWREGN OF THIS DAARA	219
THE FOUNDATION OF KHABANE	220
THE METHODS OF THE TARBIYYA DURING THIS PERIOD	221
KHABANE'S DIAWREGNS	222
THE FOUNDATION OF NDIAPANDAL	223
THE RETURN TO NDIAPANDAL	224
THE FOUNDATION OF THE NDIOUROUL SCHOOL	225
THE DEVELOPMENT OF NDIOUROUL	229
THE FOUNDATION OF THE NDOKA SCHOOL	230
THE SCHOOL OF LAGANE	231
THE SCHOOL OF GNIBINGUELLE	233
THE SCHOOL OF NIAROU	233
THE SCHOOL OF NGUEDIANE	234
THE SCHOOL OF GUELOR	235
THE SCHOOLS OF TOUBA AND SURROUNDINGS	235
THE KHELCOM FOUNDATION	235
KHELCOM'S GEOGRAPHICAL LOCATION	235
THE AWARD OF KHELCOM	236
THE HISTORY OF KHELCOM'S DEVELOPMENT	237
MODERNIZATION OF AGRICULTURAL EQUIPMENT	238
CONSTRUCTION OF SCHOOL BUILDINGS AND HOUSING	238
WATER AND FACILITIES	239
KHELCOM'S FIRST VISIT	240
START OF ACTIVITIES AT KHELCOM	242
ITS METHOD OF ORGANIZATION AND MANAGEMENT	244
THE OPERATING COSTS OF THE *DAARAS*	245
THE HEALTH CARE SYSTEM	248
CLOTHING EXPENSES	250
AGRICULTURAL PRODUCTION	253
EDUCATION IN THESE DAARAS	254
CHAPTER VIII - SPIRITUAL EDUCATION	**256**
ITS PHILOSOPHY AND PEDAGOGY	256
THE CONCEPT OF BENEFICENCE (SALAH) IN THE QURAN	257
THE GOODNESS OF ACTS	257
THE GOODNESS OF PEOPLE	258
THE RENOVATING MISSION OF SERIGNE SALIOU	261
SERIGNE SALIOU AS SHEIKH TARBIYYA	264
CRITERIA FOR THE FUNCTION OF SHEIKH	265
SERIGNE SALIOU SHEIKH TARQIYYA	267
THE PRINCIPLES OF SPIRITUAL EDUCATION: HIS PEDAGOGICAL PHILOSOPHY	270
THE SUFI VISION OF EXISTENCE AND THE HUMAN BEING	271
THE DIFFERENT MODALITIES OF HUMAN PERFECTION	272
THE LINGUISTIC AND CONVENTIONAL MEANING OF TARBIYYA	274
THE MEANING OF EDUCATION AMONG PHILOSOPHERS	275
THE SPIRITUAL EDUCATION OF THE SUFIS	276

THE AIMS OF SPIRITUAL EDUCATION	279
THE PRINCIPLES OF SPIRITUAL EDUCATION IN SHEIKHUL KHADIM	281
KHADIMOU RASSOUL'S GOALS OF SPIRITUAL EDUCATION	284
THE METHODS OF SPIRITUAL EDUCATION OF SHEIKHUL KHADIM	285
VARIETIES OF METHODS ACCORDING TO DIFFERENT ABILITIES	287
SERIGNE SALIOU'S METHOD IN SPIRITUAL EDUCATION	289
THE THREE PRINCIPLES OF SPIRITUAL EDUCATION	290
THE FUNDAMENTAL AXES OF SPIRITUAL EDUCATION OF SERIGNE SALIOU	292
ONE: BENEFICIAL KNOWLEDGE	293
SINCERITY IN MOTIVATION	295
THE USEFULNESS OF KNOWLEDGE IS IN ITS PRACTICAL RESULTS	296
THE IMPORTANCE OF THE EDUCATIONAL SYSTEM IN MOURIDISM	297
DIFFICULTIES AND TRIALS IN BUILDING SCHOOLS	298
THE RECOMMENDATION OF THE QASIDAS READING	299
THE QASIDAS CHOIRS (KORELS)	300
THE TEACHING OF RELIGIOUS SCIENCES	301
THE METHODOLOGY OF THE SCHOOLS OF SERIGNE SALIOU	302
TWO: WORK (A'MAL) AND SERVICE (KHIDMA)	303
THE MEANINGS OF THE WORKS IN THE QURAN	303
THE RESULTS OF THE SPIRITUAL EDUCATION OF SERIGNE SALIOU	304
THREE: THE RULES OF PROPRIETY AND THE NOBILITY OF THE SOUL	305
THE REALITY OF THE RULES OF DECORUM (ADAB)	306
THE IMPORTANCE OF THE RULES OF DECORUM IN MOURIDISM	306
CATEGORIES FOR RULES OF DECORUM IN MOURIDISM	307
THE IMPORTANCE OF (ADAB) IN SERIGNE SALIOU'S PEDAGOGY	310
THE AIMS OF SPIRITUAL EDUCATION	311
DISCIPLINE IN SCHOOLS	314
THE IMPORTANCE OF DISCIPLINE	314
OBEDIENCE TO AUTHORITY	314
THE IMPORTANCE OF A HEALTHY ENVIRONMENT	315
THE IMPORTANCE OF EXEMPLARITY	315
THE IMPORTANCE OF MERCY AND CARING FOR CHILDREN	317
THE IMPORTANCE OF THE PUBLIC INTEREST	318
THE IMPORTANCE OF AVOIDING INJUSTICE	318
A FEW WORDS OF WISDOM	319
THE NEED FOR COMPANIONSHIP	320
THE RULES OF PROPRIETY OF THE COMPANIONSHIP BETWEEN THE SHEIKH AND THE DISCIPLE	321
THE DIFFERENCE BETWEEN THE STUDENT (TALIBÉ) AND THE ASPIRANT (MOURIDE)	321
THE SECRETS OF THE BARAKA AND THE SPIRITUAL FLOW (MADAD)	322
TARBIYYA AND THE MOURIDE	323
MERCY TOWARDS CHILDREN	324
TIPS FOR A SUCCESSFUL TARBIYYA	325
TIPS FOR PATIENCE	326
REASONS FOR MOURIDE EMANCIPATION	327
HIS AFFECTION FOR HIS DISCIPLES	327
SOME PERSONALITIES EDUCATED IN THE *DAARAS*	328
SALIOU TOURÉ SIGN	329

THE SUFI SPIRITUAL DIMENSION OF SERIGNE SALIOU TOURÉ	330
SERIGNE SALIOU SY	331
CONCLUSION	**334**
BIBLIOGRAPHICAL REFERENCES	**338**
INTERVIEWS	**346**

DEDICATION

For the one who, through his life experience, personified sincere will and high aspiration, as well as *khidma, patience,* and a sense of *sacrifice.*

He had remained constant in his principles, in addition to his humility and compassion for humans.

He who educated me for the love of Allah and his Prophet Muhammad (peace and salvation be upon him), as well as for the love of Khadimou Rassoul and the virtuous saints.

He who inscribed in my soul the attachment to Good, Truth, and Virtues, and who also taught me the truthfulness in spiritual commitment and the quest for high aspirations through the values of *khidma* and sacrifices, as well as patience and perseverance.

He who taught me that life is a struggle for principles and faith.

I want to name Serigne Saliou Mbacké (upon him the approval of Allah): my sheikh, my educator, my master, and my guide in the spiritual journey, to whom I dedicate this book to pay homage.

I humbly acknowledge that it is impossible for me to thank him in the measure of his illustrious rank, but I still hope to benefit from his benevolent gaze, his love, and his pleasure.

ACKNOWLEDGEMENT

I thank Allah for the completion of this work. I also thank all those who participated in its elaboration; either through encouragement, rereading, correction, or through observations or suggestions on the substance and form of the book.

I would like to thank the venerable 'sheikhs' who have given me valuable and sometimes unpublished information about Serigne Saliou Mbacké, notably his Khalif Serigne Sheikh Saliou Mbacké as well as Serigne Fallou Chouhaybou Mbacké and also Serigne Hamza Mbacké Abdoulahad, as well as Serigne Moustapha Abdoulkader Mbacké and Sheikh Abdessamad Ibn Sheikh Chouhaybou Mbacké.

I would also like to thank the late Sheikh Mustapha Diaw as well as Sheikh Mbacké Abdoul Ahad Diakhaté and many others that I will quote in the book.

My heartfelt thanks go to the eminent scholars who corrected the original work in Arabic, especially my brother Serigne Sheikh Waalo who also prefaced the book.

I also thank Inspector Mouhammad Lo, Pr Mor Faye, Serigne Mbacké Dieng, Mr. Omar Ba, Sokhna Fama Toure and Mr. Moustapha Diop.

I must thank those who helped me in the translation and publication of this book in French, including Serigne Mbaye Ndaw, Abdourahmane Ba, and Sheikh Abdallah Fahmi. I also must thank Shiloh Shaeed El who helped me to publish the book in English. My sincere thanks to His Excellency the Minister Mr. Madické Niang who is a great mouride and who also prefaced the book. May Allah amply reward them and those who, from near or far, contributed to the publication of the book.

SATISFACTION OF THE KHALIF OF SERIGNE SALIOU MBACKE

Bismillah Ir Rahman Ir Rahim

In the name of Allah, the Clement, the Merciful

Glory be to Allah the Lord of the Worlds and greetings on the most Noble of the Envoys, our Master Muhammad, and his family and Companions.

I am very happy and proud to see that one of my sons, who is in charge of research, fulfilled his duty by producing a biographical book on our Enlightened Guide Serigne Saliou Mbacké, who has educated generations of disciples.

May Allah be pleased with him and grant us the benefit of his lights and blessings.

Our sheikh was one of the most illustrious guides in the spiritual path as well as in piety and conformity to the precepts of religion.

Throughout his life, he embodied the noble values of Islam and noble character in its finest expression.

Both his sons and his disciples should consider this book as a reminder and a sermon that further motivates us in the continuity of our sheikh's work.

This sheikh has dedicated himself to the service of Islam and Muslims by spreading the teachings and exercising spiritual education while manifesting through his person noble values and virtues.

It is as if the sheikh manifested himself again through certain passages of this book and visited us through the different chapters, to give us lessons in the fields of 'Iman', 'Islam' and 'Ihsan' as well as in beneficial knowledge and rules of propriety.

The sheikh also calls upon us to perfect the worship and characterization by the Quranic characteristics by enhancing our aspirations and fulfilling the duties of the path, including the sheikh's consideration and perpetual commitment to divine service and the education of aspirants to produce exemplary generations that conform to the values stipulated in "Matlaboul Fawzein."

I ask Allah to bless this prestigious work and to grant it approval on earth and in the heavens. I also hope that this work will be translated into all living languages, so that everyone can benefit from it.

I would like to finish by saying to my son, the author of this book; "This is what those who want to work must work for" and also "this is what the competitors must compete in."

Serigne Sheikh

Khalif de Serigne Saliou Mbacké

Wednesday 18 Dhul Hijja 1439 H

PREFACE

In the name of Allah, the Merciful.

Praise be to God, the Lord of the Worlds, and blessings and peace be upon him who has been sent as a mercy to the worlds.

First of all, I want to express from the bottom of my soul my thanks and gratitude to my nephew Serigne Souhaybou Kebe for his tireless efforts that resulted in the publication of this precious book, which has enjoyed unprecedented success and achieved many spiritual, educational, and social goals.

It is a book full of generous lessons, which have awakened our memories and made us relive them with Serigne Saliou the reformer and spiritual guide who was a pious sufi with unshakeable faith and relentless determination.

Serigne Saliou had an extraordinary memory and vivid intelligence, but he also possessed encyclopedic knowledge. Our sheikh was imbued with his father, both in his asceticism and in his relations with the rulers, whom they feared in no way because he coveted nothing from them. He was kind and generous during his caliphate and he defended the oppressed by watching over their rights.

He was interested in all the central issues of the Islamic nation, such as the Palestinian question to which he attached particular importance. He constantly informed himself about the situation of the Palestinians and prayed that they would obtain justice and build their country in peace.

He advocated unlimited support for the Palestinians for whom he had a real affection and wished them to regain all their national and international rights and to be able to reach a peaceful, final, and lasting solution.

Serigne Saliou was pious and righteous in accordance with the teachings of his illustrious father whose way of life he followed by furnishing his time with the Quran and Awrads (litanies) as well as Qasaids', Eulogies and Prayers on the Prophet Muhammad (sallallahu alayhi wa sallam).

However, this in no way prevented him from fulfilling his function as a khalif with all the related responsibilities.

He was wise and measured and made his decisions only after consultations, patiently listening to opinions without rushing into taking positions. He only rarely got angry and only on important religious issues.

All noble and virtuous souls are grateful to him for his tireless work in the educational and spiritual field as well as for his courageous fight against corrupt systems and indecent morals. He tirelessly faced the challenges of his time.

Finally, one can talk endlessly about the qualities of this exceptional sheikh to the point that several books would not be enough to exhaust the material. I think that the way is open for researchers and intellectuals to dig deeper and discover wonderful aspects of Serigne Saliou Mbacké's personality.

It is perhaps necessary to mention that obedience to Allah and respect for religion is surely the beneficial trade and protection against the evils of our times, it allows as well the renewal of our societies so that they impose it upon themselves before others.

Seyidna Omar Ibn Khattab said: "We are a people whom Allah has valued through Islam, and whoever seeks to be respected outside Islam will be humiliated by Allah."

Allah says: "They seek dignity from them, and the true dignity is with Allah."

Allah also says: "Dignity is with Allah and His Messenger and the Believers" Sura Al-Munafiqun 63:8

Preface to TOUBA THE SAINT

Thursday 27 Safar 1442h

October 15, 2020

Sheikh Mohamed Mustapha Ibn Sheikh Abdelkader Mbacké

DEFINING THE LIFE

"To the well-born souls, the value of a man does not wait for the number of years," said Cornelius.

What courage it took for Serigne Chouaïbou Kébé to dare to undertake to define the life of a man whose every facet could have amply constituted a whole life for an ordinary man!

What recklessness to pretend to describe the colossal work of art of this man, Serigne Saalih Mbacké ibn Khadimou Rassoul, that an encyclopedia would certainly not have succeeded in exhaustively telling!

Serigne Aboo Madyana Kébé, as a worthy heir to his namesake and grandfather Serigne Chouaïbou Mbacké ibn Khadimou Rassoul, has nevertheless managed to condense into about three hundred pages a life placed in a predestined trajectory of aspiration to divine closeness and earthly greatness.

With this work, Serigne Chouaïbou ibnou Sokhna Waalo Binetou Serigne Saalih Mbacké has admirably succeeded in recounting, through a scientifically elaborated historical account, the singular life of this personality created by Allah to fulfill a particular destiny dedicated to the completion and universalization of the titanic work of Sheikh Ahmadou Khadim.

"Saalih, to whom the task of completing my work will be entrusted" (As salihou lazzi youkammiloul amal) came, as Khadimou Rassoul had announced, lived as an exemplary ascetic universally admired and loved and elevated to a divine proximity (apotheosis) among the list of Khalifs, sons of Khadimou Rassoul as the Khoutbu Zamman (Pole of the Poles).

Indeed, Serigne Chouaïbou reveals that after preaching of his Lord, Sheikh Ahmadou Khadim had consoled Sokhna Faty Diakhaté, mother of Serigne Saalih who lost several children, in these terms: "GOD (You) will give a healthy and blessed son who will have a long life; this son would also be famous and distinguished among his contemporaries like the sun in broad daylight."

Organized in nine chapters, this goldsmith's work returns to the history of the introduction of Islam in Africa and Senegal before plunging us into the family environment of the Holy Man. Traveling with us, Serigne Chouaïbou Kébé makes us discover, in turn, Serigne Saalih's childhood, his religious education, his intellectual formation, and his virtuous character traits which were the leaven of a completed spiritual ascent.

Like every disciple, Serigne Saalih has taken the priestly path of the true aspirant (murid sadikh) to put himself at the service of Allah (Khidma) and become an unquestionable and undisputed master in spiritual education, philosophy, and Islamic pedagogy.

Throughout its reading, this work allows us to bring to life unpublished, authentic, and instructive anecdotes, among others, on:

- the exemplary relations between the Diakhaté and the Mbacké-Mbacké were born from the historical allegiance of Serigne Modou Asta Diakhaté to Sheikhul Khadim in these terms: "I want to make my allegiance by offering you my person, my goods, and my children while remaining at your service all my life";
- the memories that Serigne Saalih keeps of his venerated father: Sheikhul Khadim received them (Serigne Saalih and Serigne Chouaïbou), sitting on the floor, preparing to write. He said to Serigne Hamza: "I did not eat or drink during these two weeks", which marked Serigne Saalih who, throughout his life, chose to serve food to "berndé" human beings instead of helping himself;

- the world geopolitics that he mastered perfectly, understanding very early on that: "The communists wasted their efforts in vain because they neglected the most fundamental axis to serve humanity, which is faith in God.";
- his perception of the reality of Sheikhul Khadim's personality: "Sheikhul Khadim cannot be confined to a station or function and no intelligence can control him. In truth, everyone will understand from the sheikh what his level of understanding will allow him to understand";
- His mercy towards children is summarized in this statement: "The Quranic teacher is like the fighter in the way of Allah as long as he does not violate children, for if he does, he will be like a coward who flees in battle."

We had the grace to witness these treasures, which are anecdotes about the life of Serigne Saalih. We were there when one of the heaviest casualties fell on the Mouridiyya: that of Serigne Mouhamadou Mourtada Mbacké, Ibn Khadimou Rassoul. All the entourage of Serigne Saalih knew the links that united him with the cadet of Serigne Touba: Goor Yallah. Everybody expected to see him strongly saddened by the event. On the second day of mourning, we were all astonished to see that despite this great loss, Serigne Saalih presented the image of a servant giving thanks to the Almighty and fully accepting His Will. Yes, he said, "Allah fades away the power to afflict every human being, but no divine decision should cause the servant any bitterness."

Everyone remembers the victory of Abdoulaye Wade in the presidential election of 2007 and especially the deep calm that the country experienced despite the apocalypse predicted by some circles. Of course, we thanked Allah, but we also knew that it was through the exhaustive prayers of Serigne Saalih that this victory came so easily.

When we came to express our gratitude to him, he did not accept any role in this victory. He attributed all the credit to Sheikh Ahmadou Khadim, the Prophet, and Allah.

Serigne Saalih was so grateful to Allah that he said "Giving thanks to God (Choukri) carries the same weight in good, as denying his existence (Koufrou) is bad." It is this vision that inspired many of his followers, who institutionalized the Thiant (Giving thanks to Allah) as the door to happiness on earth and in heaven.

We can never express our gratitude to Serigne Aboo Kébé enough for providing us with a bedside book that will accompany us every day in our reflections to remain always in the path traced by Sheikhul Khadim to be at the service of Islam in general and Mouridiyya in particular.

May God grant him long life to complete this colossal work through the volumes that are announced to continue this instructive and educational story.

To Serigne Saalih ibn Khadimou Rassoul, we address our fervent prayers so that his divine retribution may be constantly multiplied and that the celestial light forever surrounds him, for the immense work accomplished in the service of Islam but also of the human species.

President Madické Niang
Counsel to the Court
Former President of the Madické 2019 Coalition
Former Minister of State Minister of Foreign Affairs
Former Minister of State Keeper of the Seals, Minister of Justice

INTRODUCTION

In this book, we will try to introduce readers to an extraordinary man, an outstanding personality, and an emblematic figure of Islam in the 20th century. He is our revered master Serigne Saliou Mbacké, son of Khadimou Rassoul and fifth Khalif of Mouridism.

He was an outstanding scholar and spiritual guide who revived the tradition of the prophets and envoys through his exemplary virtues and noble character. He devoted his entire life to teaching the Islamic religion and educating the souls of the aspirants to lead them to spiritual perfection. Sheikh Muhammad Lamine Diop Dagana in a poem dedicated to Serigne Saliou said:

"He was a sun in the sky of his contemporaries to illuminate the darkness of his time."

His Quranic skills and prophetic virtues, which he inherited from his illustrious father Khadimou Rassoul, enabled him to carry out immense works in favor of Islam and Muslims and, beyond that, all of humanity. He valued immense lands and initiated numerous disciples, but above all, he rose in spiritual realization to perfection and settled in the station of the Muhammadian heritage: "a witness who is a harbinger and a warner who calls to Allah by his permission while being an illuminating torch."[1]

He illuminated the sky of his time and guided his generation and later generations and thus fulfilled the hopes of his miraculous father through his achievements in teaching, educating, and reviving the spiritual path. Indeed, Khadimou Rassoul said in his poem "Nourou Daarayni": "Grant

---

[1] The Holy Quran, Al Ahzab 33-46

me the true knowledge and action (salah) that will complete my hopes."

In the following pages, we write the biography of Serigne Saliou Mbacké and record some edifying stories in an easy-to-read book that will help disciples to better know this exceptional man so that his action remains radiant and his exemplary nature can inspire present and future generations.

Sheikh Muhammad Bashir Mbacké [2] in "Minan al Baqi al Qadim" stated that his illustrious father lived in perfect conformity with the stations of evidence (maqamat al yaqin) and he had therefore classified the spiritual itinerary of Khadimou Rassoul according to these nine stations: repentance (tawba), patience (sabr), gratitude (shukr), hope (raja'), fear (khawf), asceticism (zuhd), confident surrender (tawakul), satisfaction (ridha) and love (mahabba).

We can also affirm that Serigne Saliou lived according to these stations by realizing through his person all the spiritual teachings of his illustrious father and by reviving the way through knowledge, action, rules of propriety, determination, as well as through generosity, and commitment in pious works. For this reason, we have classified this work on the principles of Muridiyya, of which Serigne Saliou was the revivifier, just as Khadim Rassoul was the revivifier of the spiritual path as a whole.

We have divided this book into two volumes. The first one will deal with the spiritual dimension of this holy man, his environment, his childhood, his intellectual and spiritual journey, his mission in Mouridism and in the service of Islam. The second will deal with his magisterium in the

---

[2] Son and Biographer of Khadimou Rassoul. He was one of the greatest intellectual and spiritual figures of Senegal and Mauritania.

Khalifat, his achievements, and his contribution to society and Islam, and will report some of his wonders.

Today, we publish the first volume which is divided into three parts, each part contains several chapters. In the first part: *Man and His Environment*, we will deal with the social and family environment in which Serigne Saliou Mbacké appeared. This part will be divided into three chapters:

- A historical overview
- The family environment
- His childhood and religious education

In the second part: *Man and His Journey,* we will shed light on the intellectual and spiritual journey of this holy man, we have treated him in three chapters:

- His intellectual background (His intellectual training)
- His spiritual journey
- His virtuous character traits.

In the third part: *Man and His Mission*, we will study the religious and spiritual mission of Serigne Saliou Mbacké. We will divide this part into three chapters:

- Portrait of a Mouride Sadikh
- His service for Islam (His Daaras of Tarbiyya)
- His pedagogy of spiritual education.

That is, each chapter will be a preliminary to the next chapter. We had tried not to exceed three hundred pages. However, in the course of the work, we realized that the subject was inexhaustible, all the more so as the testimonies and anecdotes multiplied.

Research Methodology

We followed the narrative method and historical analysis which is the compilation of written and oral sources. We then analyzed and critiqued them before selecting, writing, and presenting the main results.

First: Compiling the Sources

On this point, it should be pointed out that the subject was very little discussed and there were very few sources available, especially written ones. In fact, there was only Serigne Khalil Mbacké's lecture during the Magal of 2007, a small unpublished work entitled "The sun of his time" and Professor Mohammed Adama Diakhaté's book entitled "The Life of the Fifth Khalif."

Although these are commendable initiatives, they are very limited in quantity and quality. Their objectives were not to deal exhaustively with the life of Serigne Saliou.

We still benefited from these works and then we resorted to fieldwork, to collect information from those who lived with the sheikh and who knew him closely.

We were able to have more than twenty meetings with personalities who were able to tell us interesting stories and anecdotes. They included scholars and sheikhs, as well as politicians and doctors or civil servants, some of whom are close family members. We were able to draw from a variety of sources.

Second: Criticism and Analysis

After collecting the information, we had to make a critical check for correction because we needed to make sure that the stories were true and to confront them, to avoid implausibilities or contradictions by choosing the most authentic stories, as law theorists operate in their discipline.

For this, we had to neglect many stories that lacked rigor and did not meet the criteria of the scientific approach used in historical criticism.

Nevertheless, we used personalities known and recognized for their integrity and scrupulousness, to avoid any implausibility in the stories.

However, when in doubt, we resorted to confrontation with other narratives to confirm or refute the stories that did not meet the criteria of our methodology.

When we found stories that corroborated the version in question, we brought them back to validate the story.

We have tried throughout the book to mention the sources of the stories or testimonies by citing the names of each narrator.

In the stories known to all, there was no need to quote a narrator. But we use expressions such as "one tells", "one says in mouride circles" or similar formulas, which nonetheless lend credence to the narrative.

Third: Narration and Composition

The compilation allows us to gather the information that is still scattered because events and facts do not give us a glimpse of the sheikh's life, which leads the researcher to have to elaborate a logical framework that allows the construction of a homogeneous literary work.

Thus, we had to combine these stories and testimonies to give them coherence and to produce a work that is historically, ethically, spiritually, and socially beneficial.

Objectivity

We have tried as much as possible to be objective in this biography. Thus, we have voluntarily chosen not to relate too much of our own experiences with Serigne Saliou but rather to relate those of our companions, some of whom lived with us in the *daaras*.

This allowed us to make less subjective and more documented analyses.

At the same time, we wanted to emphasize the theological and spiritual significance of Serigne Saliou's personality and highlight his knowledge and experiences, instead of being satisfied with a purely biographical study that would be chronological or historical.

We wanted to shed light on an Islamic personality who had a great weight in our time and who was a model to guide and direct generations on many levels, especially on the ethical and spiritual levels.

We also made a point of presenting this work methodically.

We have made an introduction for each chapter or section. We have analyzed the religious vision with reference to the main works of *tasawwuf* and Islamic gnosis (irfan), as well as Quranic commentaries, ethics, history, and biographies, to highlight the objectives of the study.

However, this work can be perfected because we do not claim to have exhausted the subject. Far be it from us to say that this study is perfect because perfection is divine.

We simply hope to have participated to the extent of our possibilities in working for the dissemination of Islam and to make known to the public the Mouridiyya and its illustrious men.

We hope that this work can be beneficial, that it brings added value to the mouride library, and that it will be one more brick in the cultural edifice of Senegal's sufi heritage.

Finally, we ask Allah to accept this modest work and to make it useful and beneficial for the readers and for all those who will participate in its publication, distribution, or translation.

"Lord grant us the blessings of this world and the hereafter, and protect us from infernal punishment."

PART ONE: THE MAN AND HIS ENVIRONMENT
1. A HISTORICAL OVERVIEW
2. THE FAMILY ENVIRONMENT
3. HIS CHILDHOOD AND RELIGIOUS EDUCATION

CHAPTER I - A HISTORICAL OVERVIEW

In this chapter, we will discuss the general history of Islamic penetration in the West African region, we chose to give an overview of the Senegalese society with its components and its cultural, social, and religious realities.

The Entry of Islam in Africa

Islam entered Africa thanks to the Prophet (peace and salvation be upon him), when he sent his first companions there before the hegira of Medina, because of their persecution at Makka. More precisely, he sent them to Ethiopia, a land of freedom and justice in East Africa where a just King reigned who welcomed them, defended them, and eventually espoused their cause. The Negus was thus the first king who embraced Islam, marking the symbolic relationship between Islam and Africa with a deep spirituality.

Shortly after the death of the Prophet (peace and salvation be upon him), Muslims set out to conquer the great empires that stretched from Byzantium to Persia, then from the Mediterranean Basin to North Africa, thanks to Oqba ibn Nafa' al Fehri. The populations of these regions embraced Islam in mass.

But as far as the West African kingdoms are concerned, it was not Muslim armies that established Islam but rather diplomacy and trade; thanks to the good neighborliness between West Africa and North Africa. Thus, saints and scholars, as well as merchants, crossed the Saharan regions for cultural and economic exchanges; this allowed the Islamic religion to spread naturally in the African kingdoms.

The great historian Al Beckri relates in his work "Al Masâlik wal Mamâlik" the conversion of the emperor of Mali and the entry of Islam into his empire. He says: "the King of Mali was nicknamed 'the Muslim'." He embraced Islam while his country was in the grip of a continuous drought despite the sacrifices that risked depleting the cattle herd.

At the same time, there was a Muslim foreigner in the country who was constantly reading the Quran and teaching the prophetic precepts (Sunnah). The King complained to his host about the situation and asked for his advice. The host said, "O King, if you submit to God and acknowledge His oneness and adopt His revealed religion (Islam), you will find a solution to all your problems and mercy will reign over the whole extent of your kingdom, so much so that both your friends and enemies will envy you."

They discussed this until the King became a Muslim in all convictions. The foreigner taught him passages from the Quran and introduced him to ritual obligations. The night before Friday, he had him do the ritual washing (ghusl) and gave him a woolen tunic to wear, and then asked him to follow him to a hill where they prayed together for part of the night. The man led the prayer and made invocations while the king imitated him by saying "Amin."

At daybreak, rain fell in abundance. The king ordered the destruction of all fetishes and the dismissal of the fetishes. He thus imposed Islam, which his heirs perpetuated, while the majority of the people remained fetishists. It is for this reason that the king had the nickname "the Muslim" [3].

Over the years, Islam spread in the region thanks to the elites because the people followed the religion of their rulers. The kings of Ghana, Mali, and Songhai played a major role in the spread of Islam in West Africa long before the arrival of Muslim contingents from North Africa.

---

[3] Al Beckri, "Al Masâlik wal Mamâlik."

The Penetration of Islam in Senegal

Senegal was one of the great African kingdoms of Sudan and was inevitably shaken by events as well as by the ideological and economic currents that were running through the region. Thus, Islamic influence extended from the kingdom of Ghana to the kingdom of Tekrour, where King Wara Diaby Ndiaye embraced Islam in 1040.

However, historians diverge on the circumstances of the entry of Islam into Senegal: "Some argue that it was the work of the Mourabitouns (Almoravids) led by Abdallah ibn Yacine in 1053, while others argue that it was rather the work of merchants from Barqa in Libya, Kairouan in Tunisia, Tlemcen in Algeria and Lemtouna in Morocco. Others argue that it was a king by the name of Wara Diaby who in 1040 decreed the Shar'ia in his country, the Fouta." [4] It would thus make this locality the first Senegalese region to undergo Islamic influence.

Professor Abdelkader Sylla says in his book entitled "Muslims in Senegal: Contemporary Realities and Future Prospects" that: "Wara Ndiaye is the first Senegalese King who embraced Islam. It is also said that his son Labi who succeeded him had largely contributed to the victory of the Mourabitouns over their opponents of the Berber tribe Doukala in 1056. Apart from the Western and Southern regions, all the Senegalese regions are dependent on Fouta for their Islamization." [5]

Moreover, Fouta was known as the country of Tekrour. However, historians diverge on the location of the kingdom of Tekrour which would be between the Senegal Basin and the Niger River and Ouellata. In his book "Fath al Shakur fi Ma'rifat Ay'an al Tekrour", Abu Abdullah Talib Muhammad

---

[4] Abdoulkadre Sylla Muslims in Senegal: Contemporary realities and future prospects.
[5] Abdoulkadre Sylla *Idem.*

Aboubacar Siddiq Bartali (m: 1804/1219 h) describes the borders of Tekrour: "it is a vast region that extends from the Adghag to the West, the sea of Beni Znequia, south to Bit and north to Adrar." [6]

The Mauritanian scholar Khalil Nahwi says on page 19 of his book "Bilad Shanguit": "The First Islamicized Kingdom in Sudan was named the Tekrour kingdom, it's King Wara Diaby embraced Islam (1040/434 h) and spread the sciences of Islam in his kingdom. Tekrour is actually the name of a city by the river mentioned by Al Bekri.

This Kingdom of Tekrour allied itself with the mouribitoun (Almoravids) in Western Sahara. Labi, son of War Diaby, emir of Tekrour, made an alliance with the emir Lemtouni Yahya ibn Omar in the year 448 h (1056/1057)." [7]

Scientific and Cultural Development

Then, around the 12th century (AD), with the emergence of the Almoravid Empire, Islam underwent a prodigious expansion in both West and North Africa, with Almoravid rule reaching as far as the Iberian Peninsula.

During this period, many Islamic schools and centers were established in different places such as Timbuktu, Ndienné, Ghana, Fouta Toro, Fouta Djallon, Ouadaguest, Wallata, Tchitt, Waddan, Tnicki, Attar, and other cities.

Dr. Ahmad Chalabi in his book entitled "The Encyclopedia of Islamic History" says: "Sultan Askia Muhammad energized the cultural and scientific movement by favoring scholars and calling on jurists (fuqaha) to come and settle in Timbuktu, Ndienne, and Gao. Some will come from the

---

[6] Bartali, *Fath al Shakur* page 46 edition Najibawayhi center for manuscripts.
[7] Khalil Nahwi, *Bilad Shanguit* page 19 edition.

Maghreb and neighboring countries. He built cultural and knowledge centers and thus spread religion and knowledge in his country.

The big cities of his kingdom will compete to attract the maximum of great scholars such as Ahmad Baba of Timbuktu who settled in Kano to teach on his return from the pilgrimage."[8]

Sultan Askia Muhammad sent scientific expeditions to neighboring regions to spread Islam and educate the people. Dr. Muhammad Salih Ba said in his book "Arab Culture in West Africa": "The Sultan attracted scholars from neighboring countries and at the same time he sent those who could be more useful elsewhere in the regions that needed their presence."[9]

It is in these positive circumstances of good neighborliness that scholars and proselytizers were able to penetrate very early into Western Sudan and approach the ruling classes, princes, and viziers, to initiate them to the spiritual message of Islam.

Through wisdom and good example, they had been able to convert the elite to the way of Allah. They taught theology and ethics in accordance with the prophetic message in its original simplicity.

The Efforts of the First Muslim Scholars in West Africa

Among the first generations of Muslims in West Africa, an elite dedicated themselves to spreading Islam by founding schools and villages to teach the Quran and science. The Sarakollé ethnic group distinguished itself by its commitment to this spiritual work which covered the empire of Mali and, later, the Songhai which included the current states of Mali, Senegal, Guinea, and Burkina Faso, and other regions.

---

[8] Ahmad Chalabi *the encyclopedia of the history of Islam*.
[9] Dr. Mohammad Salih Ba: *Arab Culture in West Africa*, p. 842.

It has been reported that it was the Sarakollés who had converted the Pulaars and who would be their sheikhs. According to Dr. Muhammad Salih Ba in his book entitled "The Arab-Islamic Culture in West Africa": "Sultan Askia Muhammad sent scholars to the cities and villages of Tekrour to teach Islamic sciences and animate the cultural life in these distant places. Their descendants in Fouta are the Maraboutic families who bear the following names: Sakho, Sylla, Dabo, Yaly, Correra, Camara, Kébé, Docke, Samory, etc. [10]

Subsequently, Tekrour scholars distinguished themselves in the propagation of Islam and played a leading role in the dissemination of Islamic science education in West Africa.

Over the centuries, the families of the Muslim religious elite became a distinguished class with its privileges and peculiarities. They passed on to their children the spiritual vocation and trained them in religious education, ethics, and good dispositions that attract the *baraka* (blessing) so much sought after by princes and ruling classes.

Thus, in all regions of West Africa and within many ethnic groups, families have sprung up in which all the children specialize in teaching the Quran and religious sciences to spread Islam. These are maraboutic families as can be observed among the Mandingue, Soninke, Pulaar, Toucouleur, Wolof, Soussou and others. In Mauritania, the religious families are called "Ahl al Zawaya", which are highly respected for their attachment to Islam and prophetic traditions.

Ibn Battouta reports in his book "Touhfat an Noudhar" [11] passages on the maraboutic families of West Africa: "They are very diligent in learning the

---

[10] Dr. Mohammad Salih Ba: *Arab-Islamic Culture in West Africa* (p. 842).
[11] *Ibn Batouta, Touhfat an Noudhar,* p. 703 edition Dar Ihya Al'ulum 1987 Beirut Lebanon.

Quran and put chains on their children if they notice that they are not diligent; they only remove them when the child finishes memorizing the Quran."

The author continued: "I entered the cadi on the day of Aid, and I saw that his children were chained. I said to him, 'Aren't you releasing them?'"

He replied, "I will do it when they memorize the Qur'an." Another time, I passed a boy with a beautiful face and dressed in elegant clothes with chains on his feet and I said to the one who was with me, "What did he do, did he commit an assassination?" He understood my astonishment and laughed and said, "He is in chains until he memorizes the Quran.

But when the child finishes memorizing the Holy Book, a party is organized in his honor during which gifts are given to him. He then bears the honorary title of 'Hafiz' in the traditions of religious education in Africa."

In the West, specialization in the Qur'an is done through memorization, comprehension, and transcription. These specialists are called in Wolof *kaaŋ*, while those who, in addition to this, specialize in legal and linguistic sciences, as well as traditional and rational sciences, are called *fóore*. Those who specialize in the Quranic sciences and the commentary of the Holy Book are called **mufassir** or **tafsîr,** such as Tafsir Mbacké Ndoumbé [12].

As for the one who brings together all his specialties, he is called **Mor** or *Mouri,* a Mandinka term meaning "the great sheikh or the illustrious scholar" (who masters all Islamic sciences). [13]

Muslims in these regions respected the traditions of religious knowledge and did not award these titles lightly. They subjected candidates to various

---

[12] He is the maternal uncle of Sheikh Ahmadou Bamba and one of his first Quranic masters.
[13] For more details on the scientific curricula of the ulema in Sudan, please refer to Dr. Abderrahmane Mohamed Maiga's book on the men and schools of jurisprudence in Sudan between the 8th and 13th centuries, p. 194. See also [Prof.] Thiero Ka, *Pir Saniokhor School: History, Teaching and Culture,* and also [Dr.] Omar Salih Ba's book on *Arab-Islamic culture in West Africa.*

examinations and tests before tying a turban on their heads to symbolize their consecration. Thus, all those who bore the title of Mor (like Mor Anta Saly or Mor Diarra) had finished proving their competence and mastery in Islamic religious sciences, which are subdivided into three categories: those called traditional, those called rational, and those called linguistic:

1. The traditional sciences mainly gather all the knowledge transmitted through the Quranic revelation or the words attributed to the prophets or the different religious authorities of history.

2. The rational sciences, on the other hand, gather the knowledge that can be acquired through the methods of logical deduction of the human mind.

3. Finally, linguistic sciences, as their name indicates, are the sciences that allow a perfect mastery of languages such as grammar, vocabulary, poetry, etc.

At the end of his studies, the student of the *daara* was honored by his family and a big party announced his promotion. He was now called *hafidh (hafiz)*, *kaaŋ, fóore, tamsir,* or *mor*.

Later, these significant traditions in West Africa will become customs far removed from the traditional and intellectual spirit, especially in regions far from the major centers of knowledge such as Timbuktu, Djenne, and Wadan. Incompetent men were named *kaaŋ* and begged in assemblies, dancing and performing.

Before colonization, this phenomenon was known as laawan. "Some people wandered through the villages, making use of their gifts in the Quran. They wore patchwork clothes with mirrors, oversized pants, and greys everywhere, even in their hair. People would gather around them and they would recite the Quran while singing and, sometimes, shouting and dancing.

Then people would clap and offer gifts." [14]

The Role of Marabout Families in the Diffusion of Islam

For centuries, maraboutic families were predominant over culture and education in West Africa as they managed the schools and institutions from which the great leaders of Islamic expansion would emerge. These families had set themselves the mission of enlightening their fellow citizens and guiding them towards bliss here below and in the beyond. They succeeded in their mission thanks to the nobility of their character.

Kings and rulers were impressed by the baraka of these pioneers and by their charisma; which assured them a venerable position among all strata of the population.

West African society was composed of the ruling class, the nobility, and the lower classes, which brought together diverse groups. Each group had its function within society, be it political, economic, subordinate, etc.

As for the maraboutique families, they were in charge of religious affairs and teaching, which gave them a special aura, especially since they were attributed with charisma and wonders. These qualities pushed the ruling classes to do everything to attract their favors. This is how the maraboutique families occupied a privileged place in the heart of the people.

Indeed, kings and emirs did everything to attract scholars and religious people to their courts for different reasons, sometimes spiritual or intellectual or commercial or diplomatic. The prodigies and charismas of certain saints were legendary in West Africa so rulers tried to take advantage of the services of famous saints.

---

[14] (*Cf.* document of the conference "Sheikh al Khadim and the Quran" of Fallu Bousso, p. 19).

Serigne Modou Bousso, eldest son of Serigne Mbacké Bousso wrote in the biography of his father that: "his grandfather Hammad, a citizen of Djoloff, left the Fouta in search of his brother Osman, son of Ali, who was at the Saloum. On arriving at the Djoloff, Hammad had been noticed by certain charisma that a Fulani reported to the King who sent an emissary to invite him. After having checked the status of his guest, the King did not manifest his intention to keep him with him, for fear that another King might discover him and benefit from his prodigies. After having asked him the purpose of his trip he proposed to stay a little time to rest and then he put at his disposal scouts. He tricked him to occupy him with requests and services until he married him into a large Muslim family and finally, he settled in the Djoloff until his death." [15]

The Major Islamic Centers

Some students who received their training in the major Islamic centers in the region were solicited by their fellow citizens for teaching. Cultural centers abounded in towns and villages. Later, they radiated by the quality of their teaching. This is the case in the schools of Fouta, Thiamene among the Wolof, Ndogal in Baol, Koki in Ndiambour, Pire, Mbakol in Cayor, and many others.

Maraboutique families had a long tradition of learning the Qur'an and spreading religious knowledge; this meant that all their children had to memorize the Holy Book and devote themselves to its teaching so that if any of them neglected this duty, they were blacklisted.

In this perspective, it seems necessary to report a very significant anecdote

---

[15] Serigne Modou Bousso "la biographie de son père Serigne Mbacké Bousso" published by Doctor Khadim Mbacké, p. 19.

that illustrates the importance that the maraboutique families gave to the mastery of the sciences of the Quran. According to Doctor Muhammad ibn Ahmad Miska in his book entitled "Karamat Sheikh Ahmadou Bamba": "Among the Karamat of the sheikh, there are many people who memorized the Quran by his baraka. He prayed for them in an extraordinary way, as I have already mentioned in Ibn Itcha's account. This was also the case with his disciple Muhammad Fall ibn Ibadh Tamaklawi when he visited him to ask for his prayers at the beginning of Ramadan. Upon seeing the crescent, the sheikh recited: "The month of Ramadan in which the Quran was revealed as guidance for humans." Then, he wrote words that he gave to Muhammad Fall who miraculously memorized the Quran. The sheikh advised him to recite it constantly and he did so in any position, walking, sitting, or riding a horse; he was nicknamed Muhammad Fall Quran for this.

Because of this devotion to the Quran, Allah has blessed this region of Africa which is full of scholars and saints.

CHAPTER II - THE FAMILY ENVIRONMENT

We have devoted the first chapter to his family origins and his grandparents and their involvement in Islamic education and the dissemination of knowledge.

The Divine Election

Regarding Serigne Saliou Mbacké, it is worth noting that his paternal and maternal families were among the most illustrious in Senegal. They had been known for centuries for their long tradition of spreading Islamic knowledge.

Allah wanted to choose this holy man among the spiritual elite of the country as the divine election according to His Word:

"Allah has chosen Adam and Nuh (Noah)

 and the family of Abraham and the family of Imran above humans, a sorted descent of the same ancestry. Allah is the All-Knowing Auditor" [Sura 3, Ayah 34]; and also: "And the pure land brings forth its flora by Allah's permission, but the impure one brings disaster; so, we show our signs to a meditating people." [Sura 4, Ayah 58].

This echoes the words of the venerable and revered Prophet Muhammad (sallallahu alayhi wa sallam) who said: "Choose for your seed because the gene pool is important." He added: "Humans are like the minerals of the earth, the best among you in the time of ignorance (jahiliyya) will be the best in Islam if they are educated." [16]

---

[16] Authentic Hadith reported by Bukhari and Muslim.

Paternal Lineage

His paternal lineage, the Mbacké, comes from a noble family in science and religion. They belong to the Cherifian lineage whose origins go back to Moulay Muhammad ibn Idriss al Azhar Ibn Moulay Idriss al Akbar ibn Abdallah al Kamil ibn Hasan al Muthanna ibn Hassan Ibn Ali Ibn Abi Talib and Fatima Zahra, the daughter of the Prophet Moulay Muhammad (sallallahu alayhi wa sallam)

There are two versions of their Cherifian descent. The first one attests to their kinship with the Modenalla family according to Sheikh Muhammad Lamine Diop in "Irwa al Nadim":

"It would be a toucouleur whose parents would have come from the Fouta Djolof and it was well known that they came from Mauritania. Their Mauritanian cousins were the Modennalla, who were the darlings. My friend and brother Mokhtar bint Lo ibn Sheikh Ibrahim Ndiomre informed me that he had heard the sheikh confirm this. He said: I was in the presence of the sheikh and there was mention of a Moorish tribe known by their Cherifian ancestry so he told me: you do not know that they are our brothers. So, we were sure of their Cherifian ancestry." [17]

Dr. Sidi Ahmad Ould al Emir the director of African research at *al Jazeera Center of Studies,* says that "the Modennalla family are Fulani sheriffs whose ancestry goes back to the Cherif Sidi Ilyes al Salihi al Waddani nicknamed Yoro of Timbuktu." [18]

Cherif Sidi Elies al Salihi was born in Ndienné, Mali. His mother was Fatima bint Waqi the governor of Djenné. His mausoleum is in Waddane

---

[17] Serigne Mohammad Lamine Diop Dagana: *Irwa al* Nadim, p. 64, edited by Rabita alkhadimiyya 2017.
[18] Interview with Dr. Sidi Ahmad ould al emir.

and he lived between the 8th and 9th centuries of the Hegira. His father is the Cherif Hilal ibn al Ayed al Kanani al Saghir ibn Abdallah al Cherif ibn Hilal al Saghir ibn Abderrahman ibn Abdallah ibn Hilal al Dimachqi ibn A'id al Kinani ibn Habibullah ibn Abdallah ibn salah ibn Abdallah ibn Moussa al Thani ibn Abdallah al Saqi nicknamed Aboul Kiram ibn Moussa al Joun ibn Adallah al Joun ibn Abdallah al Mahdh ibn Hasan al Muthanna ibn Hasan ibn Ali ibn Abi Talib.

Allah blessed his descendants who spread out in several branches "including Mahdina Lillah of Salem Oueled Ghilan. The Modenalla family were the commentators of the Quran in western hawdh. Ahl Baba Mody in Oueled Ghilan. Ahl Awiss in Trarza. Ahl Mody Malik in Oueled Deyman. Ahl al Talib Ajouad. Ahl Oubek. Ahl Rached. Ahl Mody Samba. Ahl A'mar Ghani. Ahl Muhammad Abdallah Souad. Ahl Boutan biskabt. Banou Jabir Kane in Niger." [19]

The scholar Khalil al Nahwi says in his book "Bilad Chinguit al Manara wal Ribat" that one of the sons of Sheriff Ilies de Wallata had married in Senegal and had children, among whom was Abdallah Dieng (Dieng means the scholar). The latter had a son Mody Malik who settled in Mauritania in the qibla where he taught the Quran to Beni Deyman in the 11th of the Hegira.

The descendants of Mody Malik gave many scholars including his son Minhana (m: 1150 h) as well as his other sons, some of whom mixed in Senegal and spread Islamic knowledge." [20]

The Modennalla families are part of them and are their cousins. Part of this family crossed the Senegal River and, through the bonds of marriage, their

---

[19] Hasan ibn Sheikh Suleiman: "Tarikh Beni Salah Churafa Koumbi Salah" published by Youssef ibn Tachfin 2009.
[20] Al-Nahwi Khalil: *Bilad Chinguit al Manara wal ribat*, p. 264.

children became full-fledged Senegalese. Other Cherifian families had done the same, such as that of Muhammad Fadel ibn Mamin and others.

As for the family of our sheikh, it continued its emigration from Fouta to Djoloff where the ancestor Sheikh Ousmane settled. This family was known for its piety and knowledge, as Sheikh Mouhammad Lamine Diop[21] relates in his book "Irwa-u Nadîm": Their nobility, even if not attested by oral or written evidence, could be detected in their character and knowledge, as well as in their courage and aptitude for good in all circumstances, as well as in their repulsion to any malevolence.

This family was renowned for its knowledge as well as for the holiness and teaching of the Qur'an which was its primary concern. Sheikh Moulay Ali Bousso said in his biography of his father Sheikh Mbacké Bousso[22], about one of his century-old grandmothers who had numerous descendants: "One could not find among his sons and grandsons anyone who had not memorized the Holy Quran." [23]

Thus, this illustrious family had devoted itself to the Quran and the spread of Islam until the arrival of the incomparable Sheikhul Khadim, who was a divine miracle, all the more so as no one is unaware of his special relationship with the Holy Book, which he had integrated by his soul and spirit.

All his life, he worked to spread the Quranic teaching and Islamic sciences among his contemporaries. He composed unique works for all generations. He devoted all his time and material means to this mission and rewarded

---

[21] A disciple and biographer of Sheikh Ahmadou Bamba, he was a fine scholar and a talented scholar. He composed several books, the most famous of which is *Irwa -u-nadim fi adhbi hubb-l- khadim*.
[22] Disciple and maternal cousin of Sheikh Ahmadou Bamba. He is certainly the greatest scholar of Senegal after his Sheikh.
[23] Quote reported by [Dr] Khadim Mbacké in his book in Arabic "Rasael Sheikh Mbacké Bousso."

those who devoted themselves to teaching, learning the Quran, or disseminating it. He said: "My treasure is the Qur'an and the hadith and ethics, not the collection and hoarding of silver or gold. [24]

By the service of the Qur'an and the hadith, my inheritance is attested, not by earthly possessions." [25]

He honored those who memorized the Qur'an as well as scholars by spending fortunes to maintain them. He encouraged them to devote themselves to science education by funding the opening of schools throughout the country. He surrounded himself with companions with proven skills in the Quranic sciences and assigned them the task of constantly reciting the Holy Book and transcribing many copies of it while educating the learners.

Maternal Lineage

As for the maternal line, it comes from the parents of one of the most prestigious religious families of the Wolof country. They were famous for their honorable positions and their devotion to Islam, through the dissemination of Islamic knowledge and values.

They were recognized for their competence in Quranic sciences since the arrival of their grandfather Omar Kaba Diakhaté who would be the first to set foot in Senegal from the north (or east according to other accounts).

Some versions trace Omar Kaba Diakhaté's ancestry to Moorish origins, more precisely to Shinguit, while others claim that he is of Soninké origin and that the family emigrated from the empire of Mali. Professor Mouhammad Diakhaté wrote in his book *The Life of the Fifth Khalifa of*

---

[24] Bamba Sheikh Ahmadou, Poem in acrostic letters from "A.B.T....."
[25] Bamba Sheikh Ahmadou, Poem in acrostic of the letters of "Yawma al Ahad Safar" in the collection of *Fuyudhat Rabbaniyya,* (Divine Bestowals).

the Mourides: "the Diakhaté family emigrated like other families from Mali precisely from Kaba Kouta, their original home.

Some historians claim that this family is Soninke, while others maintain that it would be Arab of Hassanite Cherifian origin; but the preponderant opinion among genealogists and even anthropologists would be the Soninke ancestry.

The Soninke were the first inhabitants of these regions [26]; they founded the old empire of Ghana in the 8th century. This empire collapsed around 1040 with the emergence of the Bambaras who founded in its place the empire of Mali which lasted until the advent of the Songhai Empire. The Berber tribes of Sanhaja appeared from the north and settled on the banks of the Senegal-Ghana River which became the Sanhaja River." [27]

Serigne Mourtadha, son of Serigne Saliou Mbacké told me that he introduced Diahanké scholars to his father, to whom Serigne Saliou said: "Our parents Diakhaté and Sylla are of Diahanké origin. They came from Mali and then settled in Cayor."

According to this account, we can affirm that the origin of the Diakhates is Soninké. One of their historical epics is the erection of the civilization of Ghana.

Whichever version is adopted, it is established that this ancestor settled in Wolof country in the Ndiambour, which at the time was part of the Wolof Kingdom before being divided into several emirates often at war.

He was the host of Lamane Wonta Saala Dieng who noticed the piety and

---

[26] Lamin Sanneh, *The Jakhanke Muslim Clerics: A Religious and Historical Study of Islam in Senegambia*.
- Eric Ross, Sufi City: *Urban Design and Archetypes in Touba* Cambridge University Press.
- J D FAG, *An Introduction to the History of West Africa*.

[27] Diakhaté Mouhammad Adam, *The Life of the Fifth Khalifa of the Mourids*.

charisma of the foreigner. The Lamane honored him and asked him to settle in his house to be his sheikh and advisor in religious and social affairs as was customary at the time. Very quickly, the grandfather became integrated into Wolof society and his host gave him in marriage to his daughter Salimata Dieng who gave him a son named Moussa Farma, father of Lamine Yoro.

The Family Tree of Mbakol

The Diakhaté family settled in the Wolof country and were linked with a few religious families through marriage. This was the case for the family of Massamba Thiam, the Mbacké family, the Touré family, and others. In the same way, matrimonial ties were established with the princely families of Cayor, Djoloff, and Baol, to such an extent that the Diakhaté family became an essential part of the Wolof social fabric. Its main activity will always remain the teaching and dissemination of Islam and its virtues.

At the same time, the family developed and its members were divided into several branches scattered between the Cayor, the Baol, the Ndiambour, and the Saloum. The branch of Mewnou, Merina Asta, and Khelcom Keur Mamom are the main families of the Diakhatés.

The family of Serigne Saliou Mbacké (on him the approval of Allah) descends from the branch of Mewnou Diakhaté, which takes its name from the village of Mbakol in Cayor, renowned in the region for the quality of its religious education.

This village was founded by Massata Baba, son of Baba Khari Ndiaye, son of Alassane Coumba Souka Dièye, son of Yéri Takou, son of Lamine Yoro, son of Moussa Farimata, son of Omar Kaba the grandfather, the first who lived in the Ndiambour.

Massata Baba had two children: Muhammad Kala, nicknamed Modou Kala Dianne, and Mokhtar Tadir, father of the famous scholar Sheikh Abdou Rahmane Diakhaté, a homonym of the illustrious scholar Sheikh Abdou Rahmane Lo, servant of the Quran and Quranic disciplines, in the way of Sheikhul Khadim.

Muhammad Kala had two children: Massata Salem and Massata Binta Doune, the father of Makhoudia Fafall and Modou Asta Diakhaté, grandfather of our Sheikh Serigne Saliou Mbacké, by his mother Sokhna Faty Diakhaté (on them all the approval of Allah).

The Pact of Allegiance of The Diakhates to Khadim Rassoul

Serigne Moudou Asta Diakhaté (on him the approval of Allah) was a disciple of Sheikhul Khadim. He had pledged his allegiance from the beginning of the Sheikh's mission in Mbacké Cayor, even before the latter's installation in Mbacké Baol.

Serigne Moustapha Saliou told us the circumstances of this allegiance in these terms: "Between Serigne Modou Asta Diakhaté and Serigne Balla Patte Touré, the father of Serigne Abdoulwahid Touré de Lappé, a relationship of friendship and brotherhood had been established, so much so that they had assumed not to undertake anything without consulting each other. Serigne Balla Patte Touré had undertaken a journey during which he met Sheikhul Khadim; he pledged his allegiance to him to engage in the initiatory path. On his return, he informed his friend Serigne Modou Asta Diakhaté who took the news badly, because, in his eyes, it broke their agreement since he had to consult him before making such a decision.

In a fit of anger, he decided not to speak to his friend again, despite the latter's apologies and efforts to reconnect. After a while, Serigne Balla Patte

Touré came to see his friend for a last proposal: "Before cutting the bridges definitively, he said, I ask you to come with me to see Sheikhul Khadim; if you judge that he is worthy of his status, you give him your allegiance like me; if you think otherwise, I break my allegiance and we forget this episode to renew our friendship and our commitment."

Their mutual friends supported the initiative and said: "What Serigne Balla Patte Touré proposes is right and wise and you should go with him and then decide what position to take, before breaking off such an exemplary relationship. Finally, he accepted and they began the journey to Mbacké Cayor, according to Serigne Moustapha."

Sheikhul Khadim subjugated them with extraordinary words that could only come from the greatest masters of esoteric knowledge. Yet the sheikh was still a young man whose hair had not yet turned white. After that, Sheikhul Khadim honored his guests by installing them in a place worthy of their rank.

Sheikh Modu Asta Diakhate felt a great inner peace in him and had the feeling that he had reached the end of his spiritual quest; he said to his companion: "I will make my allegiance but I will not do as you did; I will not be content to do the deed and leave; I give him my person, my goods and my children and I put myself at his service for the rest of my life."

When Sheikhul Khadim received them again, Sheikh Modou Asta Diakhaté said to him: "I want to make my allegiance by offering you my person, my goods, and my children while remaining at your service all my life." After that, the two friends told him what had happened between them. Sheikhul Khadim ordered them to return to Mbakol and continue teaching the Quran and science.

The Matrimonial Ties between Sheikhul Khadim and the Diakhaté Family

It is said that the reasons for the sheikh's marriage to the Diakhate family were that Sheikhul Khadim had asked Allah to give him a perfect son, capable of reviving the religion and spreading the authentic teaching of Islam as he will see in "Matlaboul Fawzeyni" in these terms:

"Bring the perfect into my property and into my home.

And strengthen him through the faithful guide [28] (the Prophet Peace and Salvation upon him)."

When Allah notified him that his wish was granted, the sheikh was in Thiéyène. He then ordered his brother Sheikh Ibra Faty (Mame Thierno Ibrahim) to go in search of a pious woman who could be the recipient of this promised divine gift.

The sheikh indicated to his emissary a certain number of characteristics in the choice of the family. The family was to be characterized by spiritual nobility and religious knowledge; its members were to be pious and among the men of the Quran by memorization and teaching. They should also not be in the habit of associating with princes and their courtiers. Above all, he insisted that the family in question should live by the sweat of their brow and should not have slaves or other equivocal elements in their paternal or maternal lineage.

Sheikh Ibra Faty began his quest within the religious families of the Wolof country up to Mbakol. He landed at the home of Serigne Modou Asta Ibn (Massata Diakhaté) who had four boys: Hamza, Abdou Rahmane, Habiboullâhi and Serigne Mbacké, the youngest who was the namesake of

---

[28] Bamba, Sheikh Ahamadou, the work is entitled "Matlab al Fawzeyni."

Sheikh Ibra Faty.

Serigne Modou also had three daughters: Fatima (Faty), Mariama, and Aicha (Astou). Fatima was the oldest, she was fifteen years old; she was the one who was given in marriage to Sheikhul Khadim.

It was customary for the sheikh, when he took a wife, to give her something to eat or drink and ask her to say "Bismillah", with the intention of purifying her heart from all the diseases of the soul (pride, jealousy, resentment, and others), but in the case of Sokhna Faty Diakhate, he said: "She does not need to purify herself, for she came pure and free from all the diseases of the soul."

The Characteristics of Sokhna Faty Diakhaté

She had memorized the Qur'an in its entirety and mastered the religious sciences while devoting herself entirely to spiritual education. She had learned the Quran from her father in Mbakol but, according to some versions, she had completed her apprenticeship with Sheikh Abdourahmane Lo in Daroul Alim al Khabir.

She mastered the Malekite fiqh and gave lessons to girls. She also took care of the spiritual education; among them, her niece Sokhna Maty Diakhaté. She also taught the fiqh and tasawwuf books of Khadimou Rassoul, including Massalik al Jinan and the Risala of Ibn Abi Zayd al Qayrawani.

Serigne Moustapha Saliou assures us that he has learned many invocations (adi'ya) and many religious texts through his holy grandmother Sokhna Faty Diakhaté.

She was truthful in her commitment and served Khadimou Rassoul (peace be upon him) not only in household affairs but also in teaching by chanting the qasaids of prayers and praise for the Prophet Muhammad (peace be upon him).

Abdul Ahad Diakhaté told us that Sokhna Faty Diakhaté had given him a collection of qasaids among which: "I have been granted wages and rewards through contraction and attraction and I am (Salah)."

She asked him to transcribe them and publish them, specifying: "They are part of the qasaids that were sung before Sheikh al-Khadim (may Allah be pleased with him). We sang in a choir and he circled us reading the qasaids."

Sokhna Faty Diakhaté was generous and constantly gave alms to the poor and needy. She distributed food to the students of Quranic schools. Every Friday, she gave to everyone, so that the poor and needy stayed at her door waiting for their share. Her multiple qualities made her a first-rate educator of souls and many pious and learned women were trained by her. Very modest, she did not look up in front of strangers.

The Installation in Thiéyène

Sheikhul Khadim was living in the village of Darou Rahman in Thiéyène Djolof when Sokhna Faty joined him. His sisters Mariama and Aicha (Astou) had also come to help him. She had two boys, Serigne Abdoul Quddous and Serigne Abdoul Bâkhi, and a daughter named Sokhna Tâhiratou, but all died early. This plunged Sokhna Faty into deep sadness and she cried constantly.

Sheikhul Khadim commanded her to be patient and trust in Allah and that she would soon have good news from God that would give her a healthy and blessed son who would have a long life; this son would also be famous and distinguished among his contemporaries like the sun in broad daylight.

He also told her that her son Serigne Abdul Bâkhi had left because he was to be an intercessor for his forefathers and for other reasons that he should not reveal.

Indeed, sometime later, the promise was kept. Three years after the sheikh's installation in Diourbel, she gave birth to a boy of sound mind and body who would live a long life; he will be the last living son of Sheikhul Khadim. This blessed son will complete the spiritual work of his father by educating the disciples and guiding them to the nearness of their Lord, thanks to this invocation of the father:

"He has given me true knowledge and work (Salah) that fills me with hope.

"Grant me true knowledge and the work (Salah) that completes my hopes." [29]

---

[29] Bamba, Sheikh Ahamadou, the work is entitled "Nour al Dareyni."

CHAPTER III - HIS CHILDHOOD AND RELIGIOUS EDUCATION

In this chapter, we will discuss the childhood and youth of Serigne Saliou based on available sources and the testimonies of people who knew him. We will also approach some esoteric subjects to understand the particular personality of our sheikh and his aptitudes and potentialities.

His Birth

Serigne Saliou (on him the approval of Allah) was born in the month of Zhul Qih'da in the year 1333H, according to the Mouridiyya historian Serigne Muhammad Lamine Diop Dagana. The author mentioned the event in his book *Irwaa-un Nadîm* where he said: "The 14th day of Zhul Qih'da in the year 1333H was the birth of our Sheikh Salih." This date corresponds to October 22, 1915, in the Gregorian calendar.

This birth took place in Diourbel three years after Sheikh Al-Khadim settled there from the locality of Thiéyène. His birth coincided with the full moon, which referred to certain signs and indications. The day before, his father had summoned the elite of the mourides, honored them, and ordered them to recite the Qur'an and to mention the name of Allah at all times. This injunction was later interpreted by the fact that Sheikh Al-Khadim was about to receive an illustrious guest: his son Salah.

Indeed, Serigne Saliou was one of the last sons of Sheikh Al-Khadim who said: *"The Prophet Announcer of Good News (Al-Bashir) has announced that any newborn child I have after my son Muhammad Al-Bashir will be among the greatest saints (Awliyas)."* [30]

---

[30] In Sheikh Ahmadou Bamba's writings about the gifts of Allah on his person, he mentioned almost all his children's names and characteristics. He also mentioned their future works and the spiritual ranks of each of them. These writings are always kept by the family.

It is well known among the mourides that the sons of Khadimou Rassoul who were born before the sea exile obtained holiness (Wilaya) through their works (Khidma); this is, therefore, a matter of the order of acquisition (Iktisab). On the other hand, those born after the maritime exile are of the order of gift and grace (Wahb wa Fadhl). That is why Sheikh Al-Khadim said: "The education (tarbiyya) of an immortal living being is not comparable to that of a living mortal."

The Blessed Consecration

On the day of the baptism (Aqiqa), the sheikh gave one of his disciples a blank sheet of paper on which he had written: "As-Salih" (the Benefactor) and ordered that the newborn be named so.

Serigne Abdou Samad, son of Serigne Chouhaybou Mbacké tells [31] that he asked Serigne Saliou if Sheikhul Khadim had chosen this name as the homonym of the Prophet Salah (Salah on him). The Prophet Salah replied that his illustrious father had written the blessed name "As-Salih" on a blank sheet of paper and had given it to a man named Mad Laam. He ordered him to give it to Serigne Hamzatou Diakhaté so that he would know the name to give to the newborn child and kept the sheet of paper afterward.

Serigne Saliou also told that the latter had one day shown him the famous sheet on which was written the first name "Salah" in the hand of Sheikhul Khadim.

Sheikh Abdou Samad son of Serigne Chouhaybou Mbacké added: "The choice of this prophetic name surely implies secrets and signs, especially since I think it is part of the names of the Prophet Muhammad (sallallahu alayhi wa sallam)."

---

[31] Serigne Tayyib Diakhaté also told me the same thing.

He goes on to say: "I personally think that this is so because Sheikhul Khadim, in many of his prayers about the Prophet Muhammad (sallallahu alayhi wa sallam)) or his eulogies refer to him by this name as in the poem *Jalibatul Maraghib* where he writes:

"Pray on the Benefactor (Salah) who is the Regenerator (Muslih).

The Truthful (As-Sàdiq) the True (As-Sidq) a prayer that regenerates."

This historical event was recorded by Serigne Muhammad Lamine Diop Dagana in the poem he composed on the occasion of the baptism. He celebrated the coming into the world of the child while conjunctivating on his wonderful destiny in the propagation of Islam and the spread of Mouridiyya. He wrote:

By His grace, He has bequeathed to us a Benefactor (Salah)

The Lord who has bestowed a blessing upon us (Salah)

He did it like a sun in the sky of his time.

In order to repair the damage of his contemporaries

He made it perfect so that he completes the guidance

In all blessing truth and intelligence.

A Name Full of Meaning

There is no doubt that this prophetic name conceals magnificent secrets and symbols. It could not be conjunctural on the part of the father, but would rather fall under the station and the spiritual function of Serigne Saliou who will become an educator, a spiritual guide, and a reformer, following the example of the prophets and envoys who had lived on earth for the needs of their mission.

Allah says in Sura *Al A'raaf* ayah 56: "Do not sow corruption on earth after it has been restored."

Thus, Serigne Saliou followed in the footsteps of the Prophets and Envoys, perpetuating their mission throughout his life, which he devoted to religious teaching, spiritual education, guidance, and good.

Entire generations have benefited from his contribution and countless pious scholars have graduated from his schools (*daara*).

Sheikhul Khadim had already announced to Serigne Saliou's mother the prodigious destiny of her son, as he will signify it in several of his poems. Indeed, in his writings, he alluded to the role of her son Serigne Saliou in the fulfillment of his hopes for the ideal community in which the mourides will be taught by true knowledge and where they will work for the good with an irreproachable ethic.

Sheikh Abdou Samad, son of Serigne Chouhaybou tells: "It happened to me one day that I said to Serigne Saliou: 'I think it is you that Sheikh Khadim was referring to in this line by Nourou Daarayni: "Grant me true knowledge and beneficial work (salah) that completes my hopes."

Serigne Saliou answered me: "Even if it was not the case, I hope that Allah by His Grace and His Kindness will make me benefit from the fragrance of His sanctity flow so that I can contribute to the realization of Sheikhul Khadim's wish. Allah is Almighty."

The passionate mouride Serigne Abo Gueye told a similar anecdote about Serigne Saliou who said: "Even if Sheikhul Khadim did not designate me by this verse, I intend to work until his wish is fulfilled by the grace of Allah."

We will limit ourselves to quoting a few passages from Muhyiddin Ibn Arabi in his book *"Al Futuhat Al Makkiyya"* to understand the meanings of the name Salah and the spiritual realities it designates. In volume 3, Ibn Arabi, also known as Sheikh Al Akbar, says: "Among the saints (Awliyas) (on them the approval of Allah) are the benefactors (salihun)[32] whom Allah has taken over through beneficence (salah) and placed in fourth place after the martyrs, but in the form of a circle. Thus, it begins with the prophecy and ends with the pious and capable benefactors (salihun) as in the figure in the margin: the prophets (nabiyun), the truthful ones (siddiqun), the martyrs (shuhada), the benefactors (salihun). In fact, every Prophet was designated as a Benefactor (Salihun) or he had asked Allah to raise him to the status of a Benefactor even though he had the status of a Prophet. This means that the station of beneficence is a peculiarity (khusûs) in prophecy and it can be a characteristic of someone who is neither a prophet (*nabi*), nor truthful (*siddiq*), nor a martyr/witness (*shahid*). Thus, the station of benevolence is the beginning of the prophets because it is characterized by this quality of prophetic ability; when they receive the signs of it, they are witnesses (*shuhada*) and when they are informed about invisible things (ghayb), they are the truthful ones (*siddiqun*). Prophets are fit for all these stations. Being benefactors (*salihin*), they have gathered all the qualities. The truthful are fit for the station of truthfulness (Siddiqiya), the witnesses are fit for the station of martyrs, so everyone is fit for his station or function, except that the benefactors whom Allah has praised are especially fit for this station (maqam). They are in the cycle of the four mentioned: the prophets (*nabiyun*), the truthful (siddiqun), the martyrs (shuhada), and the benefactors (salihun). The benefactors (salihun) are perfect, their knowledge, knowledge of Allah, and their faith can never be subject to any deficiency, for if they were, they would not be perfect. It is this benevolence (salah) that the Prophets (peace and salvation be upon them) sought.

He who has no deficiency in his truthfulness (siddiqiya) is a Benefactor

---

[32] Salihun – the pious, virtuous and capable ones

(salah); he who has none in his testimony (shahada) is a Benefactor (salah) and he who has none in his Prophecy (nubuwwa) is a Benefactor (salah). In truth, man is potentially fit for any station; but he must strive for perfection in all circumstances, for no one is immune from deficiency.

A prophet is not a prophet because of his humanity when every human could be. A prophet is a human whom Allah has chosen. Imperfection being human, it is possible that a deficiency may appear but it can be repaired; that is why the chosen ones covet from Allah to be among the benefactors who do not suffer from any deficiency. He is one of those benefactors (salihun) to whom we refer in this text." [33]

His Early Childhood

Serigne Saliou grew up in the village of Daroul "al Alîm al Khabir" in the home of Sheikh Abdourahmane Lo where part of Sheikh Khadim's family lived. He then joined his father in Diourbel to live happy days. The latter loved him very much and asked to see him every three days to pray for him and to pass on the baraka.

One day, the tutor who was taking care of Serigne Saliou came to introduce the child to his father while wearing a garment that did not cover his whole arm. Sheikhul Khadim tore a piece of the cloth off of his boubou and gave it to him to cover this part of his arms.

Sheikhul Khadim's love for his son was as strong as his love for his father, since every time he saw him, he would run to him to lift him with his arms and embrace him with affection.

Serigne Saliou used to say: "Allah gratified me with the love of Sheikhul Khadim even before I knew him."

---

[33] Ibn Arabi, *Al Futuhat Al Makkiyya* vol. 3, p. 40-39.

Serigne Saliou often remembered these happy moments. He recounts being used to running to his father to hug him every time he saw him, he was surprised when one day he did not receive him as usual with tenderness and joy. On the contrary, he pulled him towards him strongly with one hand. In the other hand, he held a copy of the Holy Quran; then the sheikh bent down to pick up crumbs of food from the ground that Serigne Saliou would unintentionally trample on. Only then did he take his son in his arms and hug him with love and tenderness as usual.

Serigne Saliou's grandson, Serigne Saliou ibn Sheikh Mustapha Saliou, told me that he experienced a similar scene with his grandfather when one day he appeared before him while Serigne Saliou was preparing coffee. Involuntarily, he was about to hit the foot of the table when the sheikh pulled him vigorously, then smiled and told him that the same thing had happened to him with Sheikhul Khadim.

Serigne Saliou distinguished himself from an early age by his perspicacity, intelligence, and efficiency. Allah had placed in him the virtues and nobility of the soul so that he was interested only in beneficial works.

Serigne Abdou Samad Shouhaïb tells that Serigne Saliou, from his early childhood, gave all the money he received as a hadiya to his father, and when he asked him the reason for this gesture, he answered: "It is a pious gift, for the Face of Allah."

His Intelligence Since Childhood

Serigne Saliou had a privileged relationship with his father and he had a vivid intelligence and a prodigious memory. His characteristics were revealed very early in the teaching period. He memorized the ayahs of the Qur'an and the eulogies about the Prophet Muhammad (sallallahu alayhi wa sallam) as soon as he heard them recited in assemblies.

It is said that Serigne Saliou memorized the qasida "Bismi Ilaahi kfinil Akdara Ya Allahu" before he even began to learn the Holy Quran.

The Period of Teaching and Education

Very early on, Sheikhul Khadim entrusted him to his maternal uncle Serigne Hamzatou Diakhaté for the learning of the Quran and education, following the example of his brothers Abdou Samad, Abdoul Ahad, and Shouhaïbou.

Sheikhul Khadim said to Serigne Hamzatou: "If I entrusted you with the education of the children it is not because you are their maternal uncle, but because I myself perfected your spiritual realization; I put secrets in you and I judged you worthy to transmit them to them. This is the only reason why I entrust them to you to teach and educate them."

Serigne Hamzatou Diakhaté took the children with him to Touba and entrusted them to Serigne Alassane Diakhaté to learn the Quran. This one was very vigilant and very competent for this mission.

Serigne Alassane was recognized as a saint (waliyou); and, for confirmation, we take from Serigne Fallou ibn Sheikh Chuhaib that his father told him: Sheikh Alassane was known for his rigor in teaching so that after the return of Sheikhul Khadim to his Lord, he gathered his students, especially the sons of Sheikhul Khadim and asked them to forgive him [for] his rigor.

Then, he told them that their father had come to see him at an unveiling (kashf) to talk to him about several subjects and that he himself would soon leave this world to join him in the afterlife. Thus, he left the world in a very short period as he had announced. May Allah embrace him in His mercy.

Serigne Saliou was brilliant in his studies and he memorized everything without any difficulty, unlike his elder brother Serigne Abdoul Ahad, whom the uncle had to bring back to his father to explain his son's difficulties in memorization. Sheikhul Khadim prayed for his son who since that day was able to memorize everything.

Our friend Abdallah Fahmi told us that Serigne Abdallah Diakhaté, son of Serigne Hamza Diakhaté, told him that during the period of learning the Quran, Serigne Abdoul Ahad had difficulties in memorizing it, such that all the students exceeded him. Serigne Hamza asked Sokhna Faty Diakhaté to inform her father so that he could pray for him.

Sheikhul Khadim asked that his son be brought to him. Serigne Abdul Ahad was washed and dressed in a new boubou and presented to the sheikh who was reading the Qur'an. He put the child on his knees and continued his reading; then he took off his turban, tore it in the middle and after removing his son's boubou, he put the turban around his neck and dressed him again. Then he recommended leaving the turban on him when he learns.

Serigne Abdul Ahad told his close friend Serigne Abdullah Diakhaté that since that day, he noticed that every time he read the Quran, it was as if the letters and words, as well as the sentences of the Holy Book, explained their meanings to him.

The uncle provided them with education according to the mouride way, which combines religious instruction with manual work and spiritual education based on virtues. Thus, the disciples went to the fields to sow and reap to become accustomed to earning an honest living with dignity and effort; likewise, they learned the rules of propriety (adab) by serving their neighbor with humility and self-sacrifice as Sheikhul Khadim teaches in his writings.

Anecdotes from The Teaching Period

Serigne Saliou told relatives about his memories during the period when he was working in the fields of Serigne Hamza Diakhaté in *Jannat al Ma'wa,* in the western part of Touba. At that time, there was a forest with marigots; he said that for him, it was the end of the world because, in the innocence of his childhood, he thought that the known world ended behind this dangerous forest. [34]

He often told the disciples about the difficult periods of childhood, such as the anecdote he told his close talibé friend Mustapha Diaw in which he said that at the time, they took ground Bissap leaves and added salt while considering it to be the most delicious dish on earth.

He also told the disciples that during the period of Quranic learning, he was with his brothers Serigne Abdul Ahad, Serigne Abdou Samad, and Serigne Chuhaib at his uncle's house, Serigne Hamza Diakhaté, who had been instructed by Sheikhul Khadim not to favor them in any way, so that one could experience the rigors of life. The father sent them nothing; and when one day they received a jar of curdled milk from him, it was a great surprise. However, for the other mouride Sheikhs life was easier, whereas for them it was so rigorous that it was very difficult to find a proper meal. However, they were certain that Sheikhul Khadim wanted for them the goods of this world and the other.

He also said that during several months of Ramadan, they could not find anything to cut the fast apart from a handful of couscous or other foods, although certainly, their father knew their situation. Probably he wanted to send them to the stations of the virtuous ascetic saints.

---

[34] Source: Serigne Moustapha Diaw.

He also told them that in their period of education (tarbiyya), they did the work like all the disciples, both cleaning and field work.

He said that while their father was alive, they were ordered to clean the rooms daily; but after the father left this world, no one ordered them to do that anymore. He added that certainly, these were the father's recommendations.

There is also the anecdote of the celebration of the first Magal, when their uncle informed them that Sheikhul Khadim had ordered them to celebrate this day, offering food, out of gratitude to Allah who showered his servant with graces and benefits, both manifest and hidden.

Sheikh Abdou Samad ibn Sheikh Chuhaib recounted that one of Serigne Saliou's maternal relatives, Mame Diakhaté N'diaye, had given him a sheep, and when the uncle informed him of Sheikhul Khadim's order, he gave the sheep to be burnt. As a result, Serigne Saliou was one of the first to celebrate the Magal.

His Frequent Visits to His Father

Sheikhul Khadim often requested the visit of his children whom Serigne Hamza Diakhaté accompanied to Diourbel in two groups, in turn. One was composed of Sheikh Abdul Ahad and Sheikh Abdallah Diakhaté and the other of Serigne Saliou and Serigne Chouhaybou.

However, among the significant anecdotes reported by Serigne Saliou, we will note the one where he said that he and his brothers respected Serigne Hamza Diakhaté who represented for them the highest spiritual authority, so much so that they were astonished to see him before Sheikhul Khadim behaving in all reverence and humility like a talibé; whereas usually, he was imposing by his charismatic stature.

It made such an impression on them that it marked them forever because they had just learned the respectable attitude of the Talibé before his sheikh and spiritual guide.

Serigne Saliou recounted certain episodes of his visits to his father, such as the one where leaving Touba in the morning, they stopped at Khourou Mbacké; then continued to Diourbel where they arrived in the evening and stayed in the house of Serigne Mbaye Diakhaté, one of the Sheikh's great disciples.

Serigne Hamza went to visit Sheikhul Khadim who asked him who was accompanying him among his children. He informed him that he was with Serigne Saliou and Serigne Chouhaybou. This time they had several interviews, some of them separately. And when they had to leave, Sheikhul Khadim received them, sitting on the floor, preparing to write. The lice were visible on his clothes and his body, and he told Serigne Hamza: "I did not eat or drink during those two weeks."

He asked his son Saliou: did you rest on the way? They answered: we took a nap at Mbaye Diakhaté's house in Khourou Mbacké. Then Sheikhul Khadim said to him: that's how you call him Mbaye Diakhaté without mentioning uncle.

Serigne Saliou who loved his uncle Serigne Mbaye very much says that from that day on he learned the rules of decorum (adab) with the elders. [35]

During this stay, Sheikh al-Khadim personally took care of the education of his children; which Serigne Saliou recounted, mentioning that he had been

---

[35] Serigne Saliou told this anecdote to his disciples to teach them these rules. Serigne Khalil Mbacké told me that one day Serigne Saliou asked him where he came from. He answered, from Sheikh Mbacké's house, referring to Serigne Sheikh Mbacké ibn Sheikh Abdoulahad. Serigne Saliou said to him: that is how you call him; you do not know that he is your uncle. Then he told her the anecdote quoted.

asked several times to serve his father; and each time he told him: "Begin with the name of Allah and say Bismillah and mention Allah every time you undertake a work."

Sheikh Hamed ibn Ishaq Al Hasani says that this anecdote holds precious secrets and meanings for the spiritual flow (madad ruhani). One day, he asked Serigne Saliou for elements of his memories of Sheikh Khadim and he answered: "I went to see Sheikh Khadim when I was a child but I had already memorized the Qur'an and he said to me: 'Say in the name of Allah and give me this. Salihou, say *Bismillah* and give me this. Salihou, say *Bismillah* and do this or that for me."

This anecdote informs us about Sheikhul Khadim's method of education through virtues and by mentioning the name of Allah in any undertaking, as in the hadith of the Prophet Muhammad (sallallahu alayhi wa sallam): "O boy mention Allah and eat by your right hand and before you" (Reported by Bukhari). Indeed, these words are a precious source for attracting divine blessings and flow.

First Sheikhul Khadim made Serigne Saliou work by giving him orders to accomplish and it is well known that the sheikh had raised many of his disciples to high spiritual stations just by giving them work to accomplish. Then, he transmitted to Serigne Saliou the secrets of the name of the Majesty and that of the Basmala by giving him the order and permission to use them in any work.

One of the stories that influenced his childhood was that of his last visit to his father in Diourbel. It was a trip with his uncle Serigne Hamza Diakhaté and his brother Sheikh Shuaibou Mbacké. It was the last time he saw his father (may God be pleased with him).

His disciple Sheikh Abdul Ahad Diakhaté, who was our Quranic master, told me this version he heard from the mouth of Serigne Saliou who said: "The sheikh invited us to Diourbel where we found him in a place infested with fleas and insects with bamboo mats (Rombu Jaan) on which were enthroned writings he had just completed. We couldn't even sit down because of the fleas and insects. He took a copy of the Holy Quran and then said, "This Quran is for you, but it is a debt that must be paid back, that is, when you memorize it, you must make copies for me by your hands. When the time comes to pay this debt, I will accompany you to Touba and I will stay there with you forever. I will guarantee you everything you want."

Serigne Saliou commented on this anecdote by saying: "God intended that when we memorized the Quran, we would wait for each other for the transcription until we were late to finish it. Our father asked us again to come and see him a few days before he was called back to God. This time we went down to our uncle Serigne Mbacké Diakhaté's house but we were unable to meet him. So, we waited there for a long time. Then, we returned to Touba by car."

The author Muhammad Adam Diakhaté mentioned in his book "The Life of the Fifth Caliph of the Mourides" a slightly different version of this visit, quoting Serigne Moustapha Saliou Mbacké. According to the latter, "Serigne Touba was on this day in a closed circle around which a large number of visitors gathered. Serigne Saliou saw him in the distance, through a porthole or a small window with his uncle, Serigne Hamza Diakhate. He was calling people to reach out to receive prayers. It was the last vision he had of his father (may God be pleased with him! ...)."

Memorization of The Holy Quran

After the death of his father, Serigne Saliou finished his Quranic studies. He mastered reading, memorization, calligraphy, and intonation, according to the narration of Imam Warsh under the authority of Ibn Nafi (may God be pleased with him). It is customary in this region, after mastering the Quran, to transcribe it from memory. This step is a sign of good memorization and the skills necessary to transmit the Noble Quran. Thus, after completing his Quranic studies, Serigne Saliou gave his elder brother, the successor of his father, Serigne Mouhamadou Moustapha Mbacké, his first copy of the Holy Quran.

Thus, Serigne Saliou completed this first stage of his career and was to open a new chapter in his life in education and spiritual formation.

PART TWO: THE MAN AND HIS JOURNEY
1. HIS INTELLECTUAL TRAINING
2. HIS VIRTUOUS CHARACTER

CHAPTER IV - HIS INTELLECTUAL TRAINING

This will be an overview of his peregrinations in the quest for knowledge, including his studies with:

- Sheikh Makhtar Dieng

- Serigne Habiboullah Mbacké (in Touba)

- Mor Sasoum and Sayar Sylla (scientists of Mbackol)

- Makhtar Sow (Tekrour scholar)

- Sheikh Muhammad Dème (in Diourbel).

Then we will discuss his intellectual curiosity and passion for Arabic literature, as well as everything related to Muslim civilization. His peregrinations in the quest for religious knowledge will begin at the end of his learning of the Quran, crowned by a certificate of aptitude for Quranic teaching attesting to his mastery of memorization, recitation as well as calligraphy, and modulation of scriptures. A new page was opened in his life as an orphan, and his determination to reach the highest spiritual stations was strengthened. He wanted to reach perfection in religious sciences and esoteric knowledge to penetrate the secrets and mysteries of God.

Thus, he began his quest by crisscrossing the country from Touba and Diourbel to Mbackol at Serigne Sayar Sylla in Thilla Daramane. He then went to the school of cadi Ma Diakhaté Kala where his son, the scholar Mor Sasoum Diakhaté, officiated.

His Studies with Sheikh Makhtar Dieng

Serigne Saliou began his studies in Touba where his elder brother Serigne Modou Mustapha, Khalife-General of the Mourides, had founded in 1339

H (1920) a school in the village of Tindoudy *Husn al Ma'ab,* (which was a few kilometers from the Mosque of Touba and which today is a district of Touba) in accordance with the directive of their father Sheikhul Khadim.

This neighborhood was two or three kilometers away from the center of Touba and Serigne Modou Moustapha used to gather there his children and brothers to ensure their quality studies with the scholar Sheikh Makhtar Dieng Goyar.

Serigne Saliou studied religious sciences there, he distinguished himself during this period by his intelligence and his faculty of memorization, as well as by his understanding of the subtleties. Moreover, he was astonished by his determination and his aspiration to assimilate everything; so many dominating factors by which he resembled his illustrious father.

Thus, after a year spent in Tindoudy *Husn al Ma'ab* he had to return with his brothers in Touba to Serigne Habiboullah Mbacké.

The Stay at Serigne Habiboullah Mbacké's House

Khalife Serigne Modou Moustapha had asked the young scholar Serigne Habiboullah Mbacké to settle in Touba at the end of 1927 in order to teach there. This illustrious scholar was only 10 years older than Serigne Saliou but he taught the sons of Sheikhul Khadim many works of theology (aqidah) and jurisprudence (fiqh), as well as sufism (tasawwuf).

Serigne Saliou also studied Malekite *fiqh* and grammar books during this period which lasted a whole year. His mother Sokhna Faty Diakhaté advised him to go to Mbackol and he asked for advice from his uncle Serigne Hamza Diakhaté; the latter asked for the authorization of Khalife Serigne Modou Moustapha so that Serigne Saliou could join his maternal parents in Mbackol, very famous for the quality of his religious education.

In this Mecca of knowledge, schools were specializing in grammar and linguistics, others in jurisprudence, and still others in Quranic sciences. Some of them, such as the school of Thilla Daraman, the school of Cadi Madiakhaté Kala, the school of Longor, and others were very famous.

This is how Serigne Saliou was able to discover other places of knowledge and enrich his knowledge because the diversity of schools and their specialization gave the opportunity to discover other thoughts while in Touba and Diourbel the studies had remained classical.

He studied in the village of Thilla Daramane with the legal scholar Serigne Sayar Sylla. He perfected his knowledge of Malekite jurisprudence, grammar, and conjugation, as well as Arabic semantics and literature.

Serigne Saliou had an extraordinary will in the quest for knowledge; every morning, he would get on his horse and leave for school. But every time he rode through a village, he would not fail to stop if there was a scientist he could benefit from. He spent his day in research and development before returning to his residence in the village of Meonou.

In the evenings, he devoted himself to other religious or family duties, and after morning prayer, he would resume his quest for knowledge until the evening. Serigne Saliou recounted that, during this period, he was accompanied by many other students who had come from all over the world to learn. This was the case of Serigne Modou Diobbe Sylla, father of the Quran teacher Serigne Hassan Sylla, Serigne Thierno Ndiaye, uncle of Serigne Abo Guèye, Serigne Sheikh Seck Takh and others.

At Serigne Mor Sasoum

After completing his studies at Thiilla Daraman, Serigne Saliou asked his uncle Sheikh Abderrahman Diakhaté for permission to join Serigne Mor Sasoum's classes at Ain Madhi to perfect his knowledge of Arabic prosody and metrics as well as other disciplines.

Sheikh Abderrahmane Diakhaté sent Serigne Saliou Touré's father to consult Serigne Mor Sasoum and see with him the conditions of accommodation. Aynou Madhi was so far away that it was necessary to reside on the spot.

After the agreement of Serigne Mor Sasoum, Sheikh Abderrahmane Diakhaté committed himself to all the charges related to the stay and had a hut built on the land given by Serigne Osman Diakhaté, brother of Serigne Mor Sasoum. Then, the inhabitants of the village as well as a Toucouleur relative named Mokhtar Sow built two other huts for the companions and visitors of Serigne Saliou.

The precise nature of the works studied during this period is not known. But it can be considered that Serigne Saliou perfected his study of grammar, prosody, and metrics.

We also think that he studied *Mukhtasar Khalil* in the Malekite fiqh because Serigne Saliou told his disciple, Imam Saliou Sylla, that during the period of Ain Madhi when he was studying Ibn Malik's Alfia with his father Serigne Hasan Sylla, he admired the method used by Serigne Mor Sasoum which consisted in defining the rules and the main lines before starting the classes and then continuing with explanations and comments.

It was customary for education to be free. But the students had to work in the teacher's fields for free; nevertheless, every Wednesday, Serigne Saliou gave 25 francs to his master Serigne Mor Sasoum.

It is also said that Serigne Mor Sasoum had wanted to evaluate Serigne Saliou by all sorts of tests to perfect him; for the Mbacké Mbacké had the reputation of wallowing in their family prestige and taking the attitudes of great Sheikhs before reaching this station.

Thus, Serigne Saliou was tested in patience and endurance until his teacher was certain that he was dealing with an extraordinary case; for this young man did not count on his lineage, but wanted to reach the highest spiritual stations through his commitment. He spared no effort to achieve this goal, which Sheikhul Khadim recommended to his son Serigne Fallou.

Here is the will as it was reproduced in *Silkoul Jawahir:*

"Bismillah ir Rahman ir Rahim. O my son, do not be deceived by the words of those who say to you O master son of our master, for true mastery is that which you acquire by yourself and not that which is acquired by your parents or your forefathers.

Nobility is that of deeds and words and not that of kinship, and prestige lies in high aspirations and not in dried bones, for the nobility of the lineage requires the nobility of morals.

For this reason, it is said: no glory for him whose lineage is noble and whose morals are light. It is also said either like Issam and is not ostentatious because Issam said:

> *Issam's soul assured him the glory by pushing him to courage and entrepreneurship and made him a noble King.*

Another said:

> *Inherited nobility cannot be useful because only what has been acquired will ultimately benefit humans.*
>
> *Rely only on your actions and do not believe that nobility is acquired through genealogy.*
>
> *The human only ennobles itself*
>
> *Even if he has noble and brave parents*
>
> *Branches if they do not produce fruit*
>
> *They will be used as logs for the fire.*
>
> *Lord guide us on the right path, it is You we worship and it is You we implore. Pray over our master Muhammad and greet him."*

Finally, at the end of his studies, the teacher gave the following testimony in favor of his student: "This boy will have a prodigious destiny if Allah grants him a long life. I have tested his character through all kinds of trials and I have seen in him only that which is pleasing to Allah and His Prophet (sallallahu alayhi wa sallam).

When Serigne Saliou bid farewell to Serigne Mor Sasoum, the latter composed a wonderful poem in his honor in which he mentioned the virtues of his pupil and his nobility of soul. Unfortunately, we could not find this poem and we are still looking for it in the family. We think it could be at Saliou Sylla's house.

At Serigne Makhtar Sow

Serigne Saliou would have studied mathematics as well as astronomy and astrology with a colorful scientist named Makhtar Sow. Although he benefited from his broad knowledge, he did not like the character and morals of his teacher who, from the outset, had asked for exaggerated conditions that the uncle had finally accepted.

During this period in Mbackol, Serigne Saliou began his rural work in the village of Ndouckmane Dieng while his disciples did not exceed six people (Sheikh Mor Ndiaye, Makhtar Sow, Abdessalam Ba, Modou Ba, Makhtar Ba, Daouda Sall, Mor Ndiaye Niang).

In 1931 the first agricultural experiment began, recounted by Serigne Saliou himself, during which 13 kg of peanuts were sown. It was a beautiful harvest by divine blessing. He offered it entirely as Hadiya to the Khalife Serigne Modou Mustapha to contribute to the construction of the Mosque of Touba.

His Studies With Sheikh Muhammad Dème In Diourbel

Serigne Saliou settled in Diourbel where he joined the prestigious circle of studies of Sheikh Muhammad Dème. He was an encyclopedic scholar and a sufi faqih, in addition to being an exegete of the Quran who composed a large commentary in Arabic and Wolof, published in two large volumes.

It is not known exactly what subjects Serigne Saliou studied with this eminent scholar, nor the precise time of the studies, but Sheikh Mustapha Dème the son of Serigne Mohamed Dème told that Serigne Saliou had told him: "I studied with your father Touhfat al Hukkam and other more specialized works."

Serigne Moustapha Abdoul Khadre Mbacké told us that Serigne Saliou considered Sheikh Muhammad Dème as his greatest teacher; for he learned with him most of the classics of literature and religious sciences.

As for the texts and sciences that were taught in Serigne Mohamed Dème's school, we can reproduce them from a letter addressed to Serigne Moudou

Khabane Mbacké in which he explained his teaching method and the number of years required for students to complete the program. He said: "I chose as a method to ignore *Aqaid al-Din* and Awfi to be satisfied with *Tazawwud al Sighar*. I left *Al Akhdari* for *al Jawhar al Nafis*. I replaced *Om al Barahin* de Senoussi with *Mawahib al Qoddous* to benefit from the baraka of the one who said:

> *He who does what he wants has gratified me with science and its blessings through his attribute of omniscience.*

Then I begin *Nahj Qadhal Haj* to acquire the rules of propriety (adab) before mastering the sciences and benefiting from its benefits. Without the rules of decency (adab), science can be a source of unhappiness instead of the happiness that Allah preserves for us. Sheikh al Kadi says:

> *A lot of science without rules of decorum*
>
> *May result in pain and misfortune.*

Then I illuminated myself by the method of illumination of the breasts "*Mounawwiru-Cudur* to acquire enlightenment then I finished by the *Risala of* ibn Abi Zayd al Qayrawani. As for Mame Mor, he has finished the whole curriculum and only part of the *Risala* remains and as soon as he finishes, he will start grammar and finish with *al Ihmirar of* ibn Bouna then he will study belles-lettres (good looking letters) up to *maqamats* and ante-Islamic poetry and semantics, rhetoric then logic and arithmetic with its different sections: inheritance then astronomy and astrology. Then *Mukhtassar Sheikh Khalil* and *Tuhfat al Hukkam* and hadith Chihab Addine and tafsir al Quran.

Mame Mor will finish his studies unchanged after five years. I hope you leave him with me until I finish training him and he will surprise you. I know that you Mbacké you have a lot of affection for your children but inchallah he will not exceed five years.

After that, you can buy him comments on the books he has studied and others so that he progresses further. However, the student if he has books during his studies will lose focus from his classes while the real knowledge is collected from the professors. The student has to learn from his professors until he has mastered the discipline and then he can continue with the comments. Usually, the one who takes directly from the books may not differentiate between true knowledge and errors. So, you see a lot of Mauritanians and St. Louisians who study a bit with professors and then start reading books and magazines and even sometimes produce writings and poems and think they are scholars even though they don't master any discipline.

The Testimony of Sheikh Muhammad Dème on Serigne Saliou

Sheikh Abdoul Ahad Ka, the grandson of Sheikh Moussa Ka, said that his teacher Sheikh Muhammad Dème was very surprised by the intelligence of Serigne Saliou and his faculty of memorization.

The master said, "I can see no one who could compete with these three in the gifts they have obtained from Allah: Serigne Saliou in intelligence and memorization, Sheikh Mustapha Sy in discernment (tamyiz), and Sheikh Maba Sy in the power of will."

Sheikh Muhammad Dème often testified about Serigne Saliou's high qualifications and his irreproachable morals, as well as his nobility of soul. He said: "I saw of him, during the whole period of study, only perfect ethics; and I never noticed any failure in his behavior, so that he never wore his sandals in my house."

During this period, Serigne Saliou was studying with his brother Serigne Abdelkader, and out of respect and reverence, he refused to live under the same roof, so they looked for a house close to that of Khadim Rassoul. It is his residence in Diourbel which is known to all mourides.

He memorized all the classics studied in schools and assemblies, so much so that, even being Khalif of the Mourides, he could recite most of them. But, most surprising of all, it was the number of Qasaids of Khadim Rassoul that he had memorized.

Sheikh Abdoul Ahad Diakhaté told us about Serigne Saliou in this reflection: "it seems, he said, that the level of studies has deteriorated at present because, in our time, we memorized the texts but also the glosses and commentaries. We were also interested in the history of the work and the stories about it, as well as the time of its composition, the context of its publication, and the debates around the work and its author."

Languages Spoken by the Sheikh

The languages and dialects that Serigne Saliou spoke were obviously Wolof and Arabic but also Pulaar and I think he also understood French. The late Serigne Élimane Diop informed me that one day he was with Serigne Saliou who was reading a medicine leaflet to explain the dosage to a talibé.

As for the Pulaar, he spoke fluently, as Serigne Sidy Mokhtar Ka, grandson of Serigne Samba Toucouleur Ka, reported to me that "Thierno Abdullahi Diallo Imam of Koumbal at Saloum near Kaolack on the road to Porokhane told him that Serigne Saliou passed through the region and asked for the Imam's house, then when he arrived, he introduced himself and said that he wanted to perform the prayer first. He did his ablutions and prayed, he got to know the Imam with whom he began a conversation in Pulaar, which he spoke as if it were his mother tongue. Then he said to the imam: "If you come to Tuba, I will introduce you to the Khalifa Serigne Fallou. But Allah wanted the Imam not to visit Touba during the Khalifat of Serigne Fallou, Serigne Abdoulahad, or Serigne Abdelkader but in the last years of the Khalifat of Serigne Saliou. When he was in front of Serigne Saliou, he declined his name as usual: Thierno Abdoullahi Diallo. Serigne Saliou said to him: "Didn't I tell you to come to Touba so that I can introduce you to Serigne Fallou? The surprised Imam said, "Yes, but Allah wanted me to come only now.

Serigne Saliou commissioned Serigne Meudou Diakhaté to take care of his host to whom he sent the best dishes. After a few days, he freed him by putting at his disposal a car loaded with all kinds of gifts from clothes and perfumes to food and provisions. The Imam said that he returned to his village in honor loaded with precious gifts.

Then he commented on this story by saying: the Wolof say that in the court no one is allowed to wear headgear outside of the judges. But I say no one has the right to wear a turban in front of Serigne Saliou.

Intellectual Curiosity and Erudition of Serigne Saliou

After completing his schooling, Serigne Saliou immersed himself in reading books on various disciplines of knowledge, from humanities and philosophy, to psychology and the history of civilizations, as well as geography and astronomy.

He was always looking for the most reliable sources in every subject and he spent a large part of his money on the acquisition of prestigious works; so Sheikh Abdul Ahad was concerned about his younger brother's lack of consideration for worldly matters and his constant quest for knowledge and learning.

Serigne Mboussobé Mbacké told us that Serigne Saliou had many Syrian and Lebanese friends who gave him newspapers and magazines from the Near East, so he was aware of what was happening in the Islamic world, from Turkey to the East.

Sheikh Mustafa Abdul Khadre informed us that "Serigne Saliou was perfectly aware of the events of the Islamic world and all intellectual and political currents, as well as studying the thought of the reformers of the "Nahdha" movement. He also read Zaki Najib and eventually memorized his doctoral thesis by rereading it. In our nightly discussions with him, he would recite whole pages of it to us."

His Interest in Arabic Literature and Civilization

Serigne Saliou was a fine scholar who had prodigious gifts for literature and poetry. Sheikh Habibou Diop reported from Serigne Saliou that he said that at first, he composed poems, but later he turned away from them. Perhaps his acts of devotion and his commitment to the education of aspirants, as well as his daily concern for the welfare of the population no longer gave him the time to devote himself to this vocation. However, he remained all his life a passionate lover of literature and linguistic subtleties. He had a great appreciation for the fine arts and savored poetry while encouraging his followers to compose beautiful poems.

We will mention later some of the great poets who came out of his schools.

As for prose, he excelled in it, as we will see, with the texts we could find in some of his correspondence with illustrious personalities of the country.

His Letter to Serigne Fallou (2nd Khalife of the Mourides)

O Sheikh and illustrious Khalife

After presenting respectful greetings worthy of your rank, we remind you of your promise to visit us this year.

However, we inform you that we intend to leave for Dakar to attend to urgent needs and we will reside there until the end of Rajab, then we will return to Mbour where we will await your instructions, by the will of Allah the Generous.

If you decide in any way, inform us by telephone call through your disciple Ibrahima Dieng with whom you are staying in Rufisque; I will return immediately to Mbour as soon as your order reaches me. Within the week I will be in Dakar; and from Monday 28th Rajab, I will be in Mbour if Allah wills it.

I beg you O Sheikh not to deprive me of your visit.

His Interest in the Four Schools of Jurisprudence (Fiqh)

Serigne Saliou was very well versed in Malekite jurisprudence, which he had studied in Mbackol with Serigne Mor Sasoum, the son of cadi Madiakhaté Kala; however, he was very interested in other schools.

Sheikh Ibrahima Mbacké, brother of Doctor Khadim Mbacké who studied with Serigne Moustapha Sy, companion of Serigne Saliou, told that after having studied passages from *Mounawwar al Soudour,* Serigne Saliou recommended him to improve his knowledge of jurisprudence according to the four schools of fiqh if possible; otherwise, he should improve his knowledge of Malekite fiqh by studying the principles (usul) and applications (furu').

His Interest in Philosophy and Theology

Serigne Saliou was well versed in philosophy and theology, dialectics and rhetoric as well. His knowledge of theology (ilm al-kalam) was perfect and he said that he could not find anyone outside himself and Serigne Saliou Touré to teach "Mahawib al Quddous."

His Knowledge of Sufi Epistemology

Serigne Saliou studied a lot of the works of the sufis, from the first generations to the last, and he had a predilection for Ghazali, Shar'ani, and Suyuti. He said that the time of Suyuti and Chara'ni was one of the most fruitful for *tasawwuf* but also for many Islamic sciences because it was also the time of Ibn Hajar Al Askalani, the emir of the hadith believers. Serigne Saliou said to his Tunisian disciple Abdallah Fahmi: "One of the most beneficial periods for Islamic knowledge was that of Suyuti and Chara'ni, and their peers."

Likewise, Serigne Saliou loved the illuminating tasawwuf like that of Jami and Firdausi and he loved the poets of divine love like Afif Eddine Tlemçani and Omar ibn al Faridh.

The Tunisian mouride Abdallah Fahmi told us that during his first interviews with Serigne Saliou, he gave him as Hadiya the *Diwan of Omar ibn Al Faridh* that he leafed through at length before saying: "Oh, the Sultan of lovers, long time I have not read it."

He was very fond of Sheikh Akbar Muhyiddin ibn Arabi, whom he considered the seal of the saints. In this sense, we report the words of our brother and fellow disciple Abdallah Fahmi, who told us: "I was talking with Serigne Saliou about the stations of the Awliyas and he explained to me that the highest station and supreme function was that of the Qutbaniya Odhma, then succeeded him by the Siddiqiya.

I asked him, "Who is the seal of the saints (khatimou al awliyas)?"

He answered: "Ibn Arabi al Hatimi."

I asked: "And Khadimou Rassoul, what would be his station or function?"

He replied, "The more you advance in knowledge, the more spiritual openings and revelations you will have in knowledge that you could not even imagine. Sheikhul Khadim cannot be confined to one station or function and no intelligence can embrace it. In truth, everyone will understand from the sheikh what his level of understanding will allow him to understand."

During the call to the Magal in 2002, Serigne Saliou expressly announced the status of Sheikh al Akbar Muhyiddin ibn Arabi, whom he described as Qutb Ghawth and Khatim al Awliya. In this verse there are obvious indications:

> *He was the seal of the saints by his adherence to the guidance of the seal of the prophets.*

Then, he quoted the words of *Futuhat Al Makkiya* where Ibn Arabi related the polemic between Sahl Ibn Abdallah al Tustari and Iblis. Sahl said, "I met Iblis and I recognized him; he recognized me and he knew that I recognized him. A polemic arose between us; he said and I said until the polemic swelled up. I was tired and so was he. I was perplexed and so was he; finally, he said, "O Sahl, Allah has said, "And my mercy embraces all things. It is unconditional and you know that I am one thing, but in *everything* there is generality and in *everything there is* indeterminacy. Therefore, his mercy embraces me too."

Sahl said, "I was mute and perplexed because he had found an argument in this verse that I had not thought of. I began to recite the verse until I came to: "I will record it for the pious who give zakat and believe in our signs. I was very happy because I thought my argument would be decisive. I said: "O cursed one, our Lord has conditioned his mercy with specific attitudes. He did say: "I will record it for the pious.

Satan smiled and said, "O Sahl, I did not think that your ignorance could reach this level. You do not know that conditioning is part of your nature, not of the absolute."

Sahl said, "I was mute and I was thinking and swallowing my saliva without finding an answer; I could no longer argue with him. He went his way and I went mine."

Sahl says, "So I thought I could take from this opponent a knowledge that is of no benefit to him according to the saying, 'meditate on the words independently of the speaker."

His Interest in The Islamic World and Reformist Movements

Serigne Saliou had subscribed to most of the newspapers and magazines that appeared in the Arab world during the 1930s and 1940s and followed with interest the intellectual and political reformist movements. He learned a lot about Turkey and the statements and sermons of Mustapha Kamal Attatutk (Ataturk) who dethroned Sultan Abdelhamid and proclaimed the republic. Indeed, Serigne Saliou was interested in the upheavals of the Muslim world and the fall of the Islamic Khalifat with the colonial consequences that followed was of concern to him.

He also followed the news of the Palestinian people and often wept with sorrow over the misfortunes of the Palestinians who were suffering the injustice of the Zionists. He constantly implored Allah to bring relief to the Palestinians and repel the misfortunes they were facing. He commanded the disciples in the *daaras* to constantly read invocative and evocative poems such as *wa kan haqqa alayna nasrou'l mouminin, wa la qad karrammna bani Adam, husnu 'l abrar al hudat an maka'id al fujjar al bughat.*

Serigne Saliou said: "Arabs are our brothers in faith and religion and Westerners are our brothers in humanity and world citizenship. Since we share faith, worship, culture and morals as well as destiny with the Arabs, and since we share the affairs of humanity with the Westerners, it is imperative to cooperate to live together in peace and well-being."

In the troubled times between Senegal and Mauritania; at first, he had asked to recite the Qasida of Ahla Badr, then, when the problems became more acute, he gave the order to recite morning and evening the three Qasaids mentioned until the tensions calm down, and that the two brotherly peoples are reconciled.

After gaining access to the Khalifat, he was constantly inquiring with those who were informed about geopolitical issues, as he was very careful with information; and he was wary of personal opinions on these matters so as not to be influenced.

He was precise even in these invocations because he did not like injustice, and he was constantly preoccupied with the affairs of the Muslims in accordance with the verse: "Believers are brethren, make concord among your brethren that you may be embraced in mercy." And also, per the Hadith: *He who does not concern himself with the affairs of Muslims is not one of them.*

Moreover, he analyzed the news from Afghanistan, the Near East, and the greater Maghreb with great caution. In this regard, we will relate a significant anecdote with his grandson Abdoul Khadre, who is our brother, when the latter asked him to pray for the Muslims of the Islamic Republic of Iran when the Bush administration was planning a military expedition. Serigne Saliou was sitting on his hammock and he stood up to listen attentively and asked about the current situation in the Middle East.

Abdoul Khadre began to give precise explanations of the aggressive policy of the United States and its Machiavellian plan for a Greater Middle East, carving up the Islamic nations through the policy of chaos whose artisan was Foreign Secretary Condoleezza Rice.

After listening to Abdul Khadre's explanations, Serigne Saliou said: "May Allah reward you for your noble enterprise because I listen to some news with a distracted ear without it affecting my judgment, while other news has a resonance and produces effects."

He prayed long and hard for the Muslims and it was found that the American geostrategic plans for Iran and the entire Middle East region all failed. We implore Allah to perfect the strategies of Muslim countries for the good of Islam and the world.

Serigne Saliou was only following in the footsteps of his illustrious father in the protection of Islam and Muslims, devoting to them invocative and evocative poems that have incredible effects in attracting good and repelling evil.

> *O Merciful One, grant to all creatures mercy that keeps evil away from all those who read your Quran.*

Lead the community of the chosen one away from all danger and embrace in your compassion all humans O you who bring them into existence.

O Master of the Throne O you who are beyond justice and punishment, embrace in your mercy all creatures without exception.

You have removed from my heart any inclination towards evil by the grace of the best of those who have served you.

Then he says:

Keep the community away from anything that is not worship and immunize them from evil.

Keep Satan away from them forever and protect them from the wickedness of humans.

He also says:

Protector, protect the community of the best prophet from those who do not believe in prophets.

Give them the imminent victory and tell them the good news.

Grant to the believers that which increases your love, O you whose graces are constantly increasing.

Enthrone Muslims so that they do not allow themselves to be dominated by your enemies and so that they do not take them as allies.

His Interest in Modern Currents of Thought and Geopolitics

Serigne Saliou lived through a period of great divisions between the two great geopolitical blocs that were fighting over the world's zones of influence.

- The Soviet bloc advocated communism in sociology and economy as well as in politics. This tendency is based on the materialist dialectic in its vision of history and humanity.
- The Western bloc was led by the United States and Japan as well as Western Europe. This tendency advocates individualism and liberalism as well as capitalism based on free trade. This bloc monopolized the economies of Third World countries for the benefit of the white man.

Serigne Saliou followed the course of events by analyzing these currents of thought that dominated the international scene and tried to attract to their camp thinkers and researchers as well as scholars from all sides.

In some of his remarks about Marxist-Leninist philosophy and the materialist dialectic that underlies the course of history, he said that it is a childish vision emanating from a good heart with sincere intentions to serve humanity; but that sincere intention is not enough to help humanity. The communists wasted their efforts in vain because they neglected the most fundamental axis to serve humanity, which is faith in God. For this reason, all their work is scattered like dust. Allah said, "Their work was opposed and reduced to dust." The people of Paradise will be in a better condition and in a more beautiful home.

As for his position on liberalism and capitalism, he said: "They know certain aspects of this low world and they are negligent towards the realities of the other world."

We will have the opportunity, later on, to return to these subjects when we deal with his interest in the different human civilizations.

But, above all, he had a constant concern for liberation and independence movements around the world, but especially in Africa.

He was particularly interested in what was happening in the French colonies in Algeria and sub-Saharan Africa, but he saw that independence should be gradual until the colonizers finished developing the colonized countries and the elites of these countries could run national affairs competently without the need for Westerners to run the economies and geopolitics.

Sheikh Hamza, son of Serigne Abdelahad, reported the words of Serigne Saliou in this sense: "African leaders who were claiming independence in their country in a very difficult period showed naivety and haste and a lack of discernment because they could let the settlers work their country and develop it before claiming their rights and eventually inevitably obtain independence."

His Interest in Knowledge and New Discoveries

Serigne Saliou was very fond of mathematics and physics, as well as astronomy, cosmology, but also geography, and geology.

He followed with interest new discoveries in these disciplines as they began to have a clear impact on the quality of human life. It has been reported that in his youth he was passionate about these disciplines and studied them so deeply that he could no longer find a person to talk to about them or deal with the intricacies.

Sheikh Anta Diop often visited Serigne Saliou in his home in Diourbel and the latter prepared tea and chatted with him. Later, when Sheikh Anta became one of the greatest scholars of our time, he continued to visit

Serigne Saliou and discuss with him various scientific and historical disciplines.

His Interest in Ethnology and Anthropology

Serigne Saliou was also very interested in the different human races whose sciences are ethnology and anthropology. He was interested in the history of human evolution as presented by Ibn Khaldun in the *Muqaddima*. He saw this as one of the greatest epiphanies of divine names and attributes for humans: "walk the earth and see how Allah began creation; then Allah will raise up future life. Allah is omnipotent over all things. He punishes whom He wills and takes in mercy whom He wills and the return will be to Him. You shall not be able to antagonize Him neither on earth nor in the heavens, and you have no protector nor support besides Him."

He had a clear vision and a proven experience of the human being, his psychology, and his nature. Allah had endowed him with a psychological acuity that sometimes seems to be the knowledge of the invisible. He said: "Notwithstanding the realities of esotericism and the invisible, my long experience in the education of children and human relationships has given me a knowledge of human nature and the depths of souls. Allah confirms this knowledge with the ayah of Sura al Hajr: "These are signs for those who are gratified with clear-sightedness." As well as the words of the Prophet (peace be upon him) (Salla Allah Alayhi wa Sallam): "Fear the vision of the believer; he sees by the light of Allah."

His Appreciation of Different Civilizations

He was interested in ancient civilizations, the history of religions as well as ancient and contemporary philosophy. Speaking of contemporary Western civilization and its technological and scientific supremacy, he said that they are abused by divine cunning and quoted the verse: "They know aspects of this lowly world while they ignore the realities of the other world."

Then he said: "Westerners are very skillful in the material affairs of this world and everything they don't know is of no importance to them. As for the affairs of the other world and of the invisible, the little they know is of no importance to them, since it has no immediate use. Then he recited this invocation: "Allah never makes the affairs of this world our only concern and do not make it the purpose of our knowledge."

The verse and the hadith quoted synthesize the intellectual and scientific orientation of Westerners, as well as their political and sociological orientation. Indeed, when they put all their aspiration into individual welfare, they are like animals; and when they reduce all knowledge to experimental and utilitarian purposes, they take this lowly world for a purpose.

As for the materialist tendency and empiricism which ignores spiritual and metaphysical realities as well as everything related to miracles and wonders, we will quote the words of Serigne Saliou reported by his grandson Serigne Khalil Mbacké: "Western man does not believe in miracles and wonders, unlike Muslims who believe in them without interfering with the course of their lives. Then he illustrated this with an anecdote in which the French settlers chose an intelligent and cunning man who mastered the Wolof language and placed him as a spy in the homes of Khadim Rassoul. This man came to see our sheikh and declared his submission to Islam while pledging his allegiance, but the sheikh recounted to him his entire conversation with the circle commander who had engineered the plan.

The man was frightened and returned to the commander to inform him, but the commander was not surprised and said, "Surely the sheikh has spies in our house who inform him as I have spies in his house."

The Western mentality is such that their pedagogical and epistemological system rejects extraordinary facts, which Serigne Saliou once explained: French settlers conceal all kinds of miracles and wonders when they deal with the Prophet Muhammad (sallallahu alayhi wa sallam) or Sheikhul Khadim, so that one of them, in recounting the episode of Suraqa *ibn Malik* when his horse sank in the sand, said: Suraqa backed down after seeing the warlike attitude of the Prophet who was experienced in military art. He could not conceive the miracle of this episode.

His Interest in Geography and Geopolitics

He was very passionate about geography and geopolitics and knew the realities of peoples and their specificities; perhaps he had studied this in the works of Muslim philosophers such as Farabi, Ibn Sina, and Ibn Rashid, as well as Ibn Khaldun. He often talked with travelers and visitors from far-away lands to get first-hand information to verify and correct his own.

Our brother Serigne Sheikh Walo Mbacké told us that when he returned from Morocco where he was studying, Serigne Saliou spoke to him about the Atlas Mountains and some very specialized geological data in which he was unaware, although he had stayed in Morocco for a long time.

The same happened with my brother Abdou Khadre Kébé after his return from Italy, the sheikh began to talk to him about geography, climate, customs, traditions, and European civilization. He also discussed with my brother Mourtada Kebe after his return from Italy the history of Venice and its powerful trading empire over the past centuries.

There are many such anecdotes and I can't mention them all, but a few examples are enough.

Serigne Habibou Diop reported to me that sometimes he would discuss with him at night subjects of precise and in-depth knowledge of the natural and human geography of the region of Senegal and West Africa. Sometimes it is precise information on the Atlantic Ocean and the region of Cape Verde and its natural characteristics. He also told him about the water tables which, from the Dakar region, cross the rich Diobass region, flow through the lands of Cayor and Baol, then Fouta, and flow outside the borders of Senegal, crossing vast areas of Mali to the Niger River.

His disciple Sheikh Bashir Khelcom reported to us: "I was once with the sheikh and Serigne Moustapha Abdul Khadre, talking to him about the natural and human geography of Turkey, then the sheikh said: The word Istanbul is a complex word of Astana and Blvd, and he said: It means the city of Astana.

We also learned that Sheikh Mustapha Abdoul Khadre, on his way to France, visited Serigne Saliou who advised him to visit the Louvre Museum and the Palace of Versailles. After his return, they discussed at length the history of France, the time of kings. Serigne Saliou told him: Europeans have changed nowadays and they have become atheists and libertines whereas before they were very religious.

His Interest in Scholarship

One day Serigne Saliou came to Ndiouroul where I was personally responsible for religious education, he sent a pupil named Samba Ka to borrow the book of Ghazali, The Revival of the Religious Sciences (Ihya Ulum Al-Din) from us while visitors from all social classes flocked in from everywhere. However, he found time to consult the books. Sheikh Abdou Samad Chouhaib often mentions Serigne Saliou's memorization skills: "I remember visiting him in the last days of his Khalifat and I found some of his relatives such as Serigne Moustapha Abdelkader. Serigne Saliou recited from memory some texts from Islamic science books and some poems from the period before Islam as well as *Maqamat al Hariri.*

Peregrinations and Travels

Travel is part of the customs of men of God. For this reason, the sufis traveled a lot in accordance with the Quranic injunctions that exhort us to contemplate the wonders and signs laid out by our Lord.

Our sheikh liked to experience various situations by himself and he traveled a lot in his youth, so much so that his uncle Serigne Hamza Diakhaté nicknamed him with his brother Abdoul Ahad "the travelers." When he would ask about them, he would say: "where are the travelers?"

Serigne Saliou moved around a lot and did not stay in place for long; he traveled all over the country and even in the subregion, in some African countries, and other areas. He knew Senegal perfectly and rubbed shoulders with all the ethnic groups of the country and all social strata.

Sheikh Abou Guèye recounted some of his travels through Senegal and elsewhere. He would have arrived in Ivory Coast and some anecdotes of his travels are pleasant. These travels were very useful to him in his erudition and the knowledge of different customs and uses of the people.

His Travels Through Senegal

He frequently visited the ancient capital, St. Louis, where he performed the two Eid prayers at the behest of Sheikh Muhammad al-Fadhil. During these visits, he was accompanied by Serigne El Hadj Bara Mbacké, the sixth Caliph who drove the car.

He used to travel to many Senegalese cities such as Thies and Dakar. He usually stayed in Dakar with my father Serigne Mor Kébé, Serigne Mor Fall, and Serigne Abdou Guèye "Mouride Sadikh."

As for the city of Thies, it had its own house that Sheikh Mouhamadou Mustapha, the first Caliph, gave him. In Thies, he had many followers including Ousmane Ngom, who was then governor of the city.

He frequently visited the villages of the great mouride figures in the Cayor region, especially the villages of the locality of Mbackol to strengthen kinship ties with them. Among the villages he visited were the village of Badar Guèye, Ndougoubène, the village of Serigne Alseye Ndiaye, and the village of Darou Same of Sheikh Massamba Diop Sam. He used to visit the town of Ndande, near Kébémer.

When He traveled, He was accompanied by groups of singers who sang the Qasaids (the poems of praise in homage to the Prophet PSL) upon his arrival. Concerning the Saloum region, he used to visit the main mouride chiefs, including Serigne Malick Bassine with whom he had a special relationship, so much so that he named his son, Serigne Saliou Sy, and entrusted him with it after the latter had memorized the Holy Quran, with two thoroughbred horses as a gift.

Among the regions he visited in the Saloum, there was the village of Affe Mourid at his friend the great Quranic master Serigne El-Hadj Willane in the locality of Kafrine. He also visited the blessed village of Porokhane. He often went to Kaolack to visit Sheikh Ibrahima Niasse with whom he had strong relations, sometimes accompanied by his nephew, Serigne Saliou Mbacké Ambassador.

Among those who accompanied him in all his travels was Serigne Bassirou Sarr. Serigne Saliou never ceased to be amazed by him. Serigne Makhtar Diakhaté told me this: Serigne Saliou said that if he gives so much consideration to Serigne Bassirou, it is because the latter was with him when he had nothing at all. At that time, his father who was a great mouride loved him very much. It was even for its namesake Serigne Bassirou Mbacké. The two rivaled in love towards him.

But he preferred to come to me while I was living in difficult conditions. In reality, I brought him almost nothing. On the contrary, I was the one who took advantage of him. For during our travels, if we ran out of fuel, he would go to his disciples to collect enough to buy fuel. Same thing if we ran out of food and so many other things. So, if I give him so much consideration, it is just as much of those things.

Among the people who accompanied him during his travels was a Mauritanian scholar called Serigne Amadou Nar, Serigne Moustapha Gaye and the father of Serigne Modou Gaye.

His Talibes and Dahiras

Serigne Saliou was much loved by all; Allah made the hearts of the people attracted to him. He had many talibés in all the big cities of Senegal. He had many Dahiras who took care of his different schools and *Daaras*.

The dahiras came from all over Senegal to celebrate the Grand Magal in his house in Touba. They brought all kinds of condiments and good food in this great festive season, especially the Dahira of Serigne Mor Kébé, who used to bring the big fish from Dakar for the preparation and distribution of meals in the house of the sheikh for the duration of the "Magal."

Later other dahiras were created by talibés to serve Serigne Saliou, among them the Kaolack Dahira led by Sheikh Bethio Thioune and Serigne Amadou Guèye, there were also Dahiras in Saint-Louis, Rufisque and other large cities in Senegal.

His Spiritual Evolution

In this chapter, we will discuss the spiritual education of the sufis, which is still the main concern of Mouridism, then we will discuss the spiritual dimension of our sheikh and the Gnostic aspect of his sufi experience, as well as his transcendental relationship with Allah.

The Sufi Environment

When Allah wants something, He predisposes it by providing justifications for it. Our Sheikh's good fortune had predisposed him to an exceptional environment both spiritually and in terms of knowledge. Serigne Saliou was born in a pure environment, where spirituality and love of Islam predominated to such an extent that everyone around him devoted their time and possessions to serving the religion. This clearly favored him in his sufi journey, especially since he benefited from a special initiation in the school of Serigne Hamza Diakhaté.

Serigne Mboussobé Mbacké revealed to us the degree of love and respect that Serigne Saliou had for Serigne Hamza Diakhaté: "Serigne Saliou loved Serigne Hamza Diakhaté deeply and he had a reverential respect for him because he considered him as his 'Sheikh' in the litanies (awrad) and in the secrets (asrar). He benefited enormously from his contribution especially since Khadimou Rassoul had initiated Serigne Hamza to many secrets by ordering him to initiate his sons whom he had entrusted to him.

Serigne Hamza Diakhaté was notoriously known as one of the greatest scholars and saints of the country. He was educated by Sheikh al-Khadim who made him an example in spiritual education (tarbiyya) and piety, as well as in detachment and holiness. Naturally, Sheikh Hamza passed on to his nephew all his qualities as he took care of him since his early childhood.

However, it is above all the innate aptitudes of Serigne Saliou that he inherited from his father that will favor him in his spiritual realization. Very early on, he showed his predilection for the spiritual exercises of the sufis, which gradually allowed the aspirant to climb the ascending ladder of the stations through spiritual will (himma) and divine service (Khidma) until full realization. In what follows, we will study the realities of *Tasawwuf* according to the masters of the discipline before presenting the experience of our Sheikh.

The Reality of *Tasawwuf* According to the Sufi Corporation

Imam Abul Kacem Junaid may Allah be pleased with him), known as the Master of the Corporation (Sheikh al Taifa), said in his definition of *Tasawwuf*: "It is purity in dealing with Allah, the basis of which is to turn away from this world, as Haritha had expressed it: my soul has turned away from this world and I have watched at night and I have been hungry and thirsty during the days."

Abu Abdullah Muhammad Ibn Khafif said: "Tasawwuf is the purification of hearts and the breaking of natural inclinations, the extinction of human desires and the mistrust of ego pretensions, but also the quest for the angelic virtues and the attachment to esoteric sciences while giving good advice to Muslims and following the Sunnah of the Prophet Muhammad (sallallahu alayhi wa sallam)."

Imam Junaid was asked about Tasawwuf and he replied, "It is a designation that summarizes ten provisions:

- to diminish earthly needs instead of being monopolized by them;
- Let the heart rest on Allah instead of resting on the means and causes;
- to love voluntary acts of obedience instead of wasting time unnecessarily;
- patience in life's difficulties instead of complaining and seeking the assistance of others;
- discernment in the goods that fail in our hands;
- make Allah our concern instead of anything else;
- be sincere in intent so as not to let bad suggestions contaminate our actions;
- to establish oneself in certainty when doubt arises;
- to settle down in Allah to flee from perplexity and anguish.

If one combines these ten characteristics one can claim the sufi name, otherwise it would be a usurpation of quality.

Shibli said: *The sufi is cut off from the world and is connected to Allah.* Thus, in the Quran Allah said to Moses: "I have fashioned you for Me." He had disconnected him from everything else. Then Allah said to him, "You will not see me."

Abu Ali Ruthabari used to say: "Tasawwuf is the fact of remaining in front of the door of the Beloved even if one is driven out of it." Then another time, he replied that *Tasawwuf* would be the delight of closeness after the bitterness of distance."

Abu Amur of Damascus used to say: "Tasawwuf is the non-perception of imperfections to contemplate perfection."

Sheikh Aboul Najib Abdelkader Suhrawardi said: "The first part of Tasawwuf is a science (ilm), the middle part is practice (a'mal) and the ultimate part is a gift (mawhiba). The science makes the subject known, while the practice helps to obtain the benefit; the gift, on the other hand, allows access to the finality. *Tasawwuf* followers fall into three categories: an aspiring student (murid talibé), a traveling initiate (mutawassit ta'ir), and a connected realized one (muntahi wasil). The aspirant (mouride) is subject to the methods (sahib waqt), the initiate (mutawassit) is in the spiritual state (sahib hal) and the realized is in the obvious (sahib yaqin).

He also said (may Allah be pleased with him): *The best thing for the sufis was the auditing of the breaths (add al anfas).*

The station of mouride is that of exercises (mujahadat) and trials (mukabadat), as well as difficulties and the fight against passions so that he can obtain the benefits of the path. The station of the initiate is that of facing dangers to reach the goal and to be sincere in his quest, but also to comply with the rules of propriety (adab) in the stations (maqamat) and, also, in the halts (munazalat). He is subject to hazards (talwin sahib) because he changes from one state to another and progresses continuously. The station of the realized is lucidity (sahw) and confirmation (thabat) because he has responded to the True Lord who summoned him while going beyond the stations to establish himself in confirmation (tamkin). He must no longer be subject to the hazards of the way (talwin). He is no longer sensitive to the reversals of the situation and he remains firm in poverty as well as in opulence, in providence as well as in deprivation, in proximity as well as in remoteness. Whether he is satiated or hungry, whether he sleeps or stays awake, he is no longer like the common man who worries about his fate, for he thinks only of his duties towards his neighbor and the rights that his Lord has over his person."

The science of *Tasawwuf is* said to be the result of right works and the fruit of immaculate spiritual states; therefore, "He who works in accordance with what he knows, Allah will teach him what he does not know."

Imam Cha'rani summarized in *tabaqat al kubra*: "Know, my brother, may Allah have mercy on you that the science of Tasawwuf is the science that springs from the hearts of the saints (awliyas) when they are illuminated by the Quran and the Sunnah, for he who puts their teachings into practice will animate in his heart science and virtues, secrets, and ineffable realities. Moreover, the scholars of the law obtain such things when they put into practice the laws they prescribe.

Tasawwuf is the substance of the believer's practice when he complies with the Shar'ia and provided that his works are free from vices and vanity."

Sheikhul Khadim explained this in his famous book *Massalik al Jinan*:

But in all certainty, the true sufi is a scientist who practices his science, with sincerity and consistency, until he becomes pure and free of all imperfections.

Concentrated on his Lord, the heart always in meditation, making no distinction between stones or silver pieces.

It must be like the earth on which all the garbage is thrown and which produces only good things.

It is trodden on by all kinds of humans, good or wretched, pious or sinners. It supports them all and provides for their needs.

It must also be like the rain clouds that water the greenery and shade indiscriminately.

The one who combines all these qualities is a sufi, otherwise, he is a suitor, perhaps in good faith.

Tasawwuf according to Sheikhul Khadim would be the progression (taraqqi) in the stations of spiritual perfection (maqam al Ihsan), walking in its degrees and dimensions to realize one's states and truths in the best conditions, when one unites beneficial knowledge (ilm nafi') and beneficent works (amal salih) as well as the agreed rules of decorum (adab mardhi').

Tasawwuf in the Life of Our Sheikh

Serigne Saliou was a true sufi because he combined beneficial knowledge and approved works, as well as the rules of decorum which are the principles of the way. He knew that the failure of those who could not reach the junction (wusul) was linked to their neglect of the principles (usul). He conformed to the teachings of his illustrious father who said in *Massalik al Jinan*:

"Knowledge and practice are two jewels that allow us to acquire the goods of this world and the beyond.

Thus, after completing his school curriculum, he began to practice in accordance with his science. His life was in line with the teachings of *Tasawwuf* by being totally oriented to Allah. As he walked along the path to pass through the different stages of the stations of Islam and Iman, he aspired to ascend in the degrees of Ihsan."

Tasawwuf is Practical

Serigne Saliou lived the *Tasawwuf*, according to the practical definition given by Imam Aboul Kacem Junaid above. His father Sheikhul Khadim had composed books on *Tasawwuf* such as *Massalik al Jinan* and others to emphasize the practice: it is not enough to study only the basic books on Tasawwuf to claim it; one must also apply its teachings.

Thus, Serigne Saliou experimented with the different stages that allow spiritual realization and reached the highest stations through assiduous and constraining efforts, at the limit of what a human being can endure.

Tasawwuf meant for Serigne Saliou the high spiritual will (ouluw al himma) as well as sincerity in the quest (sidq al irada); the total orientation towards Allah (tawajjah ila Allah bil kuliya) and the search for its proximity by acts of supererogatory as indicated by this Hadith Qudsi where the Prophet (sallallahu alayhi wa sallam) of Allah says: "Whoever fights one of my chosen ones (waliyou), I declare war on him, and my servant cannot approach Me better than I command him; and the closer he comes to Me by supererogatory acts, the more I love him; and when I love him, I become his hearing by which he hears, his sight by which he sees, his hand by which he acts, and his foot by which he moves. And if he asks me, I give it to him; if he calls me to his aid, I help him."

Since the path indicated by Allah is marked by obligations (faraids) and recommendations (sunan), and then by supererogatory works, we will mention some practices of Serigne Saliou by which he came closer to Allah so that those who are negligent like us may find guidance. As for the noble character (akhlaq) and the rules of propriety (adab), as well as the stations of evidence (maqamat al yaqin), we will explain them in the sixth chapter.

His Awrad (Litanies), Adhkar (Evocations) and Ahzab (Collection of Ayahs)

Serigne Saliou was assiduous in reading the Quran and practicing the litanies so that he was constantly in divine closeness through the mention (tadhakur) or mediation (tafakur) which he considered to be the food of the heart and the life of the spirit.

He was constant in the spiritual exercises and practiced morning and evening all the litanies and other activities that he had imposed on himself before becoming Khalif of the Mourides. He used to say: "I have never used a technique or a litany unless it was for the Face of Allah and I have never used a practice without persevering; nor have I ever forsaken a practice I have persevered on.

Serigne Omar Diakhaté son of Serigne Hamza Diakhaté informed me that when he was sometimes in the company of Serigne Saliou, the latter was so constant in the evocations (adhkar) that he forgot his guests during these exercises. Serigne Mboussobé confirmed this in an interview at his home in Daroul Alim al Khabir:

"Serigne Saliou used a lot of Wirds that he had taken from Serigne Hamza Diakhaté, in accordance with his father's will, especially during the illness that kept him bedridden for months in 1945. From then on, he did not have much time to devote to people until his ascension to the Khalifat. All of his time was devoted to spiritual exercises. His language was devoted to the evocation of Allah as Khadimou Rassoul mentioned in the qasida 'Huqqa al Buka': Their purpose was the evocation of the Absolute Master of Providence and not the speeches about Hind or Salma.

Serigne Saliou didn't like idle talk, let alone debates on politics, because he found time precious and didn't want to waste it on trivialities.

We remember that one day, Lamine Guèye came to see him in Khaban while the sheikh was in the fields. When the delegation arrived, Serigne Saliou began his prayer and absorbed himself for a long time until the delegation became impatient from waiting and left the place. Serigne Saliou did not stop his prayers until they left the area."

The Practice of the Ma'khouz Wird

Serigne Saliou received the authorization of the *wird ma'khouz* from many illustrious personalities who had taken it directly from Sheikhul Khadim, such as Serigne Hamza Diakhaté, Sheikh Mbacké Bousso, and others.

Serigne Sheikh Mbacké son of Serigne Mbacké Fajama told us that, "Serigne Saliou told us that he had taken the Wird from many people, including Serigne Hamza Diakhaté and Sheikh Mbacké Bousso, through Serigne Abdoulkadre Mbacké." He added: "I also heard this version from Sheikh Abdoul Khadre himself who said that Sheikh Mbacké Bousso expressed his astonishment at the elevation of the spiritual will of Serigne Saliou."

Then, he added that Serigne Saliou wanted to have Mame Thierno Brahim's authorization, but when he was about to go to see him for that, he learned of his death. May Allah be pleased with him and sanctify his soul.

Serigne Sheikh Fajam also said that Serigne Saliou wanted to take the Tijane wird from Sheikh Aliou Seck Wanar because the latter had the authorization directly from Khadimou Rassoul. However, we do not know whether Serigne Saliou had taken it or not.

The Wird Shadhili

Serigne Saliou wanted to benefit from the baraka of everything related to Khadimou Rassoul, that's why he took Wirds even from people the age of his children, out of respect and love for Sheikhul Khadim. From this perspective, we can understand what his grandson Serigne Sheikh Walo tells us: "Serigne Mbacké Daba Sarr told me that Serigne Saliou had taken from him the permission to use the Wird Shadhili because he just wanted to benefit from the blessing (baraka) of this chain of transmission which would go up to Sheikhul Khadim by his brother Mame Thierno Ibrahim (Ibra Faty Mbacké)."

Serigne Habibou Diop told me: "At the end of the seventies, I was studying in Touba, and I lived in the house of the Sheikh. I remember staying with him for a whole night, and he told me about tasawwuf and the history of the sufi Tariqas, their origins, their evolution, their secrets, their litanies, and how they entered Mauritania and our West African region. Then he spoke at length about the Qadiriyya, which was the first to arrive in Senegal, then he spoke about the Shadhiliyya, its secrets, and origins, then the Tijaniyya and its branches and conditions, etc. He also spoke about the Tijaniyya and its branches and conditions. We continued the conversation until we heard the voice of the muezzin."

Prayers and Supplementary Works

Serigne Saliou was particularly keen to perform the prayers on time, and one indication of this was his good listening to the muezzin. When he heard the call to prayer, he would interrupt his speech with the people even if he was with the minister or the president. One day President Abdou Diouf had come with his delegation including Ousmane Tanor Dieng who was explaining an important issue, when the muezzin began the call to prayer, then Serigne Saliou began to listen, Tanor Dieng, realizing this, was forced to cut his speech until the muezzin finished his call to prayer.

Serigne Saliou had a constant preoccupation with the prayer times and he observed his watch at every moment of prayer while ensuring its accuracy. His driver, Gora Dièye, scrupulously watched over the accuracy of the schedules and repaired the watches whenever necessary.

In the same way, Serigne Saliou taught his relatives how to observe the sun to know the prayer times with precision. Some of his relatives such as Serigne Fallou Seck and Serigne Habibou son of Serigne Muhammad Lamine Diop Dagana informed us that our sheikh told them: "To know precisely the times of prayers, simply observe the solar disc at sunrise and sunset; you take note then you divide the hours and minutes in half to get the median time, then you add thirty minutes as a precaution to be able to make the call of the Dhuhr prayer. Three hours later, you have the schedule of Asr. As for the Maghrib schedule, you only have to observe bedtime, and then you add four minutes as a precaution. For the Ishâ prayer, it will be exactly seventy-five minutes afterward. For the Fajr, you must also add seventy-five minutes to get up."

Serigne Saliou always prayed in groups; he led the prayers in the mosque of his house. It was only when he had reached a very advanced age that he could no longer lead the group prayer. He was well known for his attachment to prayers and supererogatory works. He built a mosque in each of his homes or schools, which was usually located in the entrance area so that visitors could pray.

When he entered the mosque, he would perform the optional prayers and then lead the obligatory prayer; then he would stay to pray the recommended prayers. After the dhuhr prayer, he would stay a long time to pray the tasbih prayer.

Tasbih Prayer

This optional prayer was very popular with Serigne Saliou who performed it every day. It was part of his daily litanies to the point that everyone knew his attachment to the tasbih prayer.

Serigne Sheikh Mbacké, son of Serigne Mbacké Fajam, told us that when he asked Serigne Saliou for clarification on his attachment to this prayer, the latter answered: "I hope to obtain through it what everyone is seeking: forgiveness and freedom from sin."

The hadith on the tasbih prayer as mentioned by Ibn Abbas is quoted: "The Prophet (sallallahu alayhi wa sallam) said to his uncle Abbas ibn Abdel Muttalib: O Abbas, O uncle, I give you, I give you, I favor you, I teach you ten acts, if you perform them, Allah will forgive you all your sins past and future, old and new, voluntary or involuntary, major or minor, apparent or occult.

Here are the ten acts: do four rakaat, reciting in each one the Fâtiha and a sura. When you finish the first rakaat, you say while standing: Subhana Allah, Alhamdulillah, la ilaha illa Allah, Allahu Akbar (Fifteen times), then you genuflect (ruku') and say them (Ten times) then you raise your head after genuflecting and say them again (Ten times) then you prostrate (sujud) and say them again (Ten times) then you raise the head of the sujud and say them again (Ten times) then you do the second sujud and say them again (Ten times) then you raise the head of the sujud and say them again

(Ten times). That makes seventy-five times in each rakaat for a total of four rakaat.

If you can do this every day once, do it; if you can't, do it every week; if you can't do it every month, and if you can't do it every year, do it at least once in your life."

The Night Watch

Serigne Saliou liked to get close to Allah through all kinds of worship and good deeds; he loved the night vigil like all illustrious saints and scholars.

Serigne Mboussobé Mbacké informed us about the night vigils and adoration of the sheikh during these precious moments: "all night long, he prayed or recited the Quran or the Qasaids of Khadimou Rassoul and he did not have a quiet room or a pleasant bed to rest in. His bed was rough, and the one he inherited from his father was only for blessing (tabarrok). He never slept in it and did not even sit on it."

The scholar Ahmadou Dame Touré, author of the book *Zad al Muslim* (The Provisions of the Muslim) who taught in the schools of Serigne Saliou and who was a close relative, said that the night vigil was a youthful habit of our sheikh who kept watch until dawn.

In an interview with *Al Azhar Touba,* he said: "I was with him in his house in Mbour and he stayed up all night. However, the house was full of insects and I could not sleep a wink, so I was watching him when he started with the Sura *al Baqara*. I thought he was going to do some rakaat and rest, but he finished the sura and continued with Sura *al Imran and* those after that until Sura *al Kahf.* In the second rakaat, he starts with Sura *Mariam* and finishes the whole Quran.

He started again from the beginning until "their bodies deserted the beds" and finished the sura; then he genuflected; then prostrated and finished with the "sallam."

When he finished, dawn had risen and Serigne Saliou prayed and then led the Subh prayer. I thought he was going to rest but I was surprised to see him sitting down to receive visitors. I told myself that this was superhuman because he showed no sign of fatigue."

Serigne Saliou and the Quran

He was very assiduous in the practice of litanies (awrad) and evocations like the great saints, but his predilection was the Quran and the Qasaids of Khadimou Rassoul which are prayers over the Prophet Muhammad (sallallahu alayhi wa sallam) and the eulogies (amadah) which were his priority, day and night.

Serigne Abdoul Ahad Diakhaté told us that he thought that the daily wird of Serigne Saliou was the full reading of the Quran. But even when he finished the Holy Book, he would read it again up to the ayah of the pedestal (Ayat al Kursi).

We also noticed that at each commemoration of the Grand Magal of Touba, he completed the entire Quran after Asr, despite the visitors.

Serigne Tayib Diakhaté also told us that Serigne Saliou completed the entire reading of the Quran on Magal Day, usually with the dhuhr prayer, and then continued with *Nourou Daarayni*.

As for the wird from the Quran, he told us that he did not know exactly but that in any case, Serigne Saliou recited a large part of the Book every day. According to Tayib Diakhaté, when Serigne Saliou was in his particular spiritual state, he would complete the entire Quran and start over; this happened occasionally, but generally, he would recite parts of the Quran.

Serigne Saliou loved the Quran like his illustrious father, from whom he inherited this legacy. One day, two children from his school came to present him with their copy of the Quran they had written, according to the custom that after memorization, a copy of the Book must be written from memory.

The Sheikh, very satisfied, said, "If I could return to your age, I would spend all my time studying and teaching the Quran."

He was told, "But you have spent your whole life doing this, founding schools, and teaching the Quran and science." He said, "Then I thank Allah for that."

Serigne Habibou Diop said that Serigne Saliou told him: "If I could regain my youth, I would use all my time to study and teach the Quran. Serigne Khalil Mbacké also said the same thing.

Serigne Habibou Diop added: "I, therefore, understood from this that he wanted to exhort me to exalt my spiritual will "Himma" and increase more and more my love and ardor in the service of the Book of God, the Almighty. For me, such a statement on his part could not mean anything else because he spent his whole life serving the Quran and personifying its values and spreading its knowledge."

Serigne Khalil Mbacké also told me the same anecdote, based on Serigne Moustapha Diaw (may God, the Almighty, have mercy on him) who told him the following: "One day the sheikh was angry with me and he told me: you have upset the educational system in my schools because you give too much priority to agricultural work and services, to the detriment of Quranic education.

So, I said to him: O Sheikh, you can now find in your libraries more than a hundred copies of the Holy Quran made by students who learned in your schools, while this has not been granted to any other son of Khadimou Rassoul. Allah has dedicated this blessing to you.

His state went from anger to joy and he thanked Allah, the Almighty, and spoke at length about praise and thanksgiving.

Serigne Bachir Khelcom reported that Serigne Mahamoudan Bousso who was teaching the Quran at Serigne Chuhaibou's house, while talking with Serigne Saliou about the teaching of the Quran, told him: "There are young people in your school who have learned the Quran and who can teach it for me so that I can take care of the teaching of religious sciences."

Serigne Saliou said to him: "One should not think about this because the teacher of the Quran has entered the house of Allah and is under His protection; as for the one who teaches religious sciences, he is outside the room and he can only describe theoretically what he knows about it, without having had to contemplate it."

This means that the teachers of the Quran are the family of Allah (ahl Allah). They are intimately close to its Omnipresence and are bathed in its lights, while the teachers of science are on the outside and can only teach the rules and prescriptions, according to their theoretical knowledge of Lordship.

He loved the Holy Quran so much and was deeply touched by its recitation, such that when he heard the voice of the reciter, he could neither speak nor do anything but think about the meaning of God's words.

Sometimes, when recitation tapes were put on the speakers of the mosque in Tuba, it attracted his full attention, to the point that his energy and thought were directed towards the Quran, so that he could not practice any of his daily activities because of the intensity of his concentration on the words of Almighty God. Sometimes he would withdraw to the inner rooms of the house so that he could continue his daily tasks.

His Attachment to the Qasaids of Khadimou Rassoul

Since his childhood, Serigne Saliou was attached to his father's Qasaids, which are prayers over the Prophet Muhammad (sallallahu alayhi wa sallam) and eulogies (salawat wa amdah nabawiya); so much so that when he was in Daroul Alim (Ndam), he liked to listen to Serigne Mouhib Guèye who sang the Qasaids with a pleasant voice.

When he was in Diourbel after the call to God of his father, he had Serigne Moustapha Sy come to him and sing the Qasaids for him with a melodious voice. Mbacké Diakhaté remained amazed and said: "If Khadimou Rassoul was still with us and heard this voice, he would have been very happy."

Serigne Mboussobé Mbacké informed me that Serigne Saliou had memorized many of his father's Qasaids; that he did not know exactly how many but that he knew he recited many of them during the night, especially between Fajr and Subh.

There is especially the Qasida *Nourou Daarayni* which he recited daily like a Wird and he asked someone to write it for him.

Serigne Mountakha Bashir the present Khalif of the Mourides (may Allah grant him long life) informed us that Serigne Saliou had asked him to recite this Qasida for him daily. He has been doing this for years; but now, with his advanced age, he used to recite it for him weekly.

Serigne Sheikh, son of Sheikh Mbacké Fajam, told us that he accompanied Serigne Saliou to Imam Serigne Bousso, to whom he asked to write some Qasaids while showing the style of writing he wanted.

Serigne Bousso told him: "I understand why you want this style; it's because it was Khadimou Rassoul's favorite style. The son resembles the father as the cub resembles the lion."

Serigne Sheikh Saliou also said, "Serigne Saliou had many Qasaids written in the hand of Serigne Hassan Bousso, son of Sheikh Mbacké Bousso; he joked that you don't have the level to see such Qasaids yet."

His attachment to the Qasaids was such that he began to listen to their chanting in the early evening until late at night with circles of singers taking turns, especially when he was visiting his schools.

Sheikh Abdul Ahad Diakhaté said: "Serigne Saliou's sleep was very light, generally from two to four in the morning. Then he would wake up for night prayers and stop on the tasbih prayer during this time as well as other supplementary prayers."

We remember the time when he woke up and asked for the Qasida in the acrostic of *Rabbi ishrah li sadri* and *Rabbil wara lakal mahamidou fasalli*. When we brought them back, he recited them and told us to recite them consistently while formulating prayers for him and ourselves.

Since that day, we used to recite them in front of him every morning during breakfast. Serigne Saliou loved reading Qasaids at night.

Sheikh Abdul Ahad Diakhaté told us that one night he was with our Sheikh who was sleeping on a hammock when, around three o'clock in the morning, he woke up suddenly and prostrated himself for a long time on the floor; then he stood up and glorified Allah abundantly before saying: "I thank Allah for having given me the gift of mercy and pity towards His creatures for whom I want nothing but good."

Many had heard Serigne Saliou say similar words during a sermon, the content of which was: "Glory be to Allah who has made no one more merciful and merciful than I am for his creatures, to whom I wish nothing but good."

This can only indicate the station of our sheikh with Allah and his Muhammadian heritage and his status of the Qutbaniya *Odhma* [36] which allows the bestowal of mercy on creatures according to the Quranic ayah:

"You have been sent only pure mercy for the worlds" and in the ayah: "There has come to you a messenger who is part of you, in honor with Allah in order to relieve you and who will take care of you because he is merciful and affectionate towards the believers."

Serigne Abdoul Ahad Diakhaté says that Serigne Saliou, during that night, asked him to look for the Qasida in acrostic of *Madhoul Nabi al Moustafa al Maqboul:* "When I brought him back, he reads it in an incredible spiritual state that disturbed me to the point that I felt a lot of pity for him. In the end, I went away because I couldn't resist any longer and started to cry."

Serigne Abdoul Ahad Diakhaté also recounted: "I remember one evening, I recited before him the Qasida in the acrostic of the Quranic ayah "Inna Allaha ichtara minal mou'minin anfusahum" which begins with *In'qadal bay'u bima dalla ala ridha ba'in wa muchtari al'a* (The pact was sealed by that which ensures the approval of the seller and the buyer exalted be it).

---

[36] Qutbaniya Al Uzma is an Arabic word which denotes the highest degree and station in sufi evolution and the meaning is the Supreme Pole of Light and Sainthood

When I came to the verse that said: *wassalat li dunia'l masaliha wa bil masalihi u'inu saliha (*the world has bestowed upon me what it contains of blessings, and by these blessings, I assist salah), he said to me: "O Abdul Ahad, I do not consider this passage to concern me but I wish to be worthy of the secret of this verse."

I replied, "But it is a cloak of light that Khadimou Rassoul made you wear; he sewed it to measure and made you wear it elsewhere in the Qasida Nourou Daarayni: *wal taj'al li dunia al masaliha qa'idatan abdan khadiman saliha* (May the world grant me the blessings by leading me a slave servant salah)."

"It's a good fit, wear it, you're worthy of it. It is for you the secret of these verses." Serigne Saliou says aloud, in a significant spiritual state: "I accept and agree." He then got up and went back to his room.

His Days

Serigne Saliou's days were devoted to the worship and service of the mourides, to the point that he forgot himself, given the large number of daily visitors that he received. He was often so tired that he could no longer enjoy the visits; the sight of a lion was then more pleasant to him than that of a visitor.

One day while he was in this particular state, he isolated himself to regain strength when one of his grandsons found him enjoying a cup of coffee. The child innocently said to him, "You're here when large crowds are waiting for you outside?"

Our sheikh was very sensitive to the child's words and promptly got up to receive the visitors. This anecdote demonstrates his humility and willingness to take the very advice of a child; like perfect masters, he did not look at appearances, but scanned hearts, knowing that truth can come out even from the mouth of a child.

His Program of The Day

He usually began his days with the litanies (awrad) and absorbed himself in the zikr from morning prayer until breakfast, when he received his students to check their needs. Sometimes there were visitors, but generally, these times were devoted to the students. The zikr would stay until 10:00 a.m. and then the doors would be opened for visitors.

The day was devoted to the visits of the *Dahiras* and individuals seeking baraka, as well as the needy. Sometimes, these were opportunities to settle disputes or needs so that all could find the necessary comfort and humanitarian or spiritual help. Then, from Asr, he returned to his litanies to the Maghrib.

His Night Program

In the evenings, he listened to the Qasaids, prayers over the Prophet Muhammad (sallallahu alayhi wa sallam), and eulogies in the choirs that sang after the maghrib or after the Ishâ. Sometimes, some of Khadimou Rassoul's family members came in the evening, and the sheikh received them affectionately.

The singing continued until dinner, which was usually served around midnight. Meals were distributed to guests and students as well as to the family, and some guests were provided with the Sheikh's dishes for baraka. After that, he would release everyone and stay with the people of his household to give instructions.

Serigne Abdoul Ahad Diakhaté informed me that the sheikh had no specific place to sleep; he spent the night doing worship, checking the needs of the students, or talking to them about religion, the Prophet Muhammad (sallallahu alayhi wa sallam) or Khadimou Rassoul. He only slept for a few hours, between two and three hours when he was tired and could no longer stay awake. But at four o'clock he would wake up, pray and recite the Quran or litanies.

In the last years of his life, he prayed the tasbih prayer at night, whereas at first, he did it during the day.

His States of Jamal and Jalal

Serigne Mboussobé Mbacké informed me that Serigne Saliou was living in the states of Jalal (majesty) where only his Lord could contain him. The Prophet Muhammad, in mentioning these states, said: "I have moments with Allah where I cannot be contained; neither a close angel nor a sent prophet."

Sometimes he was in such a state when a visitor came with gifts, while the sheikh was absorbed by his Lord and, noticing nothing around him, he took his prayer mat and settled down in the distance under the sun. Then he would tell the doorman to bring everyone out so that he could be alone with his Lord.

When some visitors insisted on waiting, he would come to them after he was out of these states and apologize so as not to offend them, and then order them to be honored with meals and marks of consideration.

Serigne Mboussobé Mbacké told us that he had accompanied Serigne Saliou since his youth and that he had not noticed any change in his practices, habits, or character. It is only in the physical aspect that there has been a change due to age. Old age has changed him in appearance but his character and qualities have remained the same, as well as his wisdom and knowledge.

Tasawwuf was for Serigne Saliou a means to climb the ladder of the stations of evidence; to obtain also the approval of Allah and his nearness by trying to have the characteristics of the resolute envoys and those of the truthful as well as the martyrs and benefactors.

CHAPTER V - HIS VIRTUOUS CHARACTER

In this chapter, we will discuss the implications of spirituality related to ones way of life, character, and relationship with others.

We have spoken in the previous chapter about his journey and experience in spiritual education and also about his vertical relationship with the Divine, and now we should speak about the effect of this spiritual experience on his behavior, morality, daily life, and horizontal relationships with human beings, based on the sufi saying: "Sufism is based on morality." Whoever is superior to you in morality is better than you in sufism.

The Place of Virtues in Sufism

Since *Tasawwuf* is conceived as a set of virtues (akhlaq), the one with the most remarkable virtues is considered the best sufi.

Aboul Hussain Ahmad ibn Muhammad al Nouri said: "Tasawwuf is neither formalism nor science but rather virtues."

In truth, Tasawwuf would be the realization and confirmation of characteristics proper to prophets, especially those gifted with resolution. This made the master of the corporation Aboul Kacem Junaid say: "The building of Tasawwuf is built on the characteristics of eight prophets (peace and salvation are upon them):

- the prodigality (sakha) of Abraham;
- the satisfaction of Isaac;
- the patience of Job;
- the subtlety of Zachariah;
- the sobriety of John the Baptist;
- the wearing of the woolen frock of Moses;

- the peregrination (travels) of Jesus;
- the destitution of Muhammad is last (salvation and peace be upon them all)."

This was indicated by Sheikh Muhyiddin Ibn Arabi in his work Al Futuhat al Mekkiya: The people of the way said: "Sufism is based on morality (moral character). Whoever is superior to you in morality, is better than you in sufism."

Aisha, the mother of the believers, was asked about the virtues of the Messenger of God (sallallahu alayhi wa sallam). She replied that his morality was the Quran.

Allah praised him in the Quran for his morality and he said, "And you are indeed of immense morality (eminent standard of character).

It is an essential condition for a sufi to be probing and gifted with wisdom, for otherwise, one cannot claim this title. It is a whole art of wisdom and morals, and it requires perfect knowledge, a preponderant spirit, presence, and strong self-control so as not to be governed by personal passions or goals.

Whoever tends to this station must have the Quran as his guide. They must integrate what Allah has bestowed on them as qualities to qualify them by those attributes. The sufi must act in the same way that his Lord would have acted with creatures. Sufism is as simple as that.

The sufi does not make provisions for himself by deviating from the rules established by his Lord, for whoever does so will be with the losers." His works will be in vain when he thought he was doing something useful. (Al Kahf 18:105).

Allah said about the Best Messenger: "In fact, it is by Allah's mercy that you are soft with them; for if your heart was hard, they would have left you. Forgive them, grant them forgiveness while being magnanimous and consult them." (Al Umran: 159).

Allah said, "You were sent only as a pure mercy for the worlds. (Al Anbiya: 107).

Allah has said: "A Prophet has been sent to you who is venerable to your Lord and considerate to relieve you, and who is loving and kind to the believers." (Tawba: 128)

The Prophet Muhammad (sallallahu alayhi wa sallam) was a perfect example for mankind by his noble character and virtues. Allah testified: "Truly, you are of such a noble soul. (al Qalam 4). Allah also said: "You have in the Prophet the best example for those who hope for Allah on the ultimate day and mention their Lord constantly." (al Ahzab 21).

The Prophet (sallallahu alayhi wa sallam) said: Truly I have been sent to perfect the noble traits of character.

This human perfection was recognized by supporters and opponents alike. The great German sage and poet Goethe said: "I have sought in history an example of perfection for mankind and it is in the Arab Prophet Muhammad that I have found it."

The Prophetic Heritage

Religious scholars and saints are distinguished by their participation in the prophetic heritage that includes virtues and qualities. Sheikh al-Khadim was granted the largest share because he inherited secrets and lights, as well as character traits (Akhlaq) and spiritual states (Ahwal), as Sheikh Muhammad Bashir said in *Minan al-Baqi*: "He would be the total heir of the Muhammadin inheritance, and he would be among those of whom the Prophet (sallallahu alayhi wa sallam) said: (The scholars of my community are like the prophets of the sons of Israel)."

Thus, he bequeathed them in turn to his virtuous sons. Some among them inherited states, some inherited science, some inherited beauty (Jamal), and some inherited majesty (Jalal).

Thus, human virtues were the prophetic legacy shared by the sons of Khadimou Rassoul who assumed the esoteric heritage for the good of humanity.

Abu Huraira reported from the Prophet Muhammad (sallallahu alayhi wa sallam) that he said, "My example among the earlier prophets is like that of a man who built a beautiful building, completed it without laying a stone in the corner. Humans would come around the building to admire the work. But they would ask, "Why don't you fill in this space?"

Prophet Muhammad replied, "I am the cornerstone and I am the seal of prophecy."

Muhammadian heirs are the perfect heirs in the esoteric domain, but they are also in the exoteric domain. They have inherited his virtues, his values, his physical and moral characteristics (may God be pleased with them all).

Commenting on the verse of Khadimou Rassoul: "Through the service of the Book and the hadith my inheritance is perpetuated and not through gold and silver." Serigne Bashir Mbacké said: This shows that the gold offered to him was neither sought nor hoarded, for if he had hoarded it, he would have inherited it. The use of the verb "to perpetuate oneself" reveals his great respect for the Law. Indeed, if, instead of this verb, he had used the verb "to consist", he would have come up against the formal Law. By using the verb "to perpetuate oneself", he wanted to indicate that his true treasure remained a heart still practicing zikr and a language still expressing gratitude to God and that pious works were his only riches.

The Prophet (sallallahu alayhi wa sallam) said: "We Prophets are not inherited." Another version adds: "...in property, but we inherit our science."

The ulemas, the only heirs of the Prophets, inherited only their science. The true heir is the one who inherited this science received from the Prophets. By science, we mean the knowledge emanating from the Book and the Sunnah. If it is true that one has inherited the goods left by the Sheikh, it is equally true that one will inherit his spiritual legacy insofar as, following his directives, one serves the Master, our beloved Prophet, sincerely and draws from his abundant and clear source which gushes forth from the light of the Lord of Existence. Khadimou Rassoul says in this respect:

"I am honored because I am aware of its honor and because I am watered from its clearest source.

"My Lord, out of consideration for him, shortened my journey, and after ambiguity, the best course of action became clear to me."

"I shortened the path of the People while praising him, who satisfied my needs easily and abundantly."

The Virtuous Character Traits of the Heirs

The heirs on the esoteric plane were also heirs on the exoteric plane because they shared the qualities and virtues of the one they inherited. As for Serigne Saliou Mbacké, he received the lion's share of this spiritual inheritance because, following the example of his illustrious father, he was endowed with great nobility of soul and courage.

His exceptional qualities made him a perfect example, whose works are as eloquent as his reverential and referential behavior. He was generous and selfless, pious and wise; his whole life was an embodiment of Quranic virtues and prophetic postures. He was very caring for humans, especially for children; he was very charitable to the needy.

Serigne Saliou put into practice all Quranic teachings, to the point that all his behavior naturally reflected the Quran. He was the image of the Prophet Muhammad (sallallahu alayhi wa sallam) whose Aisha (salvation be upon her) said: "His character, was the Quran."

His sufi journey had deeply marked his personality; it became so translucent that it was a reflection of his pure and immaculate soul that deciphered the hearts and consciences of his interlocutors.

The Importance of Repentance (Tawba) For Serigne Saliou

Repentance is one of the most important characteristics of Serigne Saliou, it is a station of evidence (maqamat al yaqin) that the Quran has magnified by praising those who possessed this characteristic. It is in fact, returning to Allah after sinning or committing a crime, deviation, or even distraction.

Repentance has conditions and realities, and degrees, the highest of which is, according to Sheikh Abu Abdullah Harawi al Ansari, author of *Manazil al Sa'irin*: "Repentance of all that is not Allah, then awareness of the cause of repentance, and finally repentance of the cause of repentance."

Khadim Rassoul explained in *Mounawwar al Soudour* the degrees of repentance:

Seven degrees of repentance have been identified in repentance

The repentance of the unbeliever who repents from unbelief by the empowerment of his Lord who guides him to the true religion

The repentance of the sincere believer (mukhliss) who repents of deadly sins

The repentance of the righteous (oudul) who repent of minor sins

The repentance of the devotee (abid) gracious of any false step in the way

The repentance of the itinerant (salik) of the vices of the heart and temptations

The repentance of the scrupulous believer (wara') of all that is suspicious

The contemplative's repentance of any distraction of the heart that may be blameworthy

Seek wisdom and be quick to repent before the door of repentance is closed.

The Sense of Repentance in Serigne Saliou's Work

In truth, repentance is but a translation of nostalgia for the return to the principle from which mankind emanates according to the verse: "We are Allah's and to Him, we return."

When man rises above his animality and his heart is purified from the effects of passion and the hardening and darkening [37] of the soul as well as from the temptations of the phenomenal world, he will feel nostalgia for his origin from which he emerged. The great sufi poet Jaleleddine Rumi expressed this in the parable of the flute:

Listen to the lament of the sad flute that became a warning siren for humans

If my heart could thunder because of the separation, I would propagate the secret of nostalgia in the universe.

This world takes us away from our principle, Spirit echoes my lament

I met people everywhere, some were sad and some were happy.

They took me as a close friend in appearance while my secret was hidden from them.

---

[37] The word scoria was used which is a highly vesicular, dark-colored volcanic rock; scoria is a hard and dark volcanic rock.

The hidden secret was in the lament while the light remained in the embryonic state.

There is no veil between body and mind and by my power, I come out of my envelope.

The breath of the flute is fire and not air and he who is not touched by fire will not know permanence.

Flames of love emanate from the reed and from the flame of love comes annihilation.

Humans have become companions for the lover while in his depths the secret becomes a horn.

Whoever sees the poison and the antidote in the flute is a lover or a madman.

In the tales of the lost valleys of the desert Kais Layla sang this madness

Who else but the madman can know our secret that the language pronounces only intimately to our hearing?

If the flute did not pronounce this lament (ah), the humans would not be and the fruits would not be either.

The cycle of days is full of sadness and shares with us the nostalgia for our homeland.

Those times are over, don't be afraid, you are the only refuge.

The heart of the aspirant is thus in repentance because he perceives the call of the Merciful Lord who calls him above the heavens and the earth: "O my servant, come, you are the beloved, the aspirant, the aspirant. I have created everything for you and I have subjected everything on earth and in heaven to you, but I have created you for me; leave everything and come to Me."

This call crosses the heavens and penetrates the heart of the aspirant who can no longer find rest until he responds with sincere repentance, to progress fully to Allah and reach perfection.

This is how one can describe the meaning of sincere repentance in Serigne Saliou and his fellow sufis among the elite of the sufis that Allah has described in Sura *al Tawba*, ayah 112: "the repentant, the worshippers, the grateful, the travelers, the prostraters, those who command good and forbid evil, those who keep the laws of Allah and proclaim the good news to the believers."

Serigne Saliou is one of the repentants mentioned by Allah in the Quran:

"Glorified repentants and prostrate travelers, who incite good and reprove evil while respecting the divine laws, proclaim the good news to the believers." (Tawba 112)

The great master Ibn Ajiba had commented on this verse in his famous Quranic commentary "al Bahr al Madid": *This verse brought together all the stages of spiritual ascension from beginning to end.*

The first station is repentance (tawba) because the soul, in making its repentance and freeing itself from its passions, will take the direction of its Lord and concentrate on exoteric worship which is of the order of Shar'ia.

When the signs of success manifest themselves and the lights of achievement become evident, the soul will glorify its Lord and give thanks for this privilege.

Next, the intellect will explore the realities of Malakut (angelic world) as well as Jabarut (world of divine names and attributes), before returning to the principles and applications of Shar'ia, for the finality in perfection is to submit totally to one's Lord in complete obedience to obligations.

Thus, the body prostrates itself in the human world and the heart prostrates itself in the spirit world, before the divine presence.

It is only in this station that the believer can be fit for sermons and can order good and forbid evil according to the laws of exoteric Islam for all, and according to esoteric realities for some.

For the former, it will be sermon and reminder (wa'adh wa tadhkir) and for the latter, it will be spiritual education and realization (tarbiyya wa tahqiq).

It is important to know that only those who respect the limits prescribed by Islamic laws and the recommendations of the prophets may be qualified to guide others and thus hope for bliss and high stations.

Serigne Saliou always insisted in his sermons and speeches on repentance; he exhorted people to repent constantly, emphasizing the value of sincere repentance (tawba nasouh), which consists in the beginning by announcing one's own repentance.

Thus, in the sermon of Eid al Fitr in the year 1412 AH, he declared: "First I address myself and then all of you as a reminder of our essential mission on earth: 'Worship Allah the One without associating anything with him."

Allah said, "Be not like those who forgot Allah and He made them forget their being." (al Hashr 19)

I recommend that you rush to sincere repentance and turn to Allah for it is high time; Allah does not neglect His promises. He says, "He is the One who accepts repentance and forgives sins." I ask you to seek intercession for the acceptance of our request for repentance by giving alms and making gifts that are pleasing to Allah.

Don't underestimate any gift, no matter how small; don't overestimate any gift, no matter how great. Above all, give to those you consider worthy to receive these gifts among the poor and needy.

We ask Allah to guide us on the path of bliss, to accept our repentance, and grant us His forgiveness.

He also said about repentance: "There is a great good in repentance, but one must not return to repentance after repenting." This means that one must not repeat the sin for which one repented, otherwise it would be a recurring trap.

The Asceticism of Serigne Saliou

Among the Quranic qualities of Serigne Saliou are asceticism (Zuhd) and contentment (Qana'a). He was an ascetic in everything from food and clothing to the household. He did not care about appearances and neglected his attire, except in exceptional cases.

Asceticism as defined by Khadimou Rassoul consists of: "Not to let the heart become attached to this world and concentrate on the Face of Allah so that what you possess does not delight you, and what you do not possess does not grieve you."

The reality of asceticism, according to the critics, is that it is not a matter of being heartily attached to the underworld:

> "Don't be enchanted with what you have and don't be sad for what you don't have.
>
> For the love (of this world) is the cause of all misfortune, and humans are not aware of it.
>
> All evil stems from there; that is why the scrupulous sages free themselves from earthly ties."

A disciple named Serigne Mbaye Ndao was questioned by Serigne Saliou about asceticism. He replied that, according to his understanding, it is a matter of fleeing from creatures to take refuge in isolation and thus avoid temptations. Serigne Saliou replied: "Asceticism is rather the fact of respecting the limits prescribed by Allah and not transgressing them, based on the Hadith which says: 'The licit is obvious, and the illicit as well. Between the two, there is the uncertainty that escapes the understanding of the majority of men.'"

He who avoids uncertainty has preserved his religion and reputation, but he who succumbs to it is like a pastor who prowls around a private estate; he risks violating the forbidden domain. Now, every King has private estates; and Allah's private estates on earth are His prohibitions.

In the human body, there is an organ which, by its perfection, makes the whole body perfect; by its degeneration, corrupts the whole body; it is the heart. (hadith sahih after Bukhari and Muslim).

Khadimou Rassoul said in this sense to one of his disciples called Serigne Muhammad Sylla de Tayba: "Whoever wants to be an ascetic in this life and the hereafter must turn away from all prohibitions; whoever loves Allah must love His prescriptions."

The sincere love of Allah has certain implications; he who claims to love his Lord and yet fails to comply with His commands is a liar.

In "Jawami' al Kalim", Khadimou Rassoul says about asceticism: "All good was gathered in a chamber whose key is asceticism; all evil was gathered in a chamber whose key is love of this world which is the cause of all sins. The love of this lowly world predisposes us to the forbidden, the detestable, and trivialities.

Sufiane Thawri said: "Asceticism in this world would rather consist in refraining from making long-term projections, but it is not a question of eating frugally or dressing modestly."

He also said: "If you see a scholar getting used to dealing with princes and rulers, know that he is a crook."

He also said: "A man can be rich while being an ascetic; a man can be poor while being greedy."

He also said: "Be an ascetic in this world and sleep with a clear conscience without being blamed or blaming others."

He also said, "I like to live in a place where no one knows me."

It is said that Serigne Saliou was in his youth a very cultured modern man who was well informed about international events. He was neat in his attire and dressed with elegance, but as soon as he began to work on the education of his disciples, he no longer attached importance to his attire and neglected his appearance.

Serigne Fadhel Diop Matar, who was a close associate of Serigne Saliou said, "The sheikh was very clean and elegant because he attached great importance to his appearance. I went to Gambia where I stayed for a while and on my return, I found that Serigne Saliou had completely changed, no longer cared about his appearance, and was living in total asceticism.

Serigne Hamza Abdoul Ahad Mbacké told me that Serigne Fallou saw Serigne Saliou elegantly dressed in a boubou with precious fabric and said to him: you don't need these precious clothes and this elegance you will be the last of the threads to work for Khadimou Rassoul and that is enough for you as ornament and honor.

Totally committed to his mission, the sheikh had completely detached himself from earthly attractions, so much so that one of his disciples, saddened to see him in dusty clothes, mentioned to him. Serigne Saliou replied, "If that is the case, they have become dusty in the way of Allah," and the Prophet of Allah had said to his injured finger, "You are but an organ that has been injured in the way of Allah."

Hassan Basri said: "The Prophet (sallallahu alayhi wa sallam) never built a house for himself, neither of hard nor of wood."

The Prophet Muhammad (sallallahu alayhi wa sallam) said: "If Allah wants to scatter someone's money, He has it hoarded in clay and water."

Abdullah Ibn Omar said, "One day the Prophet (sallallahu alayhi wa sallam) found us repairing a water basin that was deteriorating and he said, 'I think things are rushing and what lies ahead is more important than that."

Abdulwahhab Shar'ani said in "al Tabaqat al Kubra" that many great saints had never built hard because they were more concerned with the afterlife than with this world here below.

This was indeed the case of Serigne Saliou who never built a permanent home for himself or his family; everything he lived in as a house was built by the Khalif Serigne Abdoul Ahad or one of his disciples; the sheikh was rather concerned about the *Daaras he* built for the education of his disciples.

One day, one of the disciples, that was very wealthy, offered him a superb villa in Dakar; he gave him the title deeds and the deed of transfer while pointing out the importance of the gift and the value of the villa. Serigne Saliou took the deeds and said to him: "Now it is my property?"

The disciple was happy and nodded, and the sheikh said, "I accept your gift, but I give you back the villa, for it is enough for me to know that one of my disciples has such a villa and that he can make a gift of it for the Face of Allah."

His Sobriety

Serigne Saliou was very sober; even during the most difficult times, he never complained and showed anyone his difficulties. Above all, he avoided soliciting government officials and influential personalities.

Serigne Abdessamad Shuaibou told us that Prime Minister Aguibou Soumaré, a long-time friend of the Sheikh, had come to visit him to tell him that the President of the Republic insisted on receiving his grievances. He added that the President had given the order to satisfy them and that he, as a friend, was willing to do so.

Serigne Abdessamad Shuaibou said that, on the arrival of the Prime Minister and members of his delegation, they found Serigne Saliou with some disciples and informed him of the purpose of their visit, telling him that even if he was content to send requests through one of his disciples, they would be satisfied.

The next day, Serigne Saliou told Serigne Abdessamad Shuaibou: "I heard what Aguibou Soumaré said about everything I want. I'm sending you to tell him: rarely will I have to communicate any needs to these people who were present yesterday and if I do have needs, it will only be for the public good. If, however, it happens that I have a particular need, I will send you personally and not someone else. Tell him too: if someone else comes to see him on my behalf, let him know that it can only be a personal initiative of someone who wants to take care of his own needs. I've heard of some people who are going to address their needs using my name when I don't even know about it."

Long-Lasting Devotion

Longanimity is one of the noble characteristics of the prophets. That is why, praising Seyidna Ayub's (Job) longsuffering, Allah said: "Mention our slave Ayub when he called out to his Lord: Satan has brought me to grief and torture. (We told him) strike with your foot (to make water gush forth) here to purify you and quench your thirst, and we gave him back his family and another one as a mercy from us and as a reminder to those gifted with intelligence. Take a sheaf and punish with it so that you do not perjure yourself. He was really patient; he is a docile slave." (Sad 41-44)

Serigne Saliou inherited an important part of this prophetic characteristic; be it in the longanimity on the adoration or in the trials or the moments of opulence. In *Massalik al Jinan*, Khadimou Rassoul divides the longanimity into two modalities:

> *There are two kinds of long-suffering: longsuffering in the worship of the Transcendent Lord, O my brother!*
>
> *And the one in events, especially during the initial shock.*
>
> *These are the teachings of our guide and teacher, on him the prayers and eternal greetings of the Lord, and on his family and companions.*
>
> *However, the perfection of longsuffering lies in ignoring the evils as if one were a lucky man.*
>
> *There is also the person's longing to renounce everything that is prohibited, as well as all superfluous desires. Be aware!*
>
> *As well as patience in the face of the assaults of the imagination during happy and favorable conditions.*

Concerning Serigne Saliou, his long-lasting devotion to the worship was shown by his persistence in the supererogatory acts and litanies (awrad), as well as the night watch and other exercises as mentioned above in the chapter on his worship.

As for his long life in trials and difficulties, I will report the words of Serigne Mboussobé Mbacké who said: "the sheikh sometimes stayed three days without eating, and without cooking in the house."

Serigne Moustapha Saliou said that they often went days without consuming meals outside of what one of the neighbors to whom Serigne Saliou had offered adjoining land, sometimes brought.

He was long in pain as well, because he suffered from several diseases in his body, including rheumatism and osteoarthritis, without letting anything show. Only those close to him were aware of the situation.

As proof of his spiritual qualities and virtues, notably patience (sabr) and trust in God (tawakkul) as well as hope (raj'a) and satisfaction (ridh'a), we can quote what Serigne Bachirou Khelcom told us:

"I came to see him one day during the rainy season and informed him about the state of the fields. I told him that at the beginning of the season it was better, but after a while pests attacked the crops."

He said: God directs the destiny; it is up to him to give the order. We must thank Almighty God for this since He did not mention the loss of crops until last in the ayah: "You will be tested by a little fear, famine, death and agricultural scarcity." (Al Baqara: 155)

We must therefore thank him because he is testing us only by the lightest of tests that he did not mention until last.

Serigne Mbaye Ndao told us that one of the disciples, an internationally renowned doctor, insisted on having Serigne Saliou treated in France. The sheikh thanked him and told him: "you don't know that Allah has more worrying evils than this."

He meant that he was giving thanks to Allah for having spared him from more serious evils and that he preferred to submit to Allah's will. In case he was healed of these evils indeed, he was not sure that others more terrible ones would not follow those that left.

As for his patience in opulence, it is evident in his ascetic and sober lifestyle, far from the pleasures and delights of this life.

His Attachment to Thanksgiving (Shukr)

This prophetic characteristic was also his. Not only was it part of his character, but he insisted that his disciples make it their own; in his sermons and speeches, moreover, he called everyone to this noble virtue. In Wolof, *Thiant* is synonymous with *Shukr,* and one of his followers named Sheikh Bethio Thioune had become so prominent in applying this characteristic that his group was called the *Thiantacone*.

Among his teachings concerning thanksgiving (shukr), his Eid al-Adha sermon of Wednesday 10 Dhu al-Hijjah 1410 AH corresponding to July 4, 1990: (As for gratitude or thanksgiving (shukr), the Lord correlated it with remembrance (zikr) in the ayah: "mention me and I will mention you and give me thanks and do not be ungrateful" (Sura al Baqara, ayah: 152).

However, gratitude is one of the most difficult virtues and for this reason, Allah recommended it to His Prophets, saying: "work in the family of Dawud (David) by giving thanks," and then because of the difficulty of this virtue, the Almighty added: "Few of my servants are grateful." (Sura Saba:13)

Gratitude or thanksgiving (shukr) is one of the greatest acts of worship and Allah has set it against its opposite, which is unbelief or disbelief (kufr). Allah says, "Give me thanks and do not be ungrateful" (Sura al Baraka 152). In Sura al Naml, Allah says: "He who is grateful does good and he who is ungrateful my Lord dispenses with it He is honorable." But in Sura Ibrahim ayah 7 Allah says: "If you give thanks, I will increase your rewards, but if you are ungrateful, My punishment is terrible." Allah also says in Sura *al Zumar* ayah 7: "If you are unbelievers Allah dispenses with you and He does not accept ungratefulness for His servants, but if you give thanks, He accepts it."

Thus, thanksgiving has as its opposite, ingratitude, and the virtues of the former have as its opposite the vices of the latter. The Prophet Muhammed (sallallahu alayhi wa sallam) said: the benefits persist when one gives thanks. Then he added: but if one is ungrateful, they disappear. Thus, the meaning of thanksgiving (shukr) has been sufficiently illuminated.

Serigne Saliou was firmly attached to this characteristic. Serigne El hadj Fadhel Lo, son of Serigne Ahmad Mansour Lo, son of Sheikh Mokhtar Binta Lo, recounted: "One-day Serigne Saliou came to his Daara in Ndiapandal and, wishing to make the children happy, he promised them a good meal; but he was surprised to find that everything was missing, from oil to condiments and other ingredients.

He sent his driver to Touba to acquire the needs. But unfortunately, he returned empty-handed due to a lack of means.

Serigne Saliou was pained but changed the situation from Sabr's longanimity to thanksgiving (Shukr). He took the students to witness that he could not give them the joy he wanted to give them and he produced a parable: "if someone follows in the footsteps of another and knows that at a certain place, the person he is following is wounded by a thorn; if, when he arrives at the precise place, he is in turn wounded by the thorn, then he will know that he is on the right track. Glory be to Allah the Lord of the Worlds."

His Scrupulous Attitude

He has this prophetic characteristic because his sufi experience was singular and his attachment to obligations and recommendations was very scrupulous.

Serigne Mboussobé Mbacké told me that Serigne Saliou had told him: "if you see me one day depart from bonds or even actions that are only recommended, you must know that I no longer have my reason, and you can mourn me."

His scrupulous attitude was evident in everything; perhaps this anecdote told by Serigne Fallou Niang who was present during the scene could edify us: "One day, one day of ziar, Serigne Saliou was sitting in the room and receiving visitors when a very old man came up to him and greeted him while asking him if he had recognized him.

Serigne Saliou smiles and quotes his name and that of his parents. His name was Dieng if my memory serves me right. The man shouted and, rising to take the people present as witnesses, said, "this year this sheikh had cultivated land in Khaban, the region I was in charge of. This year's harvest was insignificant and I suggested that he consider the quantities that he used to produce as a great farmer known to all, and pay him the sums that he would ask for. He replied: I only want to be paid the three francs that my product brought me.

And the man added: "If you had accepted my proposal at the time and I find you sitting here today with all the people who hope to benefit from your prayers and baraka, I would not have said anything, but I will know in my heart of hearts what you really are.

Serigne Saliou rejected injustice and warned against coveting the property of others or abusing people's generosity or credulity. He watched over everything he received as pious gifts (hadiya) and used them only after he was sure that they were lawful. He said to Serigne Hamza, son of Serigne Abdoul Ahad: "Even if I cannot do as my father did who buried suspicious money, I can at least make sure of the legality of what I consume."

Serigne Hamza Abdoul Ahad reported comments that Serigne Saliou confided to him: "a disciple came to see me in the company of the person in charge of weights and purchases of Baol agricultural products; he wanted to make his act of allegiance but he had a bad reputation among farmers because he cheated in weights and accounts.

This manager finally told me that he could put large amounts on the books and get paid accordingly, and then give me some of that money if I agreed to cover it. I said, "You actually want to make me a thief or a crook; you'd better leave me because I can't help you if you keep this mentality."

His Modesty

This trait is part of faith because the Prophet Muhammad (sallallahu alayhi wa sallam) said: "Faith (iman) is divided into more than seventy branches; the highest would be ilaha illa Allah and the lowest would be to remove obstacles on the roads, and modesty is a branch of faith" (Bukhari).

Now, Serigne Saliou was very modest before Allah, not like it was immediately noticeable on his face.

Imam Nawawi explained that out of modesty, he did not want to offend his companions when he saw something he did not like, but his face changed, and his companions understood.

This virtue of modesty is commendable as long as it does not lead to permissiveness.

Among the traits of modesty of Serigne Saliou, here is what our mother Sokhna Walo, his eldest daughter, told us: "A corpulent and strong disciple approached until he was on the feet of the sheikh to ask for prayers; he remained for a long time to express grievances without the sheikh showing the slightest embarrassment.

After his departure, the sheikh was suffering from osteoarthritis, but he asked that the disciple not be told so as not to distress him." This other anecdote was also told to us by Serigne Tayeb Diakhaté.

The modesty of our sheikh was notorious and it manifested itself in many situations, as in the case of an elderly disciple who liked to make the announcement for prayer when he did not do it properly.

Serigne Saliou, out of modesty, silently repeated the announcement (iqama) so as not to offend the disciple. He said to Serigne Sheikh ibn Serigne Mbacké Fajam when this disciple gets up for the announcement of the prayer, I only think of repeating it without offending him so as not to humiliate him because, I think that myself, despite my faults, Allah covers me; then, I must do the same with the others.

One of his disciples that was an attorney (lawyer) told how some of the Sheikh's relatives had told him about the services he was providing to the mourides who were having legal difficulties. Serigne Saliou called him to thank him and to tell him that given his modesty, he did not dare to ask for services; but that he considered any service rendered to the mourides as a service rendered to his own person and that this was part of the Khidma (divine service) and the service of the Muslim to his co-religionist.

As a testimony to his subtlety and modesty as well as his modesty, I mention what his talibé Serigne Mbaye Ndaw told me: "I came one weekend to visit him and I was wearing a gold bracelet on my wrist. When I came to ask him for some du'a before I went home, I reached out my hand and he saw the bracelet. He looked at me and then he looked at the bracelet without saying anything. But when I was leaving, he called me and ordered me to carry a bag of rice to Serigne Moustapha Sy.

So, I took the bag from my car and dropped it off at Serigne Mustapha Sy's house, telling him it was from Serigne Saliou and I asked him to pray for me. When I reached out my hand to him, he looked at the bracelet and said: What is this? No doubt Serigne Saliou did not send you here just for the bag of rice, but rather because he cannot do what he wants to do with you as long as you are wearing such things. Get rid of it immediately.

I executed myself on the spot in complete obedience."

To Love for the Face of Allah and to Hate for the Face of Allah

Serigne Saliou Mbacké was one of the saints (awliyas; Friends of Allah) who are annihilated in their Lord and lost in the lights of beauty and majesty so that he loved only for Allah and hated only for Him.

His feelings towards people never stemmed from personal resentment, but rather from their relationship with Allah and His Prophet (sallallahu alayhi wa sallam). That is why he hated slander and the slanderer.

Serigne Mboussobé Mbacké told us that when someone was slandered in front of him, he got angry and if the slanderer was one of his disciples, he scolded him severely. If the slanderer was a stranger to him, he would find a stratagem to teach him a lesson without offending him.

He would call one of his disciples and scold him, pointing out the evils of slander, and then get up and go away angry. Thus, the disciples understood that he actually wanted to teach a lesson while sparing the slanderer out of modesty.

Serigne Mboussobé Mbacké also told us that the sheikh said to him: "I hate slander by nature, especially when it concerns a relative."

The Softness of His Heart and His Sensitivity

The sheikh was very sensitive; he often wept when he recited the Quran, spoke of the Prophet (sallallahu alayhi wa sallam), Khadimou Rassoul, certain great saints or the companions of Khadimou Rassoul and the sacrifices they made in their companionship.

One day, a mouride disciple introduced him to his two sons, saying that one of them was named Sheikh Ibra Fall; the Sheikh began to weep tears until the disciples were grieved.

Sheikh Hamid Ibn Ishaq al Hasani told us that one day, he recited before Serigne Saliou poems from the Mauritanian collection of praise for Sheikhul Khadim when our sheikh began to cry. He asked him why he was crying, and the sheikh replied, "I think of all the gifts and privileges that Khadimou Rassoul has obtained."

His grandson Serigne Khadim Mbacké Absa told us that the Mauritanian scholar Cherif Habiboullah al Ikhtiri was watching one evening with Serigne Saliou, with whom he was very close, when the sheikh began to cry and said: "O Lord, may you forgive me and save me from your wrath!"

Cherif Habibullah said to him: "If you are not saved, who will be? Haven't you spent your life working through the Quran and helping your neighbor? Is there any work nobler than the work you are doing for Islam and Muslims and your father Khadimou Rassoul?"

Serigne Saliou gave thanks for this and praised Allah.

His Mercy to All

Mercy is a cardinal virtue of the Prophets and the envoys. Allah said to His Prophet Muhammad (sallallahu alayhi wa sallam) in the Quran: "You have been sent nothing but [as a] pure mercy for the worlds."

Among the proofs of his mercy towards the creatures, is the anecdote told to us by Serigne Bassirou Abdoulkarim: "I told Serigne Saliou one day that we pitied him because of the uninterrupted visitors he receives daily. He replied: What you feel for me... I feel immensely more towards these people who come from everywhere to see me. When the visits are over and I see these people leaving I hold back my tears because I know that some of them have gone through a lot of difficulties to get to me and some have not even been able to get to my person. If they were able to endure all this out of love for Khadimou Rassoul, how can I not bear to devote my time to receive them."

Moreover, Serigne Saliou said: "No one is more merciful than I am towards creatures after their Lord." After a long prostration, he raised his head and said, "I give thanks to Allah who has graced me with mercy and leniency and for what He has bestowed on me intending good towards His creatures."

Thus, whenever he sensed hardships or disasters that might befall the country or the Muslims, he ordered good and forbade evil, starting with himself. He began with sincere repentance to which he invited all believers, then he prescribed the reading of the Quran, charity, and finally help for the needy.

He put into practice this Quranic ayah: "Take from their money and alms that purifies them and atones for their faults and pray over them, your prayer is peace over them. Allah is an all-knowing listener. Do they not know that Allah accepts the repentance of his slaves and accepts alms and that he is the magnanimous repentant? Say, work Allah will see your works and the Prophet and the believers and then you will return to the Omniscient Lord of the Unmanifest and the Manifest and He will inform you of your works" (Tawba 103-105).

Serigne Saliou was very concerned about the humanitarian dimension and urged people to do good, especially during the holidays. He gave a lot of alms and donations which he ordered to be distributed to the poor in Touba and its surroundings.

Thus, he repelled the fatality of misfortune following the hadiths of the Prophet Muhammad (sallallahu alayhi wa sallam) who said according to Abu Humama: "Doing good protects from misfortune, secret alms calm the divine anger, parental piety increases the life span."

The Prophet (sallallahu alayhi wa sallam) also said: "Good character is happiness, while bad character is a misfortune; parental piety ensures longevity, almsgiving wipes out sin and protects from death in atrocious conditions."

Abderrahman Ibn Awf reported that the Prophet (sallallahu alayhi wa sallam) said: "Alms for the Muslim lengthens his life and protects him from an unhappy end and through it, Allah dispels pride and complacency."

Serigne Saliou was very attentive to the well-being of both Senegalese and Muslim populations in general; he felt responsible for everyone, and prayed unceasingly for believers in the Middle East and elsewhere, especially for Palestinians whose rights had been violated.

During the traumatic events that took place between Senegal and Mauritania, his daughter, Sokhna Moumy, had prepared a hearty meal in her house in Daroul-Mouhty and sent it to Touba with one of her daughters to give it to Serigne Saliou. The daughter found him in a state of supplication and invocation to Almighty God, yet as she approached him to speak to him, he beckoned not to do so.

He could not bear or tolerate anyone when he was immersed in his prayers to ask Allah, the Almighty, to free the nation from distress and misfortune. Thus, he was only following the example of his father, may God be pleased with them.

Serigne Saliou and Divine Wisdom

Our sheikh considered that everything in creation was a divine order, apparent or hidden, for Allah says: "The heavens and the earth and all that is between them were not created for fun; they were created only for truth, but the majority of people do not know it."

The sheikh believed that humans must free themselves from the bonds of rationality to appreciate the secrets and wonders of Allah and the creation, for only then can they enjoy the benefits of this creation and the creatures as well as they, in turn, can benefit others with their skill or experience.

Serigne Habibou Diop, son of Serigne Muhammad Lamine Diop Dagana, told us that the sheikh had told him: "No creature is devoid of usefulness and benefit, especially humans and the earth. Only the human being is unaware of the means of benefiting from the blessings that Allah has created, whether in himself or around him."

Thus, Serigne Saliou had consideration for all creatures; first humans, then animals, and then plants and earth.

He had consideration for the creator through his creatures as indicated by his father Khadim Rassoul: "Preserved in every creature are the rights of the one who created it."

Thus, he respected both children and the elderly, and he had consideration for everyone, from the most destitute to the most respectable.

He asked forgiveness even from the children and assured them of his repentance for not being able to do more for them despite his best intentions towards them.

His Love and Mercy for Children

As for his love, mercy, and compassion for the children, his disciple, Serigne Moustapha Diaw, may God have mercy on him, told me: "He commanded mercy and compassion for the children and tried to guide them with kindness and gentleness, and he used to say: each of you went through childhood, and you desperately needed the one who accompanies you, helps you and takes care of you during this period."

Serigne Mboussobé Mbacké told me that Serigne Saliou told him in 1953: "in general, one only follows the path of the sufis in the age of maturity when one can make the difference between good and evil, and especially after having opted for celestial life to the detriment of earthly life.

But those who entrust us with their children from a young age want us to take care of them as our own children, and to be merciful and good to them. That's why I can't tell the difference between them and my own children."

Serigne Mboussobé Mbacké also told us that Serigne Saliou had bought a car at a time when cars were scarce; it was in a lot sold by the French military who were leaving the country.

The sheikh traveled to all parts of Senegal, and whenever he saw children on foot, he would pick them up out of pity and give them the joy of riding in a car.

However, his main concern was the education and teaching of children, so when parents entrusted their children to him, he put them in good conditions until they could take care of themselves; then he entrusted them to teachers to learn the Quran and religious sciences.

In the beginning, around the 1940s, he sent children to the Al haj Wilane school in Saloum, the school of Serigne Mor Mbaye Cissé in Diourbel, or other schools until they mastered the obligations and recommendations.

As for those who were old, he sent them to the fields to learn agriculture and to do Khidma (divine service).

Serigne Dam Touré told us that the sheikh told him: "We must not take advantage of the sweat of the disciples, but rather reward them by teaching them their religion.

That is why I am asking you to go to the fields with them to teach them as soon as they finish the work in the fields."

One of his ndongo tarbiyya told me: One of the students' parents entrusted his child to Serigne Saliou, and after a while, the father died. The child avoided school and was going back to his mother's house in the village, so the sheikh sent a car to pick him up, and this happened several times until the mother was embarrassed. Eventually, she told those who came to pick him up to leave him, as she feared that Serigne Saliou was wasting his time and money on her son from whom nothing good would come of it. Except that the sheikh put up with the child's behavior and was kind to him until he began to work seriously and succeed in life.

Later, he became aware of Serigne Saliou's efforts and felt the weight of his debt to him, and with each visit, he apologized more and more. But the sheikh told him: "The relationship that binds me to you is much greater than a mutually beneficial relationship between us, but rather a relationship of alliance and allegiance."

There is no doubt that this relationship between him and his followers goes back esoterically to the primordial covenant quoted in the Quran:

When your Lord drew forth from the Children of Adam - from their loins - their descendants, and made them testify concerning themselves, (saying): "Am I not your Lord (who cherishes and sustains you)?"- They said: "Yea! We do testify!" (This), lest ye should say on the Day of Judgment: "Of this we were never mindful": Or you should say: Only our fathers associated others (with Allah) before, and we were an offspring after them: Will you then destroy us for what the vain doers did? Thus do We explain the signs in detail; and perchance they may turn (unto Us). (Surat Al-'A`rāf 172-174)

Khadimou Rassoul explained this by commenting on the hadith: spirits are like enlisted legions. He said: do you know when our companionship began?

They say: we don't know.

He said: since the spirits were like legions enlisted. Those who have sympathized in the spiritual world have assembled incorporeal existence.

Those who had antipathy repelled each other. It was from this reality that our companionship began.

Without a doubt, the love of children is indeed a divine gift that some chosen ones are gratified with. Serigne Abdessamad Shuaibou Mbacké told us a very beautiful anecdote where he told Serigne Saliou a story by Khadimou Rassoul: "Allah has raised me to Paradise and I was walking there when I was in front of a door; I wanted to enter but an angel took me by the hand and asked me to look above the door; I saw written: "Enter here only the one who makes the children happy. I asked the Holy Spirit what was the reason for the refusal? I asked the Holy Spirit what was the reason for the refusal, and he said, "You were completely absorbed in fighting against the enemies of Allah, you had no time to take care of the children to make them happy, but I have already decreed the order. All you have to do is try to make up for it by bringing joy into the hearts of the children.

The next day, Khadimou Rassoul asked to open the doors and let in only the children whom he surrounded with all his benevolence by presenting them with all sorts of delicacies all day long."

Serigne Abdessamad Shuaibou Mbacké added: "When I have finished telling the story, I say to Serigne Saliou: no doubt you represent Khadimou Rassoul in this quality since his fights did not leave him time to make the children happy."

Serigne Saliou was overcome with joy and entered an extraordinary spiritual state.

The Stations of Majesty (Jalal) and Beauty (Jamal)

Serigne Saliou moved between the stations of the Jalal and the Jamal, so that sometimes the lights of domination (qahr) and the power of majesty radiated in him to such an extent that no one dared to approach him. At other times, the lights of benevolence and mercy shined in him so brightly that no one would dare go away from him.

This was how he combined the reverence of Majesty with the beauty of benevolence, yet these are contradictory qualities that can only be combined by those who are characterized by the Quran: "humble to the faithful and proud before the unbelievers" or "Muhammad the Messenger of Allah and his firm companions against the unbelievers and merciful among themselves."

Sometimes visitors would come to Serigne Saliou to offer him pious gifts and they would find him in full concentration, in such reverential states that he was not even aware of their presence.

Other times, he would walk away in the sunlight and give an order to leave the doors closed so that no one could enter. When visitors would complain later, he would apologize and honor them with hospitality and kindness.

By his humility and the brightness of the lights of beauty that illuminated his face, he was so charismatic that all those who knew him sincerely loved him with all their hearts and preferred him to any other personality, no matter how prestigious. His influence was due to his noble person (may God be pleased with him).

Anyone who came into contact with him found his humanity and humility. His major concern was the worship of Allah in servitude. His leniency towards the believers was identical to what Allah said to His Prophet (sallallahu alayhi wa sallam) in the Quran: "Be humble and gentle towards those who follow you among the believers. If they disobey you, say, "I am innocent of what you are doing." (Sura al Chu'ara 215- 216)

Serigne Saliou (may Allah be pleased with him) was so humble that he always tried to hide his good deeds and never showed his status. He honored everyone according to his dignity and addressed everyone according to his understanding, according to the prophetic method. He always tried to put himself on the level of the masses to convey the message of Muhammad's compassion and mercy.

He thus wanted to help all to perfect themselves and benefit from his contribution as heir of the function of his father Khadimou Rassoul who said:

"ALLAH assists me and the creatures follow me on land and sea for their benefit without any harm."

His humility was not due to weakness or hesitation but rather the result of piety and divine fear; moreover, if the situation forced him to be strict, he showed strength and rigor.

Serigne Khalil Mbacké told me, quoting the sheikh himself: "The President of the Republic Abdoulaye Wade asked him one day during one of his visits to change the curriculum in the *daaras* and to include vocational training while mentioning that he discussed it with Serigne Mourtada.

Serigne Saliou flatly refused and said to him: don't you know that we raise them there by a religious education based on beneficial knowledge, which produces good deeds and rules of decorum approved by Allah. But we also train them in all agricultural arts and professions. And you know that agriculture is the greatest source of income for the citizens of this country.

In this rainy season, we have produced tons of peanuts. The president says: it is the equivalent of so many millions of francs."

In spite of his modesty, he did not accept that others interfere in his private work where he spent more than seventy years and acquired many experiences mainly focused on spirituality and religious education. Since he did not interfere in the way the president conducted the affairs of the country, nor did he ask him for privileges and services such as the appointment of a person, he did not allow him to interfere in his educational tasks, which he clearly knew and which had their secrets and purposes.

Pure Servitude (Ubidiya Khalisa)

Moreover, like all great saints, he considered that the highest spiritual station was that of pure servitude (ubidiya khalisa), and that magnificence was the Lord's undivided possession. Thus, he wanted to be a devoted servant like his father who said:

"My station is that of a slave of Allah and the servant of his slave the Prophet of Allah."

Serigne Saliou, may God be pleased with him, made humility his characteristic to obtain the highest positions in servitude (العبودية), and he was sincere in his humility, simplicity, and asceticism. He was naturally so as Allah had predisposed him. These were not the qualities he was looking for because his naturalness was so simple and humble and even touching. We heard him in his sermons in the Magal ask all mourides to ask forgiveness for him from his Lord, and this is the height of fear and humility before the Creator and His creatures.

He combined in his generous personality majesty and humility, and despite his high spiritual degree, he humbled himself in front of everyone and showed compassion towards those, among the believers, who followed him to love the Messenger Muhammad Peace and Salvation upon Him.

Serigne Hamza Abdoul Ahad told us that one-day Serigne Saliou was visiting his *daara in* Ndiapandal and, noting the scarcity of rainfall, he said: "I believe that the cause comes from my own sins."

Then he ordered the students and readers of the Quran to gather together and asked them to pray to Allah for the absolution of their sins.

Serigne Hamza Abdul Ahad told him: "If you want the rain to start falling, surely Allah will send it to satisfy you."

The sheikh asked, "Do you think this year's harvest will be good?"

Serigne Hamza answered: "surely, by your baraka, it will be good and blessed."

After the departure of Serigne Saliou for Touba, the rain watered all the *daaras* for a week. Serigne Hamza on his way back to Touba, visited Serigne Saliou who was about to meet Serigne Abdoul Ahad. The sheikh said to him: "Hamza, I have seen the realization of all that you had announced to me. I thank Allah for that."

Serigne Hamza Abdoul Ahad, in recounting this anecdote, mentioned that although Serigne Saliou's baraka was obvious to everyone, the sheikh never took any credit for it. On the contrary, he emphasized his own alleged sins and obscured his gifts and wonders at a time when others were clamoring for alleged powers and secrets to assert themselves or find customers.

It happened that a certain disciple was expelled from the *daara* for a serious fault and, despite all the interventions, Serigne Saliou was adamant; later, he asked to call him back saying: "who am I to expel anyone from the *daaras that* belong to Khadimou Rassoul?" And since the service (Khidma) belongs to Allah, I cannot drive out "those who implore their Lord morning and evening, hoping for His face."

The returning disciple was very happy after receiving a formal lesson, but the sheikh was even happier because the lesson had been successful and the disciple had made sincere repentance.

This is reminiscent of the Hadith reported by Anas ibn Malik who said, "The Prophet (sallallahu alayhi wa sallam) said: Allah is happier with the repentance of his servant than one of you whose camel fled into the desert with food and water. In despair, he lies down under a tree and falls asleep; when he wakes up, he finds him before him and, holding it by the bridle, he shouts with joy: "Allahumma you are my servant and I am your Lord", thus committing a slip of speech in his joyful expansion."

Respect for Human Dignity

Serigne Saliou was known for his humanism which expressed itself with his visitors, regardless of their race or social position; he gave everyone respect due to his rank.

Serigne Fallou Shuaibou testified about this quality of Serigne Saliou in the following terms: "Serigne Saliou had experience and deep knowledge of human society and also had a great interest in individuals. He respected everyone and valued people. When he was talking to someone, you could feel that he cared about the person he was talking to and that he gave him such importance that if the person was not wise, it could mislead him into believing that he was really important, or that he had reached a high spiritual station."

In this regard, Serigne Habibou Diop said: "I don't think anyone could compete with our sheikh in the legacy of the Prophet (sallallahu alayhi wa sallam) and his father Khadim Rassoul, whether in the field of virtues, ethics, behavior or respect for human dignity.

I could bear witness to this and Allah is enough as a witness. Anas ibn Malick said, "I served the Prophet (sallallahu alayhi wa sallam) for ten years and he never said a bad word to me. He never told me why you did this or why you did not do that." In another version: "The Prophet (pbuh) had the most beautiful character."

For me, this hadith was enlightened by the behavior of our sheikh because I lived with him for more than thirty years and I never heard violent or hurtful speech from him and he never used intimidation. During all the time I lived with him, since the age of ten, he was very concerned about guiding and advising me and he corrected me when necessary and rectified my mistakes but he never offended or humiliated me. This is one of the greatest proofs of his inheritance of the qualities of the Prophet Muhammad (sallallahu alayhi wa sallam) and Khadimou Rassoul.

He was at everyone's service; he welcomed his visitors with consideration and listened to their grievances despite their number. He made superhuman efforts to fulfill his duties as a host and spared no effort to satisfy everyone. He prayed for them and said that they were Khadimou Rassoul's guests and should be served and satisfied.

Out of respect for the human being, he used to continue serving guests and visitors throughout the day, barely resting from the interviews. Even when he was very tired, he would continue to receive visitors and listen to their complaints, and requests; he would pray for them and respond to their requests.

He assumed that they came for Khadimou Rassoul and not for himself. So, he considered them as the protégés of his father whose khalif he is and they deserved all kinds of services, veneration, and honor.

Serigne Moustapha Diaw, his talibé (may God, the Almighty, have mercy on him), in showing his respect for human beings, said: Serigne Saliou had a love for everyone. He was deeply respectful of people. Through his love and respect for humans, he forgot his person and his specific needs to meet the needs of others. He always inspected the conditions of the people in the house, guests, visitors, students, and educational staff.

He did not neglect anyone and often said about the visitors: "If these visitors endure all these difficulties to get here for Khadimou Rassoul, then how could I not endure the difficulties of moving from here to the Great Hall to receive them."

Serigne Khadim Moustapha Hafsa told us that his uncle Serigne Sheikh Saliou had intervened one day to relieve Serigne Saliou who was receiving an impressive number of visitors. That day, indeed, many dahiras had come.

He proposed that only the presidents of the dahiras come to shake hands with the khalif. Then Serigne Saliou said: "they made a lot of effort to come to us, we must also make efforts to receive them with dignity."

Sheikh al-Khadim said to his elder sons: "All kinds of efforts must be made to be beneficial and helpful to Allah's creatures."

Serigne Sheikh Mbacké son of Serigne Mbacké Fajam [informed] us [that he] learned that during a Magal, the visitors were so numerous that the police, overwhelmed, began to use violence.

Serigne Saliou intervened to say that one should respect his visitors who have made a difficult journey to come to him, just for Allah and out of love for Khadimou Rassoul, and not for tourism or fun.

We must bear the difficulties of crowd management and show them respect because I heard Serigne Mbacké Madina say in such cases: "we must put ourselves in their shoes and imagine that we are outside the door waiting for our turn. We must therefore be grateful to Allah who has put in us what makes these crowds attached to us, when he could have left us outside the doors waiting for our turn like them."

Among the proofs of his respect and affection for his neighbor, there is the anecdote told us by one of his disciples who had emigrated to Europe after finishing his spiritual education in the *daaras*. He stayed in Europe for a long time before returning to Senegal and when he visited Serigne Saliou, he thought that the sheikh did not remember his name but he was surprised by the warm welcome and the attention paid to his person. When he wanted to take time off to visit his classmates in the Ndiapandal *daara*, the sheikh told him: "Apparently you didn't feel as much nostalgia for me as I felt for you."

Then the disciple was moved and stayed longer and the sheikh prayed for him so that he could leave. He went to Ndiapandal and was surprised to be joined by a car that brought food and all kinds of fruits and drinks sent by Serigne Saliou as hospitality. He was very happy with this attention to his humble self.

Serigne Saliou was very subtle in human relationships and he had the gift of activating the energies and potentialities of his disciples by surrounding them with affection and attention.

He had great sympathy and remarkable care for his disciples, and he shared their suffering and concerns with them.

In this way, he could mobilize the forces of the mouride talibés, and increase their enthusiasm and courage in the service of Serigne Touba.

Serigne Bassirou Khelcom told me: "I came one day from the *Daara of Khelcom*, so Serigne Saliou began to inquire about the situation of the Ndongo and their health and well-being as well as their morale. And he added: Are they still in their "sabr" (patience) station?

I replied: on the contrary, we always progress in the station of "shukr" (thanksgiving). Then Serigne Saliou said: We thank Allah, the Almighty, for this, and we are aware of all the efforts you make in these schools for the Face of Allah."

Serigne Bassirou Khelcom also told me that one day he said to the Sheikh: "We thank God, the Almighty, that he has not made our mission to raise and educate children in the *Daaras* difficult.

Serigne Saliou said: Have I ever mentioned this line in any of the poems of Sheikhul Khadim. I said: Which verse? He said: "During my service, I was accompanied by the satisfaction of our creator who inspires good and removes ignorance and suffering." I say to him: surely you have gratified us with the baraka of this verse. He says: I never do anything without using the baraka of this verse. We cannot exhaust all the anecdotes that we know on the subject, there are so many of them, they are numerous, but what has been said sufficiently attests to the humanism of Serigne Saliou Mbacké.

PART THREE: THE MAN AND HIS MISSION

1. PORTRAIT OF THE MOURIDE SADIKH
2. SERIGNE SALIOU AND DIVINE SERVICE
3. SPIRITUAL EDUCATION

CHAPTER VI - THE PORTRAIT OF THE MOURIDE SADIKH

In this chapter, we deal with Serigne Saliou's commitment to the spiritual path and his respect for the principles of Muridiyya as well as his relations with all those who had blood or spiritual ties with Khadimou Rassoul.

The Importance of the Spiritual Will in the Journey to Allah

It is generally accepted in the sufi way that the path to Allah is only made with sincere will and powerful determination (himma a'liya).

Anas ibn Malick (May Allah be pleased with him) said that the Prophet (peace be upon him) said: "When Allah wills good to his servant, he makes him work." He was then asked, "How does He make him work, O Prophet?" He said, "He favors him for a beneficial work at the end of his life," he replied.

Sheikh Abdelwahab Cha'rani said in "al Tabaqatal Kubra", after Sheikh Ali ibn Wahb Sinjari (May Allah be pleased with him): "Allah places the will in the heart of anyone who enjoys His love and consideration."

The aspirant (al murid) is indeed a lover who yearns for his Lord, with a nostalgic heart and a keen intellect.

The aspirant (al muurad) is rather loved and requisitioned without a will of his own, he is nostalgic but satisfied because he has found what he was looking for after having gone through the stages of the path by attraction; and this, without any effort of his own since he has annihilated his ego and detached himself from the material world.

In the same work, Cha'rani reports from Sidi Ahmad Rifa'i: "When the Lord takes hold of the heart of his servant, all humanity disappears and only that which is Allah's share remains." This is how the servant returns to the state of clay that he was initially. He no longer has any activity of his own, acting only through his Lord: no more will, no more science, no more action on his part.

Sidi Ahmad Rifa'i also said: "When the heart is filled with light, every veil between the servant and the Lord disappears."

Hakim Tarmadhi said: "The key to all blessings (baraka) is patience in the spiritual will, until the will is firm and sincere. It is then that the premises of blessing appear."

What about the spiritual will (Irada)? What are its realities and implications? We propose to develop this topic to understand how Serigne Saliou lived the principles of Tasawwuf and how he applied them.

The Reality of The Spiritual Will

There are multiple definitions of the spiritual will (irada), including the one that says it is going against the flow of habits or the one that advocates awakening the heart for the quest of the Lord.

According to Jurjani in "Ta'rifat": "Spiritual Will is a sincere heart searching for spiritual nourishment."

The spiritual will is also defined as: "The act of preventing the soul from running after its pleasures and desires while conforming to divine imperatives with adherence."

It is also apprehended as: "A brand of the flame of divine love that incites the servant to respond to the Lord's call."

All these definitions refer to a single truth: that of emptying the heart of all that is not God and stripping oneself of customs and societal habits (A'da).

Societal habits (a'da) would be the fact of getting involved in social constraints to the point of not being aware of divine constraints. It is also the fact of letting oneself go into pleasures and trivialities.

The aspirant (al mourid) must free himself from these social constraints to devote himself to the quest for God, perseverance being a guarantee of sincerity in this quest.

This is how Sheikh Ahmad Bamba (peace be upon him) explains the phenomenon:

"The definition of the spiritual will, according to the masters of the Way, would be for the aspirant to turn away from customary habits. But if he resumes these habits before reaching the end of the Way, he risks apostasy."

Sheikh Abdelkarim Quchairi agrees with this because according to him: "The spiritual will is the beginning of the Way for the itinerant; it is the first step for those who are on the way to Allah. It is called the spiritual will (irada) because it is the beginning of every act, for the servant must want something to obtain it.

It is therefore the first step in the path of Allah, so that the "aspirant" (al mourid) etymologically means: "He who has the spiritual will", just as the scholar (alim) would be the one who has knowledge (ilm). Even if the masters have given multiple definitions of what the spiritual will (irada) is, each according to his own experience, they mostly agree on this point: the spiritual will consist in separating oneself from societal habits (generally represented by unconsciousness and the pursuit of desires and temptations, without any concern for our posthumous becoming). However, the aspirant must completely separate himself from these attitudes, this separation being proof of the veracity of his aspiration. For this reason, this state is called the spiritual will (irada), which is precisely the fact of turning away from habits. The reality of this state would be an awareness that leads to the search for Allah. It is also an intuition that alleviates all fears.

The spiritual will would comprise three degrees, according to the masters of the way, as Sheikh Abdullah al Harawi states in "Manazil al Sa'irins": "The first is to move away from societal habits by investing in religious sciences and accompanying those who have embarked on the spiritual path with sincerity of intention and concentration in action. The second is to live the spiritual state in all intimacy and to walk between concentration (qabdh) and exaltation (bast). The third one: amazement (dhuhul) in all rectitude (istiqama) and perfect adequacy with the rules of propriety."

Serigne Saliou, An Example of the True Mouride

Allah has favored Serigne Saliou with innate gifts, certainly in inheritance from his illustrious father Khadimou Rassoul. This is all the truer since he was raised in the love of Allah and the Prophet Muhammad (sallallahu alayhi wa sallam) and Khadimou Rassoul, in whom he saw the lights of beauty (jamal), majesty (jalal), and perfection (kamal). He considered the service of Allah and conformity to the Sunnah, as well as the work in the path of Khadimou Rassoul as the noblest mission of the aspirant.

His disciple Sheikh Abu Madian Chouhaibou Gueye reported these words of Serigne Saliou: "Nothing will be useful in the Hereafter except the sincere aspiration towards Allah and the work for Sheikhul Khadim." This is reminiscent of Sura Ash-Shu'ara (26:88-89): "The day when neither property nor children will be useful except those who come to Allah with a healthy heart."

Serigne Saliou was a perfect example of the sincerity of the aspiration to Allah and the powerful spiritual will that was not fanaticism or conformism, such as showing his brotherhood or claiming extraordinary status without any consequent action.

According to him, the spiritual will means the sincerity of the quest, and the right intention and total concentration in Allah; in addition to detachment from this world and its artifices. Moreover, he learned the meaning of the spiritual will very early in his father's writings:

The definition of the aspirant (al murid) is summed up in the fact of stripping oneself of one's own will (irada) for that of the Lord who does what he wants.

He who wants nothing else besides his Lord will be gratified with the joining (wusul) and will obtain the best benefits from Him.

In all his acts, the true aspirant wants nothing except the pleasure of his Merciful Lord.

These words were the viaticum of Serigne Saliou, who often recalled the Quranic words of Sura al Kahf: "Whoever hopes for an encounter with his Lord must perform good deeds and refrain from associating anything with the worship of his Lord."

The Characteristics of The True Aspirant (Mouride Sadikh)

We will not only explain the realities of the spiritual will from a theoretical point of view, but we will also try to see the applications according to the teaching of Khadimou Rassoul and the practical application of the principles by Serigne Saliou.

Serigne Saliou devoted his entire life to applying the teachings of his illustrious father and teaching them in his *daaras* which are educational centers that teach Islamic knowledge and spirituality.

This is how Khadimou Rassoul explained the characteristics of true aspirants. The characteristics of the true aspirants are all in synthesis to the number of four that I am verifying to avoid any misunderstanding:

"Sincerity in the love of the sheikh and obedience to his orders without hesitation.

And never express reservations even intimately, as this is highly recommended.

Then the renunciation of one's own choices for the choice of the sheikh by good opinion without uncertainty."

Sincerity in the Love of Sheikhul Khadim

Serigne Saliou had immeasurable love for Sheikhul Khadim; he was the perfect example of the mourides and their model.

He had great affection for Sheikhul Khadim's companions and tried to follow in their footsteps. He often shed tears when the name of Khadimou Rassoul was mentioned, as his sensitivity was so great.

Serigne Mboussobé Mbacké recounted the following: "I was with Serigne Saliou in his house in Thies when a singer arrived and began to sing about the maritime exile of Khadimou Rassoul, according to the poem of Sheikh Moussa Ka, until he recited verses relating the wonders of the Sheikh.

Then Serigne Saliou was taken by rapture and cried warmly to the point that I took pity on him and asked the singer to stop.

He would simply stand in front of the large tree in his house and, facing the mausoleum of Sheikhul Khadim, he would make wishes that came true.

During the rainy season, water sometimes flowed from the mosque and formed puddles in his house.

But, despite the women's complaints, he let the waters stagnate until grass grew. He would then say, "This is the baraka of our Sheikh's mosque; we must give thanks to Allah who chose our house to collect this water with which we receive the baraka."

Serigne Mboussobé Mbacké told me this anecdote: "When the Khalif Serigne Fallou learned that water was pouring into the house of Serigne Saliou, he wanted to dig a ditch to collect the runoff but Serigne Saliou refused and said that we should leave things as they were because he was collecting the baraka."

Serigne Hamza Abdelahad used to say: "Serigne Saliou is incomparable in his spiritual will and his determination in divine service, because his acts and thoughts, as well as his intention, are firm and unshakeable.

He thinks only of the common good and the interest of Islam and Muslims; concerned only with the unity of all and the resolution of problems and disputes between believers."

Serigne Saliou was so attached to Khadimou Rassoul that as soon as people started talking about him, he entered into incredible spiritual states and his eyes watered until he could no longer stay with the people. He would get up and go home to ease his state. He venerated the name Khadimou Rassoul to the point that no one could speak of him unless he took every precaution to say only sensible things.

Serigne Abou Madian Guèye said that Serigne Saliou warned against being indelicate or irreverent with Khadimou Rassoul or his mother Sokhna Diarra Bousso, or perjuring in their name or stealing money from the Hadiyas because it could lead to sudden death, and even a bad end (May Allah protect us from it).

He also said that the name of Sheikh al-Khadim should always be pronounced with reverence, for it is a name given by Allah, and no such name is known in history, so that when one hears the nickname, one immediately recognizes that one belongs to the Mouride Way. In fact, this nickname designates an exceptional station that the sheikh had reached after the incredible trials he was confronted with. This is why one must be courteous and reverential in pronouncing it.

Serigne Saliou avoided calling the homonyms of the sheikh by the name "Khadim" but called them "Sheikhouna." He forbade the disciples to swear by the name of Khadimou Rassoul and told them: "If it is really necessary, swear by my name or that of Serigne Saliou Touré and not by Sheikhul Khadim."

The Discussions of Serigne Saliou

Whenever Serigne Saliou discussed with a scholar, the subjects revolved around Islam, Allah, the Prophet Muhammad (sallallahu alayhi wa sallam), his venerable companions, or Sheikhul Khadim and his pious companions. One day, he was talking with Serigne Saliou Touré who brought back some sublime verses from Sheikh Sidia in homage to Khadimou Rassoul where he said:

> "The sheikh is a blessing offered by Allah to all creatures without exception. He has no concerns other than the continuous worship of his Lord and making himself useful to all, morning and evening."

However, Serigne Saliou said that Khadimou Rassoul was more moved when he heard the following verses:

> "He is satisfied with the order of things in all submission because he is aware that Allah manages everything without sharing."

Khadimou Rassoul said then: "Now he really compliments me."

Then, taken by rapture and reverential fear, Serigne Saliou said:

> "These words should challenge us because we are far from being satisfied in all circumstances."

We have the opportunity to report here an extraordinary conversation recounted by his Tunisian disciple Abdallah Fahmi:

"I was discussing with Serigne Saliou about the words of the sufis, particularly the maxim that states that you necessarily need a sheikh who personifies Him" (the budda laka min sheikh yourika shukusuhu).

I said the sufi masters mean by this that the contemplation of the divine theophany (tajalliyat ilahiya) by the attributes of the Jamal and the Jalal as well as the epiphanies of the Haqiqa Muhammadia by the noble characteristics and transcendental knowledge are done in the perfect sheikh (Sheikh Kamal).

Since everything in creation is only a reflection of the divine names and attributes and the Haqiqa Muhammadia is the reality for which and through which Allah created creation. I see that the mourides contemplate this reality when they speak of Sheikhul Khadim and even today they contemplate these realities in your person as well.

Sitting on a bed, Serigne Saliou listened to me, then he lay down without saying anything. I asked him: "Do you confirm or deny what I said?"

He stood up and said to me: "I will recite a verse of Khadimou Rassoul that will clarify further for you:

Produce "Kun" for me today and set the price for me. Then give me back what I dedicate to you after this in the same way as he did."

I said, I understand the words but I don't understand the meaning. He repeated it to me again, and since I didn't understand the meaning, he wrote the verse on a notebook that I often had when we were talking about spiritual realities; then he said, "I'll explain the meaning to you so that you understand exactly. It is as if Allah has a store that holds everything and when He wants to send a messenger or a prophet, He tells him to choose from the store what he wants for himself and his followers. However, everything has its price in the sight of Allah, the price being hardship.

Therefore, the most tried of humans are the prophets and then the most exemplary; the reward is commensurate with the trials. For each people, there is a guide (li kulli qawmin hadi), so in the intermediate periods without a prophet Allah sends guides who confirm and restore the religion of the prophets and when it was the turn of Khadimou Rassoul, Allah asked him to choose. So, he chose the store which is "Kun", which is clear in the beginning of the verse: *Produce for me today "Kun."* But as everything has its price, the sheikh said: *"Set me the price."*

For this, our sheikh has faced the trials of all the prophets from exile to assassination attempts. Then he said, "give me back what I dedicate to you after this by the same as he did."

That means that he not only obtained the "*Kun*" but then dedicated it to the service of Allah and the Prophet Muhammad (sallallahu alayhi wa sallam). So, in rewarding him, Allah created things for him exclusively, as well as gifts that had never been given to anyone before.

Respect for the Status of Sheikhul Khadim

Serigne Saliou put into practice the writings of the Sheikh, namely the rules of decorum (adab) which, according to the corporation, are five in number and which provide a booty for anyone who observes them:

"Respect for status (horma), elevation of the spiritual will (uluw al himma) correct service (husnul khidma), recognition of benefits (shukr aal ni'ma), and, fifth, determination to succeed (nufudh al azima)."

According to Serigne Hamza Abdoulahad, "Serigne Saliou consolidated his relationships with all those who had ties of kinship or spiritual affiliation with his father, and above all, with his brothers and sisters.

On this subject, we can testify that we have never seen someone as respectful and devoted in blood and spiritual ties as Serigne Saliou.

Serigne Hamza Abdoulahad told us that during a cholera epidemic in Senegal, Serigne Saliou sent him to the Khalif Serigne Abdoulahad Mbacké to ask for blessings. He added that he brought him a bottle of water in which he had prayed to the Khalif, he drank it and distributed it to the children of the *daara* so that they could have their share.

Still according to Serigne Hamza Abdullahad, despite the large number of his disciples and all the graces and benefits he had at his disposal, in addition to his prodigious knowledge, Serigne Saliou constantly sought the approval of his brothers and his illustrious father's companions and sent them gifts. Moreover, he reserved for his brother Serigne Shuaibou the fruit of the Ndiouroul harvest.

His High Aspiration in Allah

It is a matter of emptying one's heart of all that is not Allah's and seeking neither reward nor status, except for the pleasure of Allah, except "a will that transcends status and stations and rises above rewards and distinctions in order to turn exclusively to Allah," to quote Sheikh al Islam Harawi in "Manazil al Sa'irins."

For his part, Sheikh Ibn Ajiba al Hasani states in "Iqadh al Himam": "The spiritual will (himma) is the determination of the heart in the quest for knowledge and concentration for the sake of Allah's pleasure.

This will be a high aspiration; but if it is a determination of the heart in the goods of this lowly world, then it will be a low aspiration.

When asked about this, Sheikh Abdelkader Jilani replied: "The servant must turn away physically from this world and spiritually from the other; he must remove from his heart all his own will to be receptive to the will of his Lord; all creation must thus disappear from his mind."

Abu Ali Hussain ibn Ahmad al Katib said: "The spiritual will is the beginning of everything; he who has a correct initiation, will benefit from a correct realization that will produce beneficial acts consequent to his spiritual states. He whose spiritual will is defective will have uncertain consequences and dubious spiritual states that will produce acts unworthy of being presented for divine approval."

Sheikh Aboubacar Abdallah Abhari said: "The spiritual will of the benefactors (salihins) is in faithful worship and obedience far from any drift. That of the learned (ulama) is in the correction and increase of their knowledge; that of the knowing (arifin) is in the exaltation of divine veneration in the heart; that of the nostalgic lovers (ahlou chawq) is to join their Lord; that of the close ones (muqarraboun) is to establish Allah (iskan Allah) in the heart."

Sheikh Dawud ibn Makhalla said: "As soon as the spiritual will of the aspirant in his progress towards Allah stops before a thing or an event, he will be challenged by the herald of spiritual realization: affirm the existence or reality of that object."

This means, that the aspirant must progress towards the one and only real (haqq) which is Allah, and not stop in front of the things or phenomena that come before him and which will be as many obstacles that he will have to circumvent.

On this subject, Ibn Ata Allah said in "Hikam": "As soon as the spiritual will of the itinerant stops in front of what he contemplates of phenomena or secrets in the revelations, he will hear the voice of truth (haqiqa) which calls him thus: we are trials, do not be unfaithful."

Ibn Ajiba commented on this wisdom in the following terms: "The spiritual will is the force that pushes along the path; and when it stops in front of something, it thinks it has reached the terminus and risks getting off at that station. The voice of truth challenges him to know that spiritual realization is still at the end of the road.

Phenomena, however extraordinary they may be, risk attracting the itinerant who must be careful not to succumb to this charm, but rather to contemplate the wisdom hidden in them and the power of his Lord who does what he wants."

Sidi Ibrahim Dasouqi said: "O my spiritual son, assemble your will in order to know the realities of the spiritual path in practice and not only in theory. Every station at which you stop will become a veil between you and your Lord. Anything other than Allah, the Prophet Muhammad (pbuh), the Quran, the Companions, and their followers, can only be a source of bewilderment. In truth, the objectives of each one can only produce consequent results."

Sidi Aboul Abbas Mursi used to say: "By Allah, I have seen greatness only in the elevation of the spiritual will."

Thus, we can see that Serigne Saliou initiated his disciples to the spiritual will, in accordance with the teaching of Khadimou Rassoul received orally from the Prophet Muhammad (sallallahu alayhi wa sallam), as reported by the Khalif Serigne Abdul Ahad in a collection devoted to this subject.

According to this collection, the Prophet (pbuh) made the following recommendation to Khadimou Rassoul: "Train your companions and disciples by theoretical teaching (ta'lim) and educate them by spiritual will (himma), according to the abilities and spiritual state of each one. Allah has taught you through me what is in the heart of each one; you must speak to them according to their understanding and honor them, each one according to his rank. This is my advice to you."

Serigne Saliou exhorted the disciples to devote themselves to Allah and to ascend to the stations of knowledge, reminding them of Khadimou Rassoul's words about the importance of spiritual will:

"Lift your will in the business of this world and that of the hereafter in trivialities intimately or manifestly."

Serigne Saliou had high aspirations, noble and virtuous, as reported in the remark he made on the verse of Khadimou Rassoul:

"Grant me the true knowledge and beneficial action (Salah) that will complete my hopes."

He had said to Serigne Abdousamad Mbacké and Abu Gueye: "Even if our sheikh did not designate me personally in this verse, I do intend to fulfill his hopes and achieve everything he wanted, by the grace of Allah.

Serigne Saliou also wanted to assemble all that was scattered among the elite and the perfect masters, as was the case of Khadimou Rassoul who said:

"Gather for me all that is scattered with benefits in my writing and purify my intellect.

And grant me that which is scattered among the venerable elite and which you majestically dispose of."

Serigne Saliou was convinced that Allah has made Khadimou Rassoul the center of lights and blessing and that in each of his sons there are specific secrets and graces. He knew that everything has its price and that to obtain blessings, one must work; this was manifested in his devotion to his brothers and sisters whom he served fervently.

We are aware of a significant anecdote reported by many people including Serigne Hamza Abdoul Ahad and Serigne Khalil Mbacké:

"In his youth, Serigne Saliou had a close friend who was often with him. But, since the recall to God of the first Khalif, Serigne Modou Mustapha, their relationship changed because this man, who came to offer his condolences, had told Serigne Saliou that he had really hoped to see Serigne Fallou in the seat of Khalif, to guide the mourides and complete the hope of Khadimou Rassoul."

These words were extremely annoying for Serigne Saliou. Later, it was thought that this man was completely irresponsible because what he hoped for was not only irreverent but also deprived him of the service due to his brothers and made him miss out on immeasurable graces and benefits.

He then decided to break up with him without offending him.

Helpfulness Towards His Brothers

Serigne Saliou had high regard for his brothers and sisters and was always at their service.

He had pledged allegiance to the first Khalif Serigne Modou Mustapha to whom he gave all that his fields produced. So, it was with Serigne Fallou the second Khalif, Serigne Abdoul Ahad and Serigne Abdoul Khadre, respectively third and fourth Khalifas.

When he became the fifth Khalifa, he continued to strengthen the blood and spiritual ties with his brothers and sisters, sending them gifts and goods regularly.

He considered the sons of Khadimou Rassoul not as his brothers but as his Sheikhs and showed them signs of reverence.

His eldest daughter Sokhna Astou Walo Mbacké came to see him in Diourbel, and he asked her where she came from; "from my uncle Serigne Bassirou's house," she answered. He then said to her: "So, you consider this illustrious man as an uncle? You must consider him as your sheikh and not as an uncle or a relative."

Availability for the Benefit of Mourides

Serigne Saliou liked to get closer to Allah by any act of charity but, in particular, by the service of Khadimou Rassoul. To this end, he devoted himself to public utility by helping the needy and by the generous offerings he gave them daily and on the occasion of festivals.

He considered, however, that the teaching and spiritual education of children was the best action, for they had to be taught the Quran and their religious obligations, to set them on the path to divine enlightenment.

He took care of the children and provided for all their food and health needs. He spent millions of dollars every month for this purpose, in addition to the assistance he provided to needy families who came from all over to settle in Touba where land and water were free.

It was a refuge and shelter for all, where everyone found spiritual and material help.

Hadiya (Pious Gift)

Serigne Saliou gave consistent hadiya because he considered that the true mouride possessed nothing and nothing can possess him.

All he is interested in is the approval of Allah and his Prophet (sallallahu alayhi wa sallam) in accordance with the ayah: "Allah bought from believers their person and their goods against paradise. They fight in the way of Allah; they kill and get killed. It is a true promise on our part in the Torah and the gospel and the Quran and is more truthful than Allah in his promises? Be happy with your pact that you have made. It's a huge triumph. (Sura al Layl:111)

Money is very important to humans because it occupies one's heart and thought; however, the "hadiya" is a barometer in the need for agreement between words and deeds, in spiritual commitment.

"Touba (blessedness) for the true aspiring servant who works by service or love or hadiya." Allah says in Sura Ibrahim 31:

"Tell my servants that they perform the prayers and spend in private and in public what they have been provided before the day when there will be no more sale or purchase."

According to Khadimou Rassoul, "Hadiya (the pious gift) attracts happiness and provides the highest stations. He makes goods grow and ensures the love of neighbors and primacy before his peers. It avoids the interrogation of Munkir and Nakir and ensures the rapid passage of the Sirat, as well as the entry to paradise without judgment.

One could add further benefits that cannot be recorded or stated, for a single Hadiya can be rewarded up to ten thousand times its value at least, while the maximum is known only to Allah the supreme master - exalted as it may be."

In Jawamai'l Kalim, Serigne Sylla reported from Khadimou Rassoul: "When a person is favored by good fortune and uses this favor in beneficial acts and assistance to his neighbor, his fortune will be a blessing for him (baraka). However, the baraka amplifies what is modest and makes majestic what is already important."

According to the Quran, in ayah 25 of Sura Ibrahim, the one who uses his fortune to do good is: "…like a good tree, whose root is firmly fixed and its branches [high] in the sky? 'always' yielding its fruit in every season by the Will of its Lord."

And, ayah 261 of Sura al Baqara similarly says, "Like a grain that produces seven ears, in every ear a hundred grains, and Allah multiplies as he pleases."

On the other hand, those who misuse their wealth and help their neighbor in prevarication while refusing assistance to the needy will have regrets and torments.

In the Quran, ayah 39 of Sura al-Nur says, "Like a mirage in the desert that the thirsty takes for water, but when he reaches it, he finds nothing."

It is well known that Serigne Saliou used to say in his public sermons to the mass of the faithful: "One of the advantages of the pious gift (hadiya) is that it brings a benefit to that which is not pure of your money, and transforms a little into a lot, and blesses the lot that is not yet blessed."

A Model in Spending for the Sake of Allah

In this respect, he was the best model for the mouride because his abundance of pious gifts and his spending for the love of God were exemplary. He was the largest agricultural producer in all of West Africa, producing thousands of tons of peanuts, millet, and other crops every year. Despite all this, he never considered the money he earned from farming as his own but as the property of Sheikh al-Khadim. That is why he recognized no rights over the profits of the agricultural crop but acknowledged that they belonged to Sheikh al-Khadim.

Sheikh Hamzah Abd al-Ahad told me, quoting the saying of Serigne Saliou: "Anyone can earn just respect by working to feed himself with the sweat of his brow. But the one who deserves the most respect is the one who earns his money by the sweat of his brow and then spends it purely for the love of God."

Serigne Saliou presented his agricultural crops to the Khalif of the Mourides, first Serigne Modou Moustapha Mbacke, then Serigne Fallou Mbacke, then Serigne Abd al-Ahad Mbacke and finally Serigne Abdul Qadir. Becoming the khalif at the head of the mourides, he gave hadiya to his other brothers, sisters, and family members and mainly spent money on the brotherhood's projects.

Said Serigne Mustapha Diaw: "At the beginning of his caliphate, the sheikh gave each family of Sheikh al-Khadim one million francs, then over time, he gave them five million francs a year, then he increased the amount to ten million, then to twenty million for men and ten million for women. As for his brother Sérigne Mourtada, he sent him every year an amount of 120 million as a pious gift."

Serigne Diaw added: "He sent me every year to deliver these gifts to Sheikh Mourtada, may God be pleased with him, so the answer of Sheikh Mortada each year: 'God was a witness of what he did, and God was satisfied with a martyr' except in the last year of his life; he would say, 'he did for me all that our father (our sheikh) would have done with me if he were alive with us, so God rewards him."

For nearly seventy years or more, the sheikh did not use the income from his fields to support his family or to spend on his own needs, such as spending for his followers in educational centers or other legitimate behaviors, but considered these as a WAQF dedicated to Allah. The profits from the fields belong strictly to Sheikh al-Khadim and should not be used except for the service of Sheikh al-Khadim, or given to those who become his khalifs:

"It was the Sheikh's custom to give his agricultural property to the khalifs, but sometimes he would accumulate debts to cover the expenses of his talibé on the farms, so he would travel and wander around to pay those debts, and he could add all his crops and that was not enough to pay the debts. This was the only reason that forced him not to offer the harvest proceeds to the khalif.

Serigne El-Hajj Lo, the grandson of Serigne Mukhtar Bint Lo, informed me that the sheikh told him: "These fields belong to Sheikh Al-Khadim, and I could not use them for my needs, because they belong strictly to Serigne Touba.

Serigne Hamzah Abd al-Ahad also told me: "The sheikh came one day to Ndiappandel and asked me to prepare something light to eat in a hurry, and he said: He did not taste the food for three consecutive days. In a hurry, I brought him pistachio nuts, the sheikh asked me where I had taken them, so I answered: 'I brought them from the fields.'"

The sheikh said, "Go and search the abandoned field, you may find peanuts that grew from the remains of the grains that were scattered last year.

Following the Model of His Illustrious Father

His disciple, Sheikh Mustafa Diaw, testified to this by saying, "The sheikh was completely annihilated in the love of his illustrious father and guide. He did not see himself as his son, but rather as a sincere aspirant who only wished to serve him and seek only to please him. He loved and revered all those who had a relationship with Khadimou Rassoul whether it was through kinship, oath of allegiance, or spiritual attachment."

Serigne Hamzah Mbacke Abdul-Ahad testified to his high level of spiritual resolve as well as his sincerity, will, and belief in his Sheikh Al-Khadim. He said: "Serigne Saliou, may God be pleased with him, used to seek the blessing of everyone who had any relationship with Sheikh Al-Khadim, be it his parents and family, his great followers and companions, and their children and grandchildren, especially those who immediately descend from the lineage of Sheikh Ahmadou Bamba. In reality, I have never seen this kind of attitude of reverence in anyone other than Serigne Saliou."

The truth is that Serigne Saliou, may God be pleased with him, used to apply the teachings of his illustrious father and guide. He had respect for all those who had a relationship with Sheikh al-Khadim as he mentions in these verses:

> *Strive to preserve the respect due to God*
> *And to those who have any kind of relationship with Him.*
> *Whether it is a prophet or a saint*
> *Whether he is a scholar or a good man*
> *And even common people,*
> *Respect them all as you should*

His Love for His Father's Companions

For this reason, he tried to further strengthen his friendship with all those who were related to his father, especially the former companions and disciples, whom he used to frequent to learn more about his father's way and method of life and his biography (sirra).

He maintained an excellent relationship with many Gnostics (Arif) among his father's disciples. He was very fond of the companions and frequently visited them and received them in his house in Diourbel.

He gathered information from them and corrected certain stories and accounts about Sheikh Khadim and his teachings and secrets.

He used to receive in his house mourides of high spiritual status, among whom was a man named Mandiaye, whom Sérigne Bachirou Mbacke particularly esteemed. He was astonished to see this holy man visiting Serigne Saliou frequently, so he wondered how he had managed to win the friendship of this strange holy man.

His love for Sheikh Al-Khadim was transcendent to the point that he loved all those who were related to him, including sons, disciples, and followers. From this perspective, we can assess his high level of love towards the apostles of the Khidma and the high symbols of the Himma such as Sheikh Ibrahima Fall and Sheikh Ahmadou Ndoumbe Khabban, whom he esteemed greatly.

Serigne Saliou considered them as the ideal of sincerity, will, and a high level of himma and khidma, he often exhorted his followers of tarbiyya to be inspired by their example and to follow in their footsteps with sincere will and unfailing determination in the service of Allah, as we will see in the next chapter, God willing.

CHAPTER VII - SERIGNE SALIOU AND DIVINE SERVICE (KHIDMA)

This chapter deals with khidma which is a fundamental action in the Mouride Way. In this chapter, we discuss his achievements in the infrastructures whether it be in agricultural fields, villages, schools and the mosques that he established (founded) from 1934 until the end of his life.

Serigne Saliou and Khidma

Serigne Saliou, on him the approval of Allah, is undoubtedly one of the greatest mouride figures who have been able to put into practice the teaching of Khadimou Rassoul, with visible impacts to this day.

Divine service (khidma) is one of the most important principles of the Mouride Path, after the sheikh emphasized it through effective work. [38]

This will give the people of his generation and the following generations a living example that will be forever remembered.

Divine service (khidma) is indeed a notion that Khadimou Rassoul revived once it was completely neglected. As a matter of fact, Anas Ibn Malik (may Allah be pleased with him) was the servant of the Prophet Muhammad (sallallahu alayhi wa sallam).

Tirmidhi reported from Anas: "I served the Prophet (Sallallahu alayhi wa sallam) for ten years and he never said a bad word to me. He never told me why you did this or why you did not do that. The Prophet of Allah had the noblest character and I never touched anything softer than his hand which

---

[38] These passages are part of a study I published on the wiki Mouridiyya website.

was softer than silk. I have never smelled anything more fragrant than his sweat which smelled better than musk."

Anas' mother entrusted him to the Prophet (sallallahu alayhi wa sallam) when he was not yet ten years old. He was raised in the Prophet's house and served the Prophet (sallallahu alayhi wa sallam) as the true mourides serve their Sheikh.

Anas also said, "My mother took me to the Prophet (sallallahu alayhi wa sallam) and said, 'O Prophet of Allah, every year men and women have showered you with gifts and I can only offer you my son who will serve you as much as you want.'" The first recommendation of the Prophet (sallallahu alayhi wa sallam) was: "O my son, keep my secrets well, so that you may be a true believer."

Although my mother and the wives of the Prophet (sallallahu alayhi wa sallam) asked me, I refused to answer them so as not to reveal the secrets of the household. The Prophet (sallallahu alayhi wa sallam) was very lenient and patient. Once, he sent me on errands and instead I stayed with the children to play. I felt behind me someone pulling me by my clothes and it was the Prophet (sallallahu alayhi wa sallam) who smiled and said: "O Anas, shouldn't you do my shopping? I trembled and said: I am leaving immediately."

His mother had told the Prophet (sallallahu alayhi wa sallam) that her son could read and write, which was already rare at the time. This would explain Anas' intelligence, as he had learned and memorized much of the prophetic teaching, to the point that he was considered one of the great traditionalists after Ibn Omar and Abu Huraira. His collection contains

2286 hadiths, 170 of which were authenticated by Bukhari and Muslim. Bukhari collected 80 hadiths from Anas and 90 from Muslim.

The Prophet Muhammad (sallallahu alayhi wa sallam) blessed Anas for his excellent service and prayed for him to have the baraka saying: "O Lord, increase his descendants and his wealth and grant him the baraka in what you grant him."

Thanks to this, Anas' wishes were granted. Thus, when he prayed for rain, the clouds piled up and the rain would pour down even during the summer.

In view of all these hadiths, it can be proved that the notion of khidma is not an innovation introduced by Mouridism in Islam. Nor is it a new principle added to the principles of religion.

Serigne Abdul Ahad said: "Sheikhul Khadim did not institute a new path in religion; he found the face of the Muhammadian Shar'ia dusty and brought it back its luster, sublimity, and wisdom to the point of making it pure and resplendent as left by the Prophet (sallallahu alayhi wa sallam)."

Our master Sheikh al-Khadim arrived at a time when the means used to spread Islam were restricted or obsolete. Some had practiced military jihad and others had chosen to ally themselves with princes and rulers (ceddo).

Our Sheikh, however, did not find these methods effective in bringing the country out of this situation of uncertainty; having understood that service (khidma) was a more effective means, he devoted his life and all his abilities to the service of the Prophet Muhammad (sallallahu alayhi wa sallam), reviving his religion and serving his community. He composed books on the various religious sciences, eulogies on the Prophet (pbuh), as well as saving prayers and invocatory petitions that served as intercessors for the believers.

The Concept of Khidma

For Sheikhul Khadim, the concept of Khidma (Divine Service) means: "Any sincere human effort by which the Face of Allah is desired, and which has as its objective individual or collective utility."

It can also be defined as any intellectual or physical effort that has a purpose or adds value in the field of religion.

Khidma is also any personal commitment or initiative that tends to do well to be useful to individuals or the community, in a spirit of self-denial, seeking only the satisfaction of Allah.

Khadimou Rassoul uses the concept of khidma within a precise framework that implies the elaboration of the virtuous and truthful human (mouride sadikh).

Khidma is a method of spiritual education (tarbiyya) that deals with faith, initiation through knowledge and practice, and spiritual realization in accordance with the sufi teachings. Continuous work is better than intermittent work.

In Massalik al Jinan, Khadimou Rassoul says:

The best works are those with lasting benefits, such as proven knowledge that keeps away ignorance and misbehavior (malfeasance).

Likewise, everything that leads to beneficence is beneficial,

As well everything that purifies the heart, even if it is minimal works as the Wise Man explained.

Thus, by developing the Islamic principle of divine service (khidma), Khadimou Rassoul was able to build the personality of the aspirant (mouride) who will thus become a virtuous and beneficial person for society and humanity.

Indeed, the mouride does not seek exclusively his interests but above all the interest of the community and even to the detriment of his own interests. He acts according to the prophetic model: "You have been sent only as a pure mercy for the worlds" (Sura 21, Ayah 107).

The mouride model is that of Khadimou Rassoul who sacrificed everything from his freedom to his own life to serve the Prophet Muhammad (sallallahu alayhi wa sallam), restore his religion, and save his people from the clutches of colonialism which sought to dissolve the African and Islamic personality to replace it with a westernized and Christianized one.

He said: "My homes were emptied and the family dispersed, while I praised the one whose praise is out of reach. [39]

May my return to my people be a blessing and save us from hell on the day of the gathering. [40]

Grant me what I ask for and make me a blessing to the creatures, O You who dispenses us from armaments." [41]

Thus, by valuing khidma as a blessing for humanity, one builds the virtuous person who does not devote himself to his passions, desires, and self-interest but seeks divine pleasure like the sahabas, the valiant companions of the Prophet Muhammad (sallallahu alayhi wa sallam) who favored religion over worldliness and the interest of the community over individual interest.

Khadimou Rassoul thus used khidma as a means and method for earthly and celestial happiness, and above all to obtain divine approval. He said:

---

[39] Bamba Sheikh Ahmadou, the poem *Assirou Ma'al Abrari*.
[40] Bamba Sheikh Ahmadou, the poem *Wa Laqad Karrammna*.
[41] Bamba Sheikh Ahmadou, the poem *Wa Kaana Haqqan*.

"I serve him until the entrance to paradise, the eternal home of bliss and benefits." [42] The service (khidma) can be done with all legitimate means: intellectual, material, physical or other.

The mouride must indeed do everything possible to satisfy Allah, by serving the Prophet Muhammad (sallallahu alayhi wa sallam) and his privileged servant; whether by his person, property, science, wisdom, advice, or otherwise.

Serigne Saliou appropriated this concept that his illustrious father had revived and applied it practically in different fields.

In this study, we will discuss the areas where Sheikhul Khadim applied this concept of service (khidma): educational, spirituality and knowledge, and then societal.

Service in the Educational Field

In the field of education, service involves initiation that enables the intellectual faculties to flourish and acquire the necessary knowledge and experiences that elevate towards spiritual perfection through the knowledge of Allah, His names, attributes, and deeds.

This is how Allah taught Adam: "He taught Adam the names and set them before the angels saying, 'Unveil the names of these things if you are truthful. They said glory to You, we have no knowledge except what You have taught us; You are the Wise Omniscient! He said, "O Adam reveal the names to them. When He (Adam) revealed the names to them, He (Allah) said: Did I not tell you that I know the unmanifest of the heavens and the earth and what you manifest and what you conceal?" (Sura al Baqara: 33).

This is the intellectual dimension in the service and essentially in the

---

[42] Bamba Sheikh Ahmadou, the poem *Minanoul Baqi Al Qadim*.

service of the Quran by disseminating its teachings and enlightenment to enlighten the human intellect and teach believers the ways to worship their Lord and fulfill their role of lieutenancy on earth. Khadimou Rassoul insisted on this in several of his poems:

By the service of the book and the hadith, my inheritance is attested and not by gold.

His right over me is to serve the book without failure or deficiency.

In the chapter on Serigne Saliou's educational service, we will discuss his achievements in this field.

The Service in its Spiritual and Intellectual Dimension

It is a matter of perfecting the human soul and purifying it through spiritual education, instilling in it the nobility of character, and elevating its spirit to the level required to be worthy of the status of divine lieutenancy.

This is indeed the original vocation of the human being. The envoys and prophets have come to remind us of this truth by their example and their message: "Allah gives to the believers by sending them a prophet from among them who recites the verses and purifies them while teaching them the book (Quran) and wisdom, whereas before they were in certain error." (Sura Al Umran: 164).

"It is He who sent a messenger from among the illiterate people to recite His verses and purify them while teaching them the book and wisdom." (Sura al Jumu'a: 2).

Serigne Saliou succeeds brilliantly in this noble mission. He revived the teachings of his illustrious father Khadimou Rassoul and trained entire generations of scholars and spiritualists who, by practicing what they learned, received divine gifts, including sciences they had not learned through didactic teaching.

For seventy years, Serigne Saliou devoted himself entirely to this noble mission. His followers belong to several generations; some of them are among the country's elite because they are characterized by Iman, Islam, and Ihsan only through knowledge and action, in addition to spiritual courtesy.

This point will be developed in chapter eight, which will deal with the methodology of the Sheikh.

Service in its Societal Dimension

It is the exploitation of arid lands to make them productive, according to a divine plan. This plan is to populate the land to make the sons of Adam exercise the role of lieutenancy (khilafa) and to merit the noble status that was conferred on them since Allah has subjected both earthly and celestial creatures to them:

"He has subjected to you all things in the heavens and on earth, and these are signs for a meditating people." (Sura al Ja'thia: 13).

"We have honored the sons of Adam, and we have borne them on earth and in the seas, as well as we have disposed of goods to them, and they have been immensely privileged over many of our creatures." (Sura al Israel 70)

"Allah promises to those who have faith and do good that He will grant them the land as He granted it to other peoples before. He will strengthen your religion which He has accepted and He will convert your fears into security. They will worship me and associate nothing with me. Those who deny the faith after this are surely vicious." (Sura al-Nur 55)

The Philosophy of Dryland Development

This is another dimension of service (Khidma) that we will explain through Serigne Saliou's career from 1934 to 1992. During this long period, he was mainly involved in the foundation of spiritual centers and agricultural fields throughout the country.

The sheikh gave fundamental importance to the land he occupied because he chose the place according to certain data related to space-time and geopolitics to reserve it for service (khidma).

He was concerned with location and orientation because the place had to be a meeting point between the absolute and the relative, the spiritual and the temporal; in short, the exoteric and the esoteric.

It is therefore easy to understand the importance given by Serigne Saliou to the foundation of the centers, through which he revived the arid lands he exploited, to put into practice, the teachings of Khadimou Rassoul for the benefit of the mourides and rural populations.

This is precisely the mission of the human being who was created to worship Allah and populate the earth by exploiting its resources.

Allah says: "It is He who has raised you from the earth and allowed you to exploit it, ask for forgiveness and repentance. My Lord is near and answers favorably." (Sura Hud 61)

"You do not see that Allah has made the heavens and the earth subject to you and has bestowed on you apparent and hidden blessings." (Sura Luqman: 20)

In Bukhari and Muslim according to Anas ibn Malik, the Prophet (peace and salvation upon) is said to have said to him: "Any Muslim who plants a tree or a plant that will be used to feed humans, animals or birds, will get common alms with it."

Nisa'i and Abou Daoud and Tirmidhi reported the following from the Prophet (peace and salvation be upon him): "A barren land that is exploited by someone is rightfully his."

Imam Ahmad Ibn Hanbal reported in his *Musnad*, as did Bukhari in *Al Adab al Mufrad*, according to Anas ibn Malik, that the Prophet (peace and salvation be upon him) is said to have said, "If the end of time comes upon you and one of you holds a seed in his hand, let him plant it if possible."

Bukhari reported in his sahih from al Moqdam ibn Ma'd Yakrab that the Prophet (peace and salvation be upon him) is also said to have said: "The best food you can eat is the food you have earned through your labor."

The Prophet Dawud ate the fruit of his labor. In Bukhari, according to Abu Huraira, the Prophet (pbuh) said, "Dawud - peace be upon him - ate only of the fruit of his labor."

Bukhari also reported from Zubayr ibn Awwam that the Prophet (peace and salvation be upon him) is said to have said: "It is better to go and fetch wood to sell it than to reach out to people who will sometimes give and sometimes refuse."

Luqman (peace be upon him) said to his son: "O my son, earn your living honestly so that you may avoid poverty. He who is defeated by poverty risks three evils: a deficiency in his faith, a lightness in his intellect, and a loss of dignity. But the most serious is that he may also suffer the disregard of people."

Omar ibn al-Khattab said: "No one should be left without work for his livelihood, saying, 'Lord, provide for my sustenance; you know that from heaven it does not rain gold or silver."

Ibn Massoud said: "I hate to see a man without activity, who does nothing in the affairs of this world or those of the hereafter."

Tabarani reports, according to Bayhaqi in Sunan and Abdulrazak after Abu Huraira, that the Prophet (peace and salvation upon him) was sitting with his companions when a strong young man passed by. Then one of the companions said, "If that man would use his youth and strength to fight in the way of Allah!

The Prophet (peace be upon him) said, "Do not say this; if he goes to work to feed his children, he is fighting in the way of Allah; if he works to feed his old parents, he is fighting in the way of Allah; if he works to protect his dignity, he is fighting in the way of Allah; but if he only seeks ostentation and boasting, he is fighting in the way of Satan."

It is well known that work is part of the principles of Muridiyya, to the extent that it is considered a part of worship when one works for the Face of Allah; however, one cannot neglect a legal obligation incumbent on every Muslim.

One can thus understand the importance given by Serigne Saliou to the exploitation of arid lands to make them arable and allow disciples to feed themselves honestly, while worshipping their Lord, and obtaining a spiritual education.

It was not for profit that he occupied the arid lands, nor for mercantile exploitation to establish a financial empire.

Rather, it was to enable the disciples to live a decent life with an efficient spiritual education.

At the same time, it gave them the means to work honestly, learn trades and use agricultural techniques that allow them to exploit the drylands so numerous in the country, in a context of acute rural exodus.

Serigne Saliou offered the country's youth an alternative to the evils of our times; he educated them spiritually and morally to put in them a piece of Khadimou Rassoul's spiritual repository that would make them examples for future generations.

This repository constitutes the two terms of the shahada, the first of which, "La ilaha illa Allah", is realized through servitude (ubudiya); the second, "Muhammad Rassoul Allah", is realized through the Khidma, approved in accordance with the Sunnah.

Khadimou Rassoul said:

"Know that knowledge and action and the rules of propriety make you achieve perfection.

Knowledge and action are two jewels that make you acquire the goods of this life and the afterlife."

Land Servicing in Mouridism

It would be useful to briefly explain the mouride philosophy in the development of arid lands as well as man's relationship with his environment, which he must dedicate to the worship and servitude of the Lord, to honor his function as God's lieutenant on earth.

In mouride literature, and particularly in the works of the founder, Khadimou Rassoul's relationship with the land and the environment is noted, and he was careful to arrange it in such a way as to create the ideal community in which the believer could live the Iman, Islam, and Ihsan by benefiting from the beneficial knowledge and charitable works, as well as the rules of decorum approved by Allah.

For this purpose, the sheikh traveled in the East of Baol and on the borders of Cayor in search of the ideal place where he will find his city, Tuba, which will be the sacred center for happiness here on earth and in the hereafter.

By analyzing the Sheikh's relationship with his environment, we understand the philosophy of Mouridism in the development of arid lands; this philosophy is based on three elements: the place, the inhabitant, and competence.

We have explained this subject in another work entitled: the theory of the two bliss (Matlaboul Fawzeyni) in Sheikhul Khadim.

The sheikh founded several schools for religious and spiritual education; schools that later became villages in Cayor and Baol among which are: Darou Salam, Touba, Darou Minan, Darou Rahman, Darou Qoddous, Darou alim Khabir, Darou Mannan, Darou Rahman Dioloff, Darou Qoddous Dioloff, Rawdh Riahin Thiéyène, and al Buq'a Mubaraka Diourbel.

In his book "Serigne Saliou the Fifth Khalifa," Mouhammed Adam Diakhaté reports that: "Serigne Touba, wanting to found this school, instructed disciples to find him a suitable place in Diourbel. An old Bambara named Sidi Ba came to see him and said: "I have a piece of land that I inherited from my father; I wanted to cultivate it, but I am old and I have no children capable of doing so; I want to work for Allah by giving it to a man of God. I was waiting to meet such a man; so, I offer this land to you." Khadimou Rassoul thanked the man for his noble feelings, but insisted that he accept a sum of money in return.

The great mouride disciples imitated the sheikh and founded religious schools throughout the country which became by following the villages producing crops and development factors for a large part of the Senegalese territory.

This mouride vocation allowed families to live in a healthy and spiritual, but also productive environment; which did not fail to upset the French colonists who saw a large part of the country escaping from the consumer society.

Eventually, the colonial administration understood that Mouridism contributed to the development of the country by making the land viable and by helping to develop demography and agricultural production.

Serigne Saliou followed in the footsteps of his illustrious father and great mouride disciples by founding religious schools and developing the surrounding land into villages with a spiritual vocation.

The initial objective of the human being is, let us recall, to be a lieutenant on earth to worship Allah and live in symbiosis with his environment.

The Daaras Foundation for Education and Agriculture

According to Serigne Abo Guèye, who learned it from Serigne Modou Sakho, Serigne Saliou's disciple, the first experience in agriculture was that of Ndouckmane towards Mbackol in 1931 while Serigne Saliou was still studying.

The peanut harvest was very good thanks to his disciples Serigne Mor Ndiaye, Matar Diaw, Abdousalam Ba, Modou Ba, Matar Ba, Daouda Sall and Serigne Mor Ndiaye Niani.

Serigne Saliou himself told that his first experience in land development was a success; with thirteen kilos of seeds, he obtained a great harvest, by the blessing of Allah.

He did not keep anything of it, however, because he offered the entire harvest to Khalif Serigne Modou Mustapha for the construction of the mosque of Touba.

It is very difficult to determine precisely the years during which the sheikh began to establish villages because in the absence of written sources and in the absence of eyewitnesses who lived these events, we can only give approximate dates.

For this, I prefer to say that it was at the beginning of the thirties of the 20th century. Just after finishing his studies in Mbackol, he thought of starting agricultural activities while performing divine service (Khidma) and taking care of the spiritual education of the disciples.

However, not having yet his own land, one of his companions from the school of Serigne Hamza Diakhaté named Serigne Seck, ibnou Serigne Modou Seck Takhi, proposed he come and settle in their village in Taiba Diakin, near Mbacké Baol, where he could farmland that belonged to him.

Serigne Saliou accepted the proposal and settled with his family and six of his disciples, as well as the famous poet Serigne Moussa Ka who accompanied him everywhere. Soon after, the sheikh founded Gotte, which was the first of his schools.

The Gotte Foundation

In 1934, the sheikh had settled in the Diobass, towards Thiès where he founded Gotte which became a village.

Serigne Habibou Diop informed us that Serigne Saliou said: "that the first school founded was Gotte."

He had told him the story of his move there and he said: "I took the train from Diourbel to Khombol and got off at Serigne Laamine Sylla's house, son of Serigne Tafsir Bobou Sylla. Then he prepared a horse for me to go to Khabane. So, I went through the village of Bousnakh and spent the day at "Gotte" in the house of a man called Mbaye Faye, Sidy Faye's father.

He offered me to reside in their village, then he consulted the Dia family who owned the village to grant me a piece of land to cultivate. After accepting his proposal, this family immediately established housing in wooden shacks."

This is how Serigne Saliou founded his first Daara in the village of Gotte. It was his first private property in the region of Diobass near Thies.

Serigne Mboussobé Mbacké told us that Serigne Saliou said that "he finished his studies in 1934, got married the same year, and started building his house in Diourbel; it was after that that Gotte was founded. He then moved to Ndiapandal where he founded another school where his eldest daughter was born. But he later returned to Gotte."

Serigne Saliou settled in this fertile region with his sincere disciples and founded a new farm. Serigne Moustapha Diaw told me that Serigne Saliou gave him a name, but the place remained known as the village of "Gotte."

The sheikh began to farm the land by cultivating it with his disciples and talibé under the direction of Serigne Sheikh Ndiaye, brother of Serigne Mor Ndiaye.

With the school, he exploited agricultural perimeters where he cultivated rice and vegetables. The harvest in his first year had reached 46 tons of rice. Serigne Saliou, as usual, offered it as a Hadiya to the Caliph of the time, Serigne Modou Moustapha Mbacké.

Serigne Sheikh Walo informed us that his grandmother Sokhna Maty Diakhaté, daughter of Serigne Abderrahman Diakhaté, told him that Serigne Saliou produced large quantities of rice; that the women worked hard in the fields with the men, and that all the production was given to

Khalif Serigne Modou Moustapha as Hadiya.

The life of Serigne Saliou was simple; he moved around a lot because his elder brother Serigne Modou Moustapha had given him a house in Mbour where he stayed often. Thus, he moved between Thies and Mbour before settling in Gotte where some of his disciples lived.

This school was blessed because as soon as the first class completed its initiation, the sheikh sent disciples to other places to train other talibés.

Serigne Moustapha Diaw told us that one day the sheikh brought them together and asked them to find him a certain amount of money. When they gathered the sum and brought it to him, he was happy and said, "You have obtained what you are looking for."

Nekhane's Foundation

In 1936, Serigne Saliou left Gotte to settle between Mbacké and Diourbel, where he founded Nekhane or Loumbel Sayal. This is where his eldest daughter Sokhna Astou Walo Mbacké was born before the sheikh returned to Gotte.

At that time, the locality was infested with wild beasts, while the school housed many children. According to Serigne Mustapha Diaw, whose father Serigne Mukhtar was an eyewitness to these events, Serigne Saliou who traveled often was absent when a large lion crossed the house, so Serigne Mukhtar marked the lion's footprints for recognition.

The lion walked to a water hole and entered it to drink, but he struggled to get out, scraping the dirt all around until he finally did get out.

When Serigne Saliou returned, he was informed of the scene and decided to move to a safer place. He had already made a big harvest which he offered to the khalif Serigne Mohamed Mustapha who was very happy. But when he learned of the lion scene and Serigne Saliou's decision to move, he granted him land in Gotte. This was how he founded the daara of Gotte.

The Foundation of the Diobass Daaras

Not only did this region have economic and geographical particularities, the water was abundant, but it also had a religious stake, as it was populated by Sererians courted by Catholic settlers and missionaries.

Serigne Saliou, by his aura and spiritual flow, Islamized a large part of this population, many of whom became attached to him. Thus, he founded several Daaras with other lands that he acquired there.

He founded Daroul Wahhab in 1941, on lands offered to him by a man named Ibra Fall; then another Daara in Keur Sheikh Maadiop on lands offered to him by Modou Guèye. In 1944, he founded a Daara in Fandag on land offered to him by Moussa Tobe. In 1945, he founded a village named Darou Sanna; he built a house there where he settled his wife Sokhna Khady Mbacké who gave him Serigne Sheikh Saliou Mbacké.

In fact, this land was rented to him; he had it for a while and then returned it to its owner.

Serigne Saliou moved constantly between Gotte and Mbour; he devoted all his time to religious education and agriculture. He rarely went to Diourbel, where his house often remained empty; he had left it to a few disciples to maintain it and he only went there on certain occasions.

The First Generation of His Disciples

The first disciples of Serigne Saliou were trained in these places of the Diombass; there were sixty-three of them, which the sheikh had divided into groups of fifteen, with a Diawregn for each group.

Among these first disciples were: Serigne Ndiaye the brother of Serigne

Mor Ndiaye, S. Osman Diakhaté, S. Bathie Diaw, S. Maléye Leye, S. Abo Fall, S. Mor Anne, S. Sheikh Dia, S. Mor Mbodje, S. Gora Diakhaté, S. Sidi Faye, Serigne Faye, S. Mase Tine, S. Yeri Diouf, S. Moudou Diack, S. Sheikh Ndiaye, Serigne Ahmad Dia, Sheikh Balla Dia's cousin, etc., etc.

In this first generation, there was his namesake Serigne Saliou, son of Khalif Serigne Modou Moustapha, who lived under the tutelage of Serigne Saliou.

At that time, he lived with him and accompanied him in his travels to his various farms and Daaras. To continue his studies, he then moved to Mauritania where he was able to do his humanities. During the whole period of his studies, he spent his vacations with Serigne Saliou. He then became one of the great intellectual figures in the Mouride Way. He was appointed ambassador to several Arab countries.

His method of spiritual education (tarbiyya) was initially through divine service (khidma) and remembrance (zikr) through the reading of qasidas. There was no precise pedagogical program, as the majority of the disciples were old and could no longer start learning sciences. It was then tarbiyya through zikr and qasidas, as well as through soul purification and divine service, away from worldly company.

The sheikh personally transcribed Khadimou Rassoul's qasidas for his disciples to chant them morning and evening and to memorize them.

In the second class, there were other eminent mouride figures, such as Serigne Moustahine Mbacké, son of Serigne Bara Mbacké. At that time, he was under the tutelage of Serigne Saliou, before he moved into the house of Serigne Bachir Mbacké. There was also in this promotion Serigne Sidi Mbacké Abdoul Ahmad.

At that time the sheikh changed his education program; he entrusted Serigne Saliou Touré with religious education because the latter had attended the school of Serigne Ahlad Dème in Diourbel.

To Serigne Abdou Ndiaye, he entrusted the teaching of the Malekite fiqh, and to Serigne Dam Diane, the teaching of the Quran.

Whereas he used to send the children to the Daaras in Mbackol, to the school of Serigne Mor Mbaye Cissé and the village of Affia in Saloum, to his friend Serigne Elhadji Willane, he began to keep them in his school, as his disciple Moustapha Diaw, who was himself sent to Saloum, told us.

The Diawregn of this Daara

According to Serigne Abo Median Guèye, the Diawregns were numerous:

1. Serigne Ndiaye the brother of Serigne Mor Ndiaye
2. Serigne Mor Diakhaté
3. Serigne Modou Sakho
4. Serigne Saliou Touré
5. Serigne Gora Diouf
6. Serigne Moustapha Bousso Ayouba the Mouride Sadikh (attested by Serigne Saliou)
7. Serigne Muhammad Dem Sy
8. Serigne Bathie Sall
9. Serigne Khadim Mbacké Bofdy
10. Serigne Abdessamad Mbacké
11. Serigne Habibou Diop son of Serigne Muhammad Lamine Diop Dagana
12. Serigne Elhadj Guèye who stayed there until the departure of Serigne Saliou.

The Foundation of Khabane

As early as the fifties, Serigne Saliou founded schools in Khabane, an agricultural region fifteen kilometers from Mbour.

Since the time of Khadimou Rassoul, this region was inhabited by mourides.

Several mouride sheikhs had founded villages all around, including Touba Dieng, founded by Sheikh Ibra Faty Mbacké (Mame Thierno Ibrahim), where his son Serigne Sheikh Khady was born.

There is the village of Keur Sheikh, founded by Serigne Abdou Mbacké of the family of Serigne Ma Ndoumbé Mbacké; the village of Keur Malamin Ndiaye of Serigne Modou Lamine Ndiaye and the village of Sheikh Issa Diene.

All these personalities are part of the mouride leaders. Serigne Saliou founded two centers in this region, Baghdad and Kébé for spiritual education and agricultural work.

Baghdad was founded in 1950 at the invitation of Serigne Diabel Leye, when Serigne Saliou had built a hut and dug a well to settle there with his wife Sokhna Khady Mbacké for three years.

In 1951, he founded the school of Kébé, three kilometers away, in lands granted to him by Mame Dame Kébé, a talibé of Serigne Touba.

The latter school would later be known by this name: the Daara of Khabane.

The region was very fertile; Serigne Saliou produced in the year 1957, more than three thousand tons of groundnuts, so that, the talibés and the villagers being unable to ensure the harvest, the Khalife Serigne Fallou sent Sheikh Ibrahim Lo and his disciples to lend them a hand.

The proceeds from the sale were donated to the construction of the mosque;

Serigne Fallou personally visited the Daara and spoke highly of Serigne Saliou. Serigne Abo Gueye informed us that Serigne Saliou became seriously ill during this season. Serigne Fallou told him that this was a divine sign and a testimony of his high status with Allah, and that, moreover, he was destined to carry a heavy inheritance.

Serigne Saliou remained in Khabane until 1957. During this period, he formed an elite of true mourides who combined religious teaching with divine service (Khidma), working the land with great skill.

He also brought in the young people he had sent to Saloum to learn religious sciences, as was the case with Serigne Moustapha Diaw and others.

The Methods of the Tarbiyya During this Period

Serigne Saliou was very rigorous in tarbiyya. He watched over the spiritual states of the disciples, following the directives of his illustrious father who said: "In the tarbiyya, the fact that the master and his disciples are together is necessary for the initiation to bear fruit." That is why the sheikh was often with his disciples in the school or the fields, as he directed the work and taught.

He would spend the rainy season in the fields to rigorously supervise the work, as well as to watch over the spiritual exercises and teachings.

He led the daily prayers and practiced wird and zikr morning and evening while accompanying the disciples into the fields and working with them all day long.

He provided food for everyone and did not allow the disciples to eat or drink. His disciples were not allowed to beg or to go looking for pittance elsewhere.

Even in difficult times, he never resorted to state aid or bank loans; rather, he resorted to invocations and said, "Whatever Allah wills will be, and whatever He decrees can only be good."

He armed himself with patience until Providence came to his aid. This was how he taught his disciples to accept the divine decrees and to be patient; but also, and above all, by a firm will and sincerity in adoration and divine service, turning away from the trivialities of this lowly world.

He placed great emphasis on rectitude (istiqama), and trust in Allah (tawakkul).

Khabane's Diawregns

According to Serigne Abo Medien Guèye, there was:

- Serigne Bassirou Kébé, the first Diawregn of this school, with Serigne Bassirou Diouf, Serigne Sheikh Anne, Serigne Daouda Beye and Murtadha Niang.
- Serigne Abdou Ba
- Serigne Modou Ba was Diawregn from 1963 to 1965. The school having then been abandoned, a few people lived there to keep the place.
- Serigne Saliou Touré took the direction of the school from 1975 to 1977. With him were Serigne el Hajji Sy, Serigne Niakhal Sylla, Serigne Modou Sall, Serigne Modou Lamine Sow, Serigne Galass Sow, Serigne Abdou Guèye. Many students were learning the Quran in this school.
- Serigne Modou Sall took over the direction in 1977; he worked with Serigne Mbacké, Serigne Khadim Gadiaga and Serigne Talla Samb.
- Serigne Saliou Sy took over from 1978 to 1982; he had under his

direction one hundred and fifty true mourides, supervised by eight Diawregn for fieldwork. Serigne Saliou Sy directed Quranic studies with Serigne Abdoul Ahad Diakhaté, Serigne Habibou Diop and Serigne Sheikh Anne.

- Serigne Saliou Sylla took the direction from 1983 to 1988; he worked with Serigne Khadim Touré, Serigne el hadj Lo, Serigne Affe Niang, Serigne Matar Kébé, Serigne Bathie Sylla, and Serigne Elimane Bousso.
- Serigne Khadim Touré took over from 1998 to 2000, when Serigne Saliou moved the students to Khelcom.
- Serigne Sheikh Diaw took over in 2003 to teach the children of the region; he remained there until he died in 2005.
- Serigne Sheikh Lèye took over the direction in 2005 until the death of Serigne Saliou.

The Foundation of Ndiapandal

This school is located in Kayel, near Mbacké, between Touba and Diourbel. Serigne Saliou already had schools in this area, notably in Nekhane and Lambel Sayal.

Ndiapandal was founded in 1956 when some Sheikhs of this region insisted that Serigne Saliou stay in their homes.

Serigne Sadiko Sall, a disciple of Sheikh Ibra Faty, granted him land that the sheikh came to visit one Sunday in the month of Rabi al-Thani.

Serigne Ibrahima Dia, also a disciple of Sheikh Anta Borom Gawan, gave him adjoining lands.

Serigne Saliou demarcated the land and went to see Serigne Abdoul Ahad to inform him. The latter ordered Serigne Bara Diène, khalif of Sheikh Issa

Diène, to build huts and to settle Serigne Sall, grandson of Serigne Sadiko Sall with a few mourides until the conditions were right to bring students from neighboring regions.

The following year, in 1957, Serigne Saliou left Gotte for Ndiapandal with many of his students. There, he taught the same classes as Gotte and Khaban; he separated the small from the big and gave each group a director. Serigne Saliou Touré received the mission to teach the Quran and religious sciences and also to educate the Talibés, while Serigne Moussa Diagne took care of the Khidma. The latter ceded his place in 1958 to Serigne Moussa Diouf, who led the Talibés until 1960, the year in which they were transferred to Ndiouroul.

Water was scarce in Ndiapandal and communication routes were very difficult; Serigne Saliou decided to move the disciples to Ndiouroul, while waiting for better conditions. The place remained deserted for fifteen years.

The Return to Ndiapandal

In 1975, Serigne Saliou rehabilitated Ndiapandal and installed Serigne Moustapha Diaw as Diawregn, with twelve assistants.

The latter remained there until 1979 and was then replaced by Serigne Saliou Diagne until 1982. During this period, Serigne Fallou Shuaibou was in charge of religious education.

In 1981, in a single day, Serigne Saliou freed a large number of his disciples after having adorned them including Serigne Moudou Fall, Serigne Ndiaga Diop, Serigne Alla Ba, Serigne Abdoul Ahad Guèye, Serigne Pape Sarr, Serigne Mbaye Diop de Mbour and Serigne Ndiogou Ndiaye.

In 1982, Serigne Saliou Sy was charged, with all his team of Khabane, to rehabilitate Ndiapandal; he will be the Director of all the sections: spiritual education (tarbiyya), teaching (ta'lim), and divine service (khidma).

One year later, the disciples were transferred to Ndoka and Lagane.

In 1983, Serigne Saliou transferred disciples of Gotte to Ndiapandal, but they were not very successful in agriculture and he reinforced them with others who were already specialized in this area.

Serigne Abo Mbacké was in charge of religious education and supervised the school until 1984.

Then Serigne Fallou Shuaibou took over until 1985 when raised to the rank of Sheikh, he was replaced at his post by Serigne Aliou Cissé, until 1986.

It was at this time that Serigne Hamza Abdoul Ahad took over the direction of Ndiapandal until 1989.

After that, it was Serigne Elhadji Bousso ibn Serigne Bousso the Imam who took the direction from 1989 with the assistance of Serigne Elhadji Fall Bathie Sylla and Serigne Khadim Sylla.

The Khidma was supervised by Serigne Saliou Diagne who had been brought up before and then recalled for this mission.

In 1992, it was Serigne Sheikh Atta who ran the school until 1996; during this time, Serigne Mame Mor Kébé directed the teaching with Serigne Abdoulkader Mbacké and Serigne Mourtadha Mbacké, sons of Serigne Saliou as well as the late Serigne Eliman Diop and Serigne Elhadji Mbacké. After the departure of Serigne Mame Mor in 2000, Serigne Sheikh Atta took over the direction; he will remain there until today.

The Foundation of The Ndiouroul School

As explained above, living conditions at Ndiapandal were harsh; Serigne Saliou had moved with his disciples to settle near Touba, fifteen kilometers to the southeast where Sheikh Ibrahima Mbacké had granted him land in

1960.

The villagers gave him other lands such as Bakoura and Gouye Mbam, then Darou Diouf and Mbelegne.

Serigne Abdoul Ahad ordered the mourides of Darou Salam Bokki Barka, under the direction of his nephew Serigne Ahmad Mbacké (Serigne Sheikh Say), to clear and prepare the land for development.

Disciples of Serigne Saliou de Gotte and Khabane also took part in the work and, when all was done, the disciples of Ndiapandal came to settle with their sheikh in the new school.

In the beginning, some of Khadimou Rassoul's sons sent their disciples to help in the fields, like Serigne Bassirou who sent his disciples in 1962 and 1963. Serigne Abdoul Ahad did the same for the fields of Darou Salam Bouke Barka.

This Daara was under the direction of Serigne Saliou Touré who supervised teaching and spiritual education. Serigne Magatte Fall was in charge of directing the fieldwork; while Serigne Saliou Sylla Thioub, known for his kindness, patience, stamina, and attention, took care of the small children, under the instruction of Serigne Saliou.

For a better organization of the Daara, the talibés were divided into eight workgroups, each group being led by a chief who supervised it.

Six years later, when everything was put in order, the new disciples were trained.

Serigne Saliou replaced Serigne Maguette Fall with Moustapha Diaw in 1966 and sent Serigne Saliou Touré back to Gotte to replace him with Serigne Saliou Sy.

Thus, Ndiouroul grew. Serigne Saliou bought several horses to give more efficiency to the work in the fields, but this was not always enough, because the disciples were too numerous.

Around the 1970s, Serigne Saliou bought many mules and gave each field Diawregn five mules for his team.

Two years later, he bought oxen to make the work even more efficient.

In 1975, he brought disciples back to Ndiapandal while leaving the younger ones in Ndiouroul to learn religious sciences and work.

He brought his son Serigne Basse and Serigne Haj Sy, brother of Serigne Saliou Sy, as well as Serigne Saliou Sylla the imam, and Serigne Modou Maamoun Bousso, current imam of the mosque of Touba. He also brought the great poet Serigne Khadim Ka, grandson of Serigne Samba Toucouleur Ka.

These illustrious personalities supervised the teaching and the khidma, giving the best example to the disciples.

In 1977, Serigne Saliou brought his nephew Serigne Saliou Ndiouroul to lead the school with, as assistants, Serigne Fallou Seck and Serigne Ndongo Dramé.

He then brought the younger ones from Gotte to study, and the older ones from Ndiapandal to supervise them.

During this period, the Quranic teaching was entrusted to Serigne Fallou Shuaibou Mbacké, assisted by others including Serigne

Sheikh Bara, son of Serigne Sheikh Maty Ly, and Serigne Khabane Mbacké, grandson of Serigne Mandoumbé Mbacké.

Here is how Serigne Fallou Shuaibou Mbacké relates his pact of allegiance with Serigne Saliou: "I was teaching in the assembly of Serigne Habibullah Mbacké when Serigne Saliou came to visit Serigne Shuaibou.

After listening to the lessons, I was giving, he appreciated and asked my father to allow me to go with him to teach in his schools. My father told him that I was under the authority of Serigne Abdoul Ahad and that I needed his authorization. Serigne Saliou went directly to Serigne Abdoul Ahad who gave his authorization; he returned to inform my father, who gave me five thousand francs and asked me to offer them in Hadiya and to pledge allegiance to Serigne Saliou.

I added five thousand francs, pledged my allegiance, and followed my sheikh to Ndiouroul.

My father told me before leaving: "O Fallou, I send you with this sheikh to represent me and to do what I personally had to do; but, as you know that my commitments do not allow me, you will replace me in this mission."

During this period, there were also serious events between the mouride disciples and the Fulani pastors; but, thanks to the wisdom of Serigne Saliou Ndiouroul, the problems were miraculously resolved without any damage.

In 1982, Serigne Saliou raised his nephew and gave him a laudatory testimony.

In 1983, he installed Serigne Haj Sy as the general manager of the school, with, as assistant, Serigne Ahmad Guèye, son of Serigne Moussa Alima Guèye, as well as Serigne Bassirou Khelcom and Serigne Saliou, son of Serigne Muhammad Moustapha Fallou. Serigne Hamza Abdoul Ahad joined them in 1985. In 1986, the disciples of Ndiouroul were transferred to Lagane and those of Lagane to Ndiouroul.

Serigne Abo Guèye became the person in charge of Ndiouroul, and all the disciples sent by Serigne Shuaibou were under his authority until 1992.

At this date, a new generation succeeded them; it will be led by Serigne Elhadji Lo, son of Serigne Mansour Lo, son of Serigne Mokhtar Bint Lo.

The author of this book lived with them for two years before they were all transferred to Khelcom, to be replaced by a new generation, led by Serigne Fallou Seck.

In 1995, after completing our religious studies with Serigne Elhadji Lo at Khelcom, Serigne Saliou ordered us to return to Ndiouroul to direct the religious studies with, as assistants, Serigne Mbaye Diaw, Sheikhouna Omar, Serigne Khadim Guèye, and others.

Serigne Mbaye Diaw later directed the school from 2000 to 2002; Serigne Gora Diop from 2002 to 2004, then Serigne Abdoul Ahad Mbacké, grandson of Serigne Saliou from 2004 until the departure of our sheikh to his Lord.

The Development of Ndiouroul

Serigne Saliou dug wells without success, so the disciples had to fetch water from nearby villagers until 1982.

It was then that the sheikh bought pipes to connect them to the hydraulic system of the village of Baila, taking care to pass the water to the village of Serigne Ibrahima to reward him for his services.

It is only around 2000, long after Serigne Saliou reached the Khalifat, that an artesian well was dug and the water problem was definitively solved in Ndiouroul.

Serigne Saliou began building buildings with wooden huts, then surrounded them with zinc, before starting to build hard in 1996.

He built two buildings with four rooms each and then gradually added more buildings until the *Daara* was completely built.

However, it was customary to build a mosque before the buildings. In Ndiouroul, however, it was the opposite, as there were some difficulties in orienting the mosque correctly toward the Qibla.

Finally, it was Serigne Muhammad al Baqer Bousso who was in charge of defining the orientation.

Usually, it was his son Serigne Moustapha Bousso who was charged by Serigne Saliou to trace the mosque and define the Qibla in all the houses of the Sheikh.

The Foundation of The Ndoka School

Since its installation in Ndiapandal in 1975, Serigne Saliou had begun to acquire land in the vicinity of the village.

Villagers offered him land until he decided to create villages such as Ndoka, Lagane, Niarou, and Gnibinguelle; there he founded schools from which mouride people were introduced to religious sciences and rural work, as well as to various trades.

Ndoka's lands were granted to him by Serigne Mbacké Ndoye, others by Serigne Mbacké Sarr, a Sheikh Baye Fall who owned Ndoka Sarr, located between Mbacké and Gossas. This school, which was founded in 1982, was 10 km away from Ndiapandal and Lagane.

In 1983, Serigne Saliou installed some of his disciples there, under the direction of Serigne Saliou Sy. Then, the school was directed successively by Serigne Muhammad Dème Sy, Serigne Same Ndoka and Serigne Abdou Diop.

As for the Quranic masters and other teachers, they were numerous to practice there, like Serigne Muhammad Dème Sy, Serigne Modou Sy, Serigne Elhadj Lo, Serigne Affe Niang, Serigne Khadim Touré, Serigne

Mbacké Ka, grandson of Serigne Moussa Ka, Serigne Saliou Kassaid, Serigne Jili, son of Serigne Fallou Shuaibou and Serigne Moustapha Mbacké Mor Maye.

As for those who directed the field work, there were Serigne Abdoulwahab Ammar, Serigne Bathie Touré, Serigne Sheikh Touré de Lappe, Serigne Abdou Ndiaye, Serigne Moussa Diakhaté, Serigne Tafsir Faye, Serigne Khayar Touré, Serigne Issa Diouf, Serigne Muntakha and the late Serigne Sheikh Diaw.

Serigne Saliou had built a beautiful building that met the standards of housing as well as those of education, with housing 85 m long from East to West, and 75 m wide, from North to South. The southern part was reserved for women.

The School of Lagane

Serigne Saliou had founded Lagane in 1976 when a Peul named Muhammad Ngari granted him land. He asked Serigne Muntakha Bachir and two of his talibés Serigne Moustapha Diaw and Serigne Tambediou to go and inspect the premises.

The land in question, being very limited, could not be used to found a school with fields; but other owners including Aldiouma Thiorro and Serigne Sheikh Ndiaye, the disciple of Serigne Abdoulchakour Fall, gave him adjoining land; which made it possible to found the school of Lagane which is 12 km from Gossas.

These lands were fertile and some mouride Sheikhs such as Sheikh Issa Diène had already settled there.

Serigne Saliou will then move to other lands that will take the name of Diéné Lagane.

Serigne Abo Gueye related in recorded testimonies that Sheikh Abdoul Chakour Fall, while passing by, had predicted that a great saint would live there and make it viable, by implanting dwellings for divine service and pious works.

Serigne Saliou informed the Khalife Serigne Abdoul Ahad of his project and the latter ordered Serigne Moustapha Bachirou to develop these lands as early as 1976.

Serigne Mustapha Saliou composed a poem on the occasion of the foundation of the daara of Lagane:

"Good news that dispels the sadness and confusion when the sheikh was able to found lagane after so much pain.

Thus, our sheikh will obtain graces through this action that his sheikh will send him."

The Ndiapandal mourides began cultivating the land in 1982. A permanent house was built the same year and the harvest was large.

In 1983, Ndiapandal's disciples were moved to Lagane and two of Serigne Saliou's wives lived in the school to take care of the meals; they were Sokhna Faty Diakhaté Diop and Sokhna Anta Diakhaté.

The direction of the school will be held successively by Serigne Saliou Ndiaye Touba and Serigne Saliou Diagne first, then by Serigne Sheikh Mbacké Abdoul Ahad and Serigne Saliou Sow, then by Serigne Saliou Diakhaté.

Serigne Abo Guèye then Serigne Khadim Touré took over and left it in the hands of Serigne Khalil Lo. Many Quranic masters and scholars that we will not be able to enumerate, have taught in this school.

The School of Gnibinguelle

With the large number of students attending his schools, Serigne Saliou had to establish more and more of them. Thus, in 1987, he founded Darou Salam Gnibinguelle in the Department of Gossas, after Serigne Mor Ba and others granted him land.

In 1988, he began cultivating the land with disciples using tractors. He relocated the disciples and settled Serigne Samba Ngom to keep the place, while periodically going there to practice agriculture.

In 2002, Serigne Saliou ordered Sheikh Bethio Thioune to build a large house like those of Khelcom where, in 2004, he installed Serigne Saliou Ndiaye Touba with the disciples of Niarou. The Quranic teaching was entrusted to Serigne Mor Lo, Serigne Abdourrahman Bousso as well as Serigne Guèye and others.

The School of Niarou

Niarou's land was granted to him by the Rural Community of Mboul under the presidency of Serigne Thierno Khouma. It was a question of abandoned lands: then he obtained other adjoining lands, which allowed him to found a new school. in 1989.

Niarou being close to Lagane, Serigne Saliou decided to take his disciples of Darou Salam Gnibinguelle to work with tractors. In 1991, he sent the disciples to Khelcom and took young students to Niarou to learn the Quran.

He also installed teachers to teach Islamic sciences; among them, Serigne Khalil Mustafa Absa Mback ", Serigne Elhadji Bousso Thioumblene, Serigne Assane Sylla, Serigne Eliman Diop, as well as Serigne Mourtadha Kébé and Serigne Saliou, grandson of Serigne Bachirou, as well as the author of these lines.

In 1992, there was an important exchange of disciples and teachers between Ndiouroul and Niarou. The following year, Serigne Saliou moved everyone to Khelcom and left Serigne Saliou Ndiaye there to oversee the affairs of this *Daara*. He had charged Serigne Bassirou Cissé, son of Serigne Mor Mbaye Cissé to take a large number of teachers to teach the Quran to the children.

The School of Nguediane

Everywhere, people worshipped Serigne Saliou who, like his illustrious father, he spread the baraka wherever he went. He took care of the needs of those who asked him for help.

Some families offered land to Serigne Saliou so that he could establish a school near their home, which was supposed to allow their children to be taught the Quran and Islamic sciences.

The brothers Diop Matar and Diall offered Serigne Saliou the lands of Nguediane that their grandfather had once occupied; they said that these lands were part of Touba and that one-day Borom Touba would come to revitalize it.

Serigne Saliou Touré composed a poem on the occasion of the foundation of Nguediane and Niaro:

"Those who have mobilized for the service of Habibullah's son in Nguediane and Niaro have obtained happiness and pleasure."

Serigne Saliou installed Serigne Moustapha Sarr as director and sent many Quranic masters including Mor Seck, Serigne Malik Sy and Serigne Galass Diattara. This school produced scholars and many poets and many students memorized the Quran.

The School of Guelor

This school is located in the fertile Diobass region where land had been owned by Serigne Saliou before he entered the Khalifat. He founded there during his Khalifat a large school where he installed the great scholar and poet Serigne Khadim Gaye as director. But in this same period, Serigne Mustapha Diaw used this land for agricultural activities.

The Schools of Touba and Surroundings

Serigne Saliou had many schools in and around Touba, such as those of Diannatoul Mahwa, Darou Tanzil, Touba Ndiarem, and Ngabou.

In each school, there were permanently more than 300 people, mainly children learning the Quran and Islamic sciences.

The Khelcom Foundation

During one of his visits to Sheikh Malik Basine Sy in Saloum, Serigne Saliou passed through the forest of Khelcom which he appreciated and thought would be ideal to create Islamic centers in the service of Khadimou Rassoul.

Upon his return, he asked Khalife Serigne Abdoul Ahad to pray for him to be able to make this wish come true, a wish that will have to be fulfilled later.

It is for this reason that he told the sons of Serigne Abdoul Ahad that this project had been materialized by their father's baraka.

Khelcom's Geographical Location

Khelcom was a classified forest that the French colonial government had reserved for pastoral livestock.

It was 73,000 ha between the forests of Mbégué to the north-east of Malem

Odar, in the region of Kaffrine in Saloum.

The Award of Khelcom

In 1991, the President of the Republic of Senegal, Abdou Diouf, signed a decree declaring 45,000 hours in the Khelcom forest for the benefit of Serigne Saliou so that he could practice agriculture there.

The state had already dug an artesian well to water the cattle and the President of the Republic promised to dig others.

One hole will be commissioned in Unit 12 and another in Mbégué. After that, Serigne Saliou started to dig wells and boreholes with his own means.

Thus, the Khelcom development project will be a true green revolution, as it will be of unprecedented economic and cultural scope.

Serigne Moustapha Diaw told us that during the Khalifat of Serigne Abdou Khadre, Serigne Saliou had sent him to the Governor of Louga, to ask for land, to create schools and agricultural perimeters. He then gave him two letterheads, to make an official request to whoever was entitled.

The Governor drafted the request, but seeing an error in the text, he wanted to take another paper, when Serigne Moustapha Diaw took out the second letterhead given by Serigne Saliou and said: "Serigne Saliou told me to give you this if you need it."

The astonished governor wrote his request on the second paper.

After the return of Serigne Abdou Khadre to his Lord, the State of Senegal signed the decree that granted the land to Serigne Saliou, despite vehement opposition from NGOs and other environmental organizations that took the matter to international bodies.

The project came into being in accordance with ayahs 105 and 106 of Sura al Anbiya: "It was written in the psalms after the reminder that the earth will be inherited by our benefactor servants."

The History of Khelcom's Development

On May 14, 1991, Serigne Saliou gave the order to all mouride sheikhs to invest in the work of Khelcom.

Each had to clear and cultivate part of the perimeter. In a fortnight, the work was completed, but only on part of the land.

In the speech he made at the end of the work, he declared: "I thank you all for the work accomplished in the forest of Khelcom. A large part of the perimeter was cleared and made cultivable in a short period of time, from the end of Ramadan to the month of Chawwal.

Completion of this work would have taken at least a year or more to completely clear the land and make it suitable for cultivation.

What has been achieved is more than enough for the moment, as it was the most difficult part to make it viable.

We will already start to work on this part; as for the rest, we will continue next year; each one will start again from where it stopped this year, but after you have finished your own fieldwork." He will also express his thanks after the mourides have finished the work: [43] "I thank you all very much. I consider less the importance of the work accomplished than the high aspiration and sincerity of intention in your commitment, as well as the serenity and enthusiasm you have shown in this noble mission."

"I had allowed you to go home, but you insisted on finishing the job. This level of achievement and determination can only be rewarded by Allah, whose pleasure you seek, by the baraka of Khadimou Rassoul. I ask Allah to

---

[43] Sheikh's speech on May 14, 1991 at the end of the work at Khelcom.

reward you beyond your expectations and to assist you in all your present and future endeavors.

I ask everyone to go home so that everyone can tend to their own fields. The wintering is approaching, it begins this Tuesday 30th of Chawwal, corresponding to May 1st."

After that, everyone left, the Baye Fall continued to work until they finished everything and left the land ready for cultivation.

Serigne Saliou had divided the land into fifteen parts, each consisting of 5 km. In each part, there was a school and agricultural perimeter, as well as houses. He entrusted the stewardship to his son Serigne Moustapha who fulfilled his mission with brilliance.

Modernization of Agricultural Equipment

The purchase of tractors and agricultural equipment in France cost several hundred million CFA. Serigne Moustapha Saliou was in charge of the activity.

Serigne Saliou had brought to Khelcom teams composed of his disciples, under the direction of Serigne Saliou Djitté. The work began in 1992.

Construction of School Buildings and Housing

Serigne Saliou had chosen to build according to sufi models, in accordance with the design of spiritual education, so that the corners and angles were traced in such a way that air circulation was permanent. This ensured hygiene and cleanliness, but in addition, the plans respected the separation of men and women as well as the isolation of the different groups.

The schools were divided into three wings. One wing, which generally consisted of twelve buildings, was reserved for teaching and housing students.

The second wing had a northern sector for teachers, a central sector for the

Sheikh, and a southern sector for women. A third wing was reserved for the Sheikh's residence.

But in Khelcom, Our sheikh changed the configuration of the premises to make the space habitable for a maximum of students.

Each school was 100 m long and 60 m wide. The eastern part was reserved for the students' housing, it was divided into three sections: the north section had 3 buildings with four rooms, making 12 rooms. The south section was also reserved for the mosque and a large classroom in the center.

The western part was also divided into three sectors: one for teachers in the northwest, another in the southwest for women and households, and the center for the Sheikh's residence; this put him in contact with everyone.

In 1992, the sheikh bought the building materials and then entrusted the Dahira with the mission of constructing the buildings, under the direction of Serigne Modou Niasse and the supervision of Serigne Mbaye Guèye. There were three phases: The first five schools were built on five concessions; the work was completed in 1993. Then there was the development in 1995 with the construction of five more schools in five other plots.

There was finally an extension with the construction of the other *Daaras*. Serigne Saliou ordered Serigne Sheikh Mariamou Ndiaye, Serigne Thierno Diouf Lambaye and Serigne Modou Aminata Fall to finish the other constructions until all the *Daaras of* Khelcom were completed.

Water and Facilities

He had a real desire to provide Khelcom with all the infrastructure necessary for its smooth operation.

Faced with the difficult situation of access to water, since there was only one available well in the area, he had considered providing the locality with an infrastructure to produce drinking water, as well as other services. Serigne Moustapha Saliou was in charge of materializing the infrastructure, the financial issue was taken care of by Serigne Saliou. It was Serigne Modou Gaye who supervised the whole process under the direction of Serigne Moustapha Saliou who had shown extraordinary courage in the materialization of the infrastructure.

In the field of health, there was already a doctor at the Touba hospital who took care of the children. Subsequently, in 1998, the construction of a health center entirely financed by Serigne Saliou began. At the time, when the government heard about this project, it had expressed its intention to take charge of it globally, but Serigne Saliou asked him to build a health center in the Diemoul neighborhood in Touba. Khelcom was then supplied with electricity in 2000.

Khelcom's First Visit

According to Serigne Saliou Djitte, the first visit that Serigne Saliou made to Khelcom was in May 1991, he was accompanied by Serigne Bachirou Sarr of Serigne Sheikh Diakhate. It was a short visit that lasted only a few hours. Since then, it was Serigne Mourtada who went there under the recommendation of Serigne Saliou. His second visit was in 1995, on a Monday in Rajab 1415. But before he went there, some dignitaries preceded him, notably Serigne Abdou Khadre Mbacké, son of Serigne Abdoul Ahad, Serigne Moustapha Qasida, Serigne Mahmoudane Bousso, Serigne Abdoul Majid Mbacké, Serigne Madd Diagne from the library of Touba, Imam Serigne Abdou Diop and Serigne Abdou Lahad Diakhaté.

They devoted themselves to reading the Quran and the poems of Serigne Touba for a whole day. The next day, Serigne Saliou arrived in Khelcom and spent the whole day there. During this period, other dignitaries came to visit him, including Serigne Moustapha Fallou (Serigne Modou Bousso Dieng), Serigne Saliou (Ambassador), Serigne Mbacké Diop, as well as other authorities of the brotherhood. Serigne Saliou was very happy with their visits. During the following week, he returned to visit the other places. Thus, he took the opportunity to honor the residents (ndongo tarbiyya), around a big meal. He had recommended to Serigne Sidy Abdoul Ahad to take care of the preparation of this meal.

Also, it was during this visit that he changed the name of the *daaras,* because before they were numbered. The toponymy chosen was taken from that of the mouride localities or the great dignitaries of the brotherhood. The list of the *daaras,* numbering 15, appears in **Table A**. It contains the names of the *daaras, as* well as the leaders (*Diawregn*) who were at the head of each of them.

TABLE A: LIST OF DAARAS

Daara Name	Names of the Diawregns
Dianatou Mahwa	Serigne Myassine Seck, Serigne Malik Sy
Darou Tanzil	Serigne Takh Sylla, then Serigne Sheikh Kane
Touba Belel	Serigne Shuaibou Fall, then Serigne Elhadji Mbacké
Daroul-Mu'ti	Serigne Saliou Djitté
Darou Rahmane	Serigne Assane Sylla
Ndindi	Serigne Saliou Djitté, then Serigne Madd Deme Sy
Housnoul Maab	Elhadji Lo, then Serigne Ibra Amar
Daroul-Khoudouss	Serigne Saliou, then Serigne Lamine Diop
Touba Khelcom	Serigne Abo Guèye, then Serigne Mbacke Niang, Serigne Bachirou Mbacké Khelcom
Darou Salam	Serigne Sheikh Diaw then Serigne Sheikh Guèye
Daroul-Minane	Serigne Mandoye Sarr, then Serigne Talla Mbacké
Daroul-Manan	Saliou Sow Sign
Oumoul Khoura	Serigne Khadim Gaye
Daroul-Alim al Khabir	Serigne Sheikh Mbacké, Serigne Khalil Mbacké, Serigne Ibra Touré
Tayba	Serigne Youssou Diop, Serigne Elimane Diop

Start of Activities at Khelcom

Khelcom started operating one year after its creation, but only plots 3 and 8 started their activities in 1991. It was in 1993 that Serigne Saliou asked the residents of some *Daaras to* deploy there, including those in Ndiouroul,

Ndiapandal, Ndoka, and Lagane.

I was one of those who had left Ndiouroul to go to Khelcom, and we occupied plot 7. The residents of Ndiapandal were at plot 13, and the people of Ndoka went to plot 6. Lagane's residents occupied plot 12, and Gnarou's residents were in plot 9.

All this deployment took place during the year 1993. During these years, the sheikh also transferred other *daaras* to Khelcom. He proceeded in this way until all the plots were occupied. For the construction did not take place during the same period.

Throughout this period, the sheikh recommended certain works at Khelcom to the mouride dignitaries.

To some, he called for the construction of buildings, to others, he recommended assisting the residents in the harvesting process. He also asked some to prepare food while the work was in progress. An example of this is Serigne Saliou Touré who was often asked by the sheikh to prepare meals for the residents during certain fieldwork. This was also the case for Serigne Bethio Thioune.

He also recommended to some of the dignitaries works such as the uprooting of trees. For some, he recommended tree uprooting, harvesting or seeding operations. Serigne Mbacké Sokhna Lo was in charge of much of the work, as were Serigne Nar Diene, Serigne Modou Aminata Fall, Serigne Amdy Khady, Serigne Modou Bousso Dieng, Serigne Mame Mor Ndendeye, the family of Serigne Massamba, as well as Darou Salam, Serigne Saliou Touré and Serigne Bethio Thioune, and other dignitaries.

Its Method of Organization and Management

In terms of organization, each daara had a minimum of 313 residents. Sometimes this number was exceeded, but only slightly. In each *daara*, he put a person in charge (*Diawregn*) who supervised the whole *daara*. This person had assistants (*top Diawregns*) as well as other sub-assistants who took care of the fields.

Thus, each room was occupied by a group of boarders with its own field to cultivate. Each room was under the direction of a person in charge (*Diawregn bu ndaw*). All the rooms had the same number of managers and each manager had a deputy (*top Diawregn*). In each daara, there was a person in charge of teaching, both the Quran and religious sciences and everything related to religion and education. There was also a person in charge of catering and taming.

Within the framework of the general coordination of Khelcom, Serigne Saliou had chosen Serigne Moustapha Diaw as general coordinator (*Diawregn*). He was in charge of all the *daara* and was in charge of their logistics, equipment, and all amenities for their operation.

In addition, he had entrusted other tasks, including pedagogy, the teaching of the Quran, and religious sciences, to Serigne Saliou Sy and Serigne Abdoul Ahad Diakhaté. They were in charge of books, the Quran, and all other educational needs. The *daara* officials would turn to them for teaching materials.

During the recent period, there was also a certain Sheikh Guèye, who was very much involved in the purchase of teaching materials.

The Operating Costs of the *Daaras*

Regarding the restoration, it was Serigne Moustapha Saliou who was in charge of it. Consequently, he bought everything the *daaras* needed. Every month, he spent millions of CFA francs. After buying the food, he entrusted the distribution to Serigne Modou Gaye. As for Serigne Moussa Niang, he took care of the couscous supply. Usually, he bought a lot of millet which he gave to women who were in charge of the process of transformation into couscous. This is how it was distributed in the *daaras*. Serigne Moustapha Guèye told me: "Every month we bought tons of coffee, rice, couscous, and smoked fish. Everything was stored in stores that belonged to the sheikh and were scattered throughout Touba. After the storage, we distribute it to the *daaras*. Each of them received a volume to ensure its food supply."

During the moments of his Khalifat, he had entrusted all the distribution work to Hizbut Tarqiyya. He bought all the operating volume and entrusted it to Hizbut Tarqiyya. He gave them all the money for renting the trucks and even the fuel for food distribution in the *daara*.

During the last moments, from his Khalifat the disciple, Serigne Moustapha Yacine Guèye, took the commitment to take care of all the *daaras'* food supplies from his own funds. The volume of food varied according to the composition of the *daaras,* as the number of people varied according to the circumstances. In the majority of cases, the volume increased, and rarely did it decrease.

Among the people in charge of food distribution in the *daaras*, I can name Moustapha Guèye and Serigne Modou Diagne Bâ. I would like to thank the latter in this case for providing me with most of the information on distribution methods.

Because of the overwhelming number, sometimes there were problems with distribution. Modou Diagne Bâ told me this anecdote: "One day, Serigne Moustapha Diaw came to complain to the sheikh about the excessive number of residents. He told him that the stock of food was ending very quickly because of the increasing number of boarders in the *daaras*. Then, he told the sheikh to make a declaration asking parents to stop taking their children for a while to avoid disorganization in the structures. And he gave an example of a *daara* that was under stress because of food supplies and that needed to be urgently addressed.

The sheikh replied: "It is easier to acquire food than to have people." It is during this moment that he tells me to go see Mayoro Dieng, so that he can give him a credit of 5 tons of rice which must be transported as quickly as possible to this *daara*. When he had finished transporting the rice, he was called to come and answer to the Sheikh.

When he came, Serigne Saliou told him: "When you had gone to bring back the rice, Moustapha Yacine Gueye came earlier to bring me back 100 tons of rice as hadiya and I want it to be distributed in all the *daaras*."

This means that God accepted the service He was doing for Him by educating Muslim children and disciples. When there is a need that gets resolved as soon as possible it is a sign that the work is accepted, as Serigne Touba said so well: "God who does what He wants has honorably consecrated me, and everything I need comes to me." To this effect, I have chosen a few receipts as examples in the Food Distribution List Every Four Months in **Table B**.

TABLE B: FOOD DISTRIBUTION LIST

Food Distribution List Every Four Months
(from Jumada al-Awla to Shaban in 1423 AH)

Names of the Centers	Number of people	Rice per kilo	Oïl per liter	Sugar per kilo	Coffee per kilo
Touba Khelcom	240	4650	900	950	180
Darou Salam	304	9120	1140	1150	228
Oumoul Khoura	340	10200	1275	1350	255
Tayba	267	8010	1001	1050	200
Daroul-Alim al-Khabir	299	8970	1121	1200	224
Daroul-Manan	286	8580	1073	1100	215
Daroul-Minane	231	6930	866	900	173
Daroul-Khoudouss	309	9270	1159	1250	232
Darou Rahmane	278	8340	1043	1100	209
Diannatoul Mahwa	180	5400	675	750	135
Darou Tanzil	275	8250	1031	1100	206
Daroul-Mu'ti	182	5460	683	850	137
Touba Belel	178	5340	668	850	134
Housnoul Maab	244	7320	910	1000	183
Ndindi	350	10500	1313	1400	262
Ndiouroul	343	10290	1286	1400	257
Ndiapandal	249	7480	934	1000	187
Nguediane	272	8160	1020	1050	204
Ndoka	340	10200	1270	1300	255
Lagane	262	7860	983	1050	197
Darou salam	318	9540	1193	1250	239
Guelor	75		281	350	56
Khabane	60		225	250	40
Total	5882	169860	22058	23450	4407

The Health Care System

Serigne Saliou spent colossal fortunes on the health and living conditions of the residents. The expenses revolved around the purchase of soaps, and all other things that made it possible to put the residents in good living conditions. In addition, he had set up a very good organization to take care of all these matters that he had entrusted to certain people. Like Serigne Moussa Samb who was the first to take care of this. Afterward, it was Serigne Saliou Diakhaté who took care of it. They bought the medicines and paid for the other health expenses.

This care for the health of the residents is longstanding, as Serigne Saliou had been taking care of residents since 1934. That's why their health was a primary concern for him. Later, when he had disciples who lived in the cities, and it happened that a resident became ill, he asked them to take care of him while he was in the hospital.

Among these disciples was my father Serigne Mor Tala Kebe, who was a very wealthy man. He was a great help to Serigne Saliou. Each time, the house was filled with residents who came for care. Serigne Saliou had been entrusting this to him for years. At least, he insured it for more than 20 years. There were also other disciples, such as Serigne Bethio Thioune, to whom Serigne Saliou asked to take care of some residents.

Then, when he became a khalif, young doctors and students from the Faculty of Medicine of the Sheikh Anta Diop University organized themselves in dahira and also assisted the sheikh in the health care of the residents. They were under the direction of Doctor Moustapha Sourang who was on duty at the Respiratory Department of the Fann Hospital in Dakar.

In this regard, they looked after the residents who came to Sheikh Bethio's house for care. Their organization has evolved to the point where it has become a large organization that was doing a tremendous amount of work in caring for the health of the residents.

When I started writing this book, in my investigations, in an interview, Moustapha Sourang explained a lot of things to me about this issue. He explained to me what the sheikh had to invest in the health sector, especially in Touba (*see* Part 2 of the book).

Moreover, when the sheikh noticed that there were many residents in the *daaras,* he anticipated the health issue to avoid any delay in care. He had asked that some of them be trained in the field of medical care. Most of them were students who had come to answer the call of the sheikh through Sheikh Bethio in 1993. As they had a level, Dr. Sourang trained them as community health workers (CHWs) in addition to being disciples in the *daaras*.

The good organization of the health care of the residents was a concern for Serigne Saliou. For this reason, Dr. Sourang had built a special pavilion at the Touba hospital reserved for patients referred by the CHWs.

This pavilion was for residents only. Other boarders stayed in the pavilion to take care of the sick people coming from the *daaras as* well.

In each *daara,* a room is created with the necessary medicines and small materials to enable the trained Community Health Worker to provide first aid before evacuating the patients to the Khelcom Health Centers or Ndoka Health Station if necessary.

These Health Structures had to refer their patients to Ndamatou, who was responsible for regulating referrals. At one point, when it came to extending the referral, the Diourbel Regional Hospital was chosen mainly for the management of traumatologies. As for the *daaras* located in the west, they referred to the Regional Hospital of Thies under the supervision of Serigne Saliou Touré.

Some of these Community Health Workers subsequently continued their training to become nurses. Lamine Dieng, who is currently in charge of the Ndongos Pavilion and who organizes the care of the residents at this level in collaboration with the doctors, informed me that others are currently doing their health training, even though they were initially residents.

Clothing Expenses

Serigne Saliou spent many millions on clothing for the residents. He bought tons of fabric and clothing. After the reception, the fabrics were distributed to the tailors. After the clothes were made, they were loaded onto trucks to be distributed to the *daaras*.

Thus, each *daara* received its share and each resident received at least three garments, whether male, female, small or large. It is for this reason that in the convention, the sizes and measures were diverse, from the smallest to the largest. For more than 70 years, he never stopped buying clothes to distribute them to the residents, after the fabrics were made by tailors. May God reward him. He was so concerned about this issue that he designated several people from among the residents to learn the tailoring trade. So, after they had learned the trade, the sheikh bought a lot of machinery so that they could be busy making clothes for the residents.

For almost a whole year, they made clothes. Then they were loaded into trucks to be distributed in the *daaras*. He also bought fabrics that he distributed to the tailors' dahiras. They too, after the tailoring phase, brought the clothes that would be loaded into trucks and transported to the *daaras*. In addition, some dahiras bought clothes that they integrated into the clothes that the tailors made.

After the grouping, the clothes were distributed in the *daaras,* and each resident received his or her share.

Being a khalif, Serigne Saliou continued in this logic, and other dahiras were created to participate in this work. When the dahiras brought back clothes, the sheikh instructed Hizbut Tarqiyya to keep them in depots. He would then give the order for distribution to the *daaras*.

By his approach, he had organized the distribution according to the following age categories: (1) children, (2) youth, and (3) married.

Each of these categories had its share of clothing in the distribution. Also, those who had children in the *daaras, in* addition to clothing, were given money to assist them in caring for their families. To get an idea of the heavy expenses he took care of, one can refer to the paper in which Hizbut Tarqiyya mentioned the data during the distribution by year. These are data-rich archives that Serigne Modou Diagne Ba gave me when I was doing my surveys for this book.

As an example, let's take this list for clothing distribution, dated September 13, 2002.

| SUPERIOR QUALITY || MEDIUM QUALITY ||
| The Size: 85 cm to 1.55 m || The Size: 85 cm to 1.55 m ||
Pieces	Total	Parts	Total
Clothing:	6080	Clothing:	11747
Pants:	5797	Pants:	2611
Sets:	5797	Sets:	2611

All these things listed were taken care of personally by him. There was no dahira or grouping that assisted him in these kinds of things. However, dahiras of tailors would come and give him their hadiya. And he gave some dahiras fabrics for making clothes.

During the last month before his death, this dahira had come to visit him (ziara), bringing 12,000 pieces of clothing. According to Serigne Abdoul Diakhaté: "the tailors' dahira came under the direction of Ibrahima Faye to give their hadiya, in the form of clothes they made. The volume of the clothes is about 12000 pieces. In addition, the sheikh had given them other fabrics. After their arrival, he told them to deposit them in the Hizbut Tarqiyya *daara* until the time of distribution. When they were about to return, their coordinator Ibrahima Faye spoke to thank the Sheikh. Among other things, he said: "We thank you for having associated us in this service to the point that we have the opportunity to serve Serigne Touba."

So, the sheikh cut him off and said, "You will not have to thank me. It is I who should thank you because you are allowing me to explain to you when I started this work and how it has worked since then. I remember the first *daara* I founded in Gotte. Then, I went on a trip to Dakar just to look for ways to take charge of the *Daara*. I stayed in Dakar for a month. It was afterward that Serigne Samb gave me 30,000 francs. So, I bought food products for the *daara*. I put it in 12 bags (malikaan bags).

After the transport and for a while it was all over. So, we took the fabric from the bags to make 12 garments. That's how we gave them to the bravest in the *daara*. They were very happy.

Right now, you're taking me up to 12,000 pieces of clothing. So, I must only thank Allah because He informs me that He has accepted my service. He did not limit Himself to acceptance but He has increased me quantitatively. What we know from the Quran is that when God increases 1 good deed (hasana), He multiplies it by 10 (Quran, S 1 V261). But rarely, He increases from 1 up to 10000. I firmly believe that such an increase means that Allah has accepted my service. For I began with 12 garments, and today He has paid me with 12,000 garments. I believe that my divine service (khidma) has come to an end. All that remains is for me to thank Allah. And, it is I who should thank you and not you who should thank me. If at first, you started with 12 and then you end up in the order of 10,000, then you must be the only person who shows gratitude. For it is a sign that God has accepted your service and that it has come to an end."

Agricultural Production

As we pointed out at the beginning of the chapter, he was only fulfilling his mission on earth to the extent of the recommendations of God in the Quran and those of the Prophet in his tradition. It is added that he was in the service of Serigne Touba in the foundation of the *daaras*. Thus, he led the people intending to put them in the service of God. It was also a way to isolate the children to educate them spiritually so that they could have access to God. So, the *daaras* allowed him to achieve several things at the same time. For, he was able to fulfill his obligations in religion, revitalize the land, and develop his country, but he also engraved the Quran in the hearts of the aspirants and revived spiritual education. Also, the *daaras* allowed him to serve Serigne Touba.

But there is also the productivity of the *Daaras* which, to our knowledge, makes Serigne Saliou one of the largest producers in West Africa. Among other things, each year it produced thousands of tons of peanuts and millet, as well as other agricultural products. The table below illustrates the volume of its production in terms of semi and crop between 1993 and 2007 for millet and groundnuts. The figures speak for themselves. They provide a good indication of the size of its production volume. We thank Serigne Modou Diagne Ba who gave us these archives and all the documentation.

Year	Peanuts Seeds Per To	Harvested Peanut	Harvested Millet
1993	310,640	1,840,689	
1994	225, 040	1,940,540	
1995	211,580	491,802	
1996	356,320	781,380	
1997	508,900	1,107,008	273,800
1998	500,200	1,327, 811	439,470
1999	522,527	4,119, 930	386,000
2000	383,000	3,081, 570	138,200
2001	not available	not available	not available
2002	not available	not available	not available
2003	not available	not available	not available
2004	not available	not available	not available
2005	not available	not available	not available

Education in these Daaras

As numerous as they are because exceeding the number of 23, if we add those of Touba, the sheikh did not establish them for an objective of agricultural production even if it is an important dimension as an economic reality especially since Islam encourages self-sufficiency and productivity. In reality, his main motivation was to serve Serigne Touba, through the *daaras* whose main objective was to serve Islam through spiritual education and teaching.

In reality, the *daaras* were only a means to create a healthy environment, which allows the residents to evolve spiritually while quietly living their religion through science, work, and the servicing of the earth to the dimension of divine recommendation.

This chapter was devoted to the foundation of the *daaras* and how the work was carried out. But as for its method of education and its content in terms of knowledge, behavior, as well as its vision on spiritual education and its philosophy of teaching, we will come back to it in the next chapter to clarify them globally. It is in this chapter that we are going to explain amply the vision of the sheikh and the way he managed to shape the human being so that he would become a virtuous man, a model, a sincere aspirant that Serigne Touba endeavored to produce (the sincere aspirant). In this chapter, we will see that God assisted the sheikh in this mission. This is how he managed to produce this type of man in thousands, who carried with dignity this torch that he bequeathed to them in the service of Serigne Touba.

CHAPTER VIII - SPIRITUAL EDUCATION

Its Philosophy and Pedagogy

In this chapter, we will discuss the mission of the sheikh which occupied most of his life, which was to spiritually educate others. He attached fundamental importance to teaching and spiritual education. We will give examples of his pedagogy and methodologies that shaped entire generations of mourides.

Serigne Saliou was the reviver of the way of his father, who was also his spiritual guide; as such, he revived the methodology of spiritual education and didactic teaching of Sheikhul Khadim.

In previous chapters, we have already discussed the development of land and the founding of schools for the training of disciples and the well-being of the people.

Now we propose to study his methods of education and teaching, as well as the purification of souls and the training of new generations of true mourides.

These results are granted by science and action, as well as by the rules of propriety, in accordance with the teaching of Khadimou Rassoul who says in "Matlaboul Chifa' ":

"Make all scientists keep their knowledge up to date.

And may their actions be sincere

And let their sincerity be coupled with asceticism.

And may this asceticism be strengthened by wisdom

And let this wisdom be beneficial

And may this blessing ensure their triumph."

We will first analyze the concepts of beneficence (salah) and reform (islah) according to the Quran, as well as the role of the Envoys and Prophets in their religious and civilizing mission throughout history, before returning to the renewing mission of Serigne Saliou.

The Concept of Beneficence (Salah) in the Quran

According to Ragheb Al Asfahani: reparation (islah) is the opposite of corruption.

The great interpreter, Muhammad Husayn al-Tabataba'i, in his Quranic commentary "Al-Mizan" explained the meaning of benevolence (salah) in the Quran, distinguishing between benevolence in beings and benevolence in deeds. He said in commenting on the ayah: (He *is in the Hereafter among the benefactors*) (2:130): "as-Salah." (أَلصَّلاحُ)) means: the good or charity.

In the divine discourse, this word and its derivatives have been used sometimes for man himself and at other times for his actions and deeds. Allah says: "...he must do good deeds..." (18: 110);

He also says, "And marry those of you who are unmarried and those who are good people among your male and female slaves" (24:32).

The Goodness of Acts

There is no clear explanation in the Book of Allah about what constitutes goodness of deeds. But some indications may help understand its meaning. For example, the following are some examples:

- A good deed is good for Allah: "And those who are patient, seeking the pleasure of their Lord" (13:22); "and you what you spend seeking the pleasure of Allah" (2:272).

- It is good for Allah's reward: "Allah's reward is best for him who believes and does good" (28:80).
- He elevates the good words that go up to Allah: "To Him go up the good words, and the good deed He elevates them" (35:10).

These descriptions show that as far as actions are concerned, a "good deed" means an action that is suitable to receive the approval of Allah. Allah says: "...but He only receives piety from you...." (22:37)"; "We all help - these and these - through the bounty of your Lord; and the goodness of your Lord is not limited."

The Goodness of People

As for persons, the following ayahs show what constitutes their goodness: "And whoever obeys Allah and the Messenger, these are with those to whom Allah has bestowed favor among the prophets and the true and the martyrs and the good; what excellent companions they are!" (4:69); "And We have brought them into Our Mercy; they were certainly among the good ones (21:86)."

Again, Allah quotes Seyidna Sulayman who says "...and bring me, by your mercy, into your servants, the benefactors."

He said: "And We gave him wisdom and knowledge, and We took him in Our mercy, and he was surely among the good ones" (21:74-75).

The mercy referred to in these ayahs is not the general Divine mercy that encompasses all things; nor does it mean the mercy that is ordained for the pious believers, as Allah says: "...and My mercy encompasses all things; therefore, I will (especially) command it for the pious." (7:156)

The great personalities mentioned in the above-mentioned ayahs were "the good ones," and they were a select group of pious believers; they were "worthy" of the exclusive mercy mentioned in those ayahs. We know that some of Allah's mercies are reserved for particular groups to the exclusion of others. Allah says: "And Allah chooses especially whom He wills for His mercy." (2:105)

Moreover, this expression does not refer to the general honor of al-wilayah in other words, it does not say that Allah has managed or is managing their affairs for them. Of course, the good ones also had this honor; certainly, they were among the honored al-Awliya ' اَلْأَوْلِيَاءُ (friends of Allah), as we explained in the exegesis of ayah 1:5 (Guide us to the right path); but this wilayah is an attribute that is also shared by the prophets, the truthful, and the martyrs.

If they had only this honor to their credit, they could not be counted as a separate group from the other three.

So, what is special about "kindness"? The answer is that Allah takes a "good" in His special mercy and grants it complete protection from punishment. These two effects are mentioned in the Quran: "Then as for those who believed and did good, their Lord will bring them into His mercy (i.e., into the Garden)" (45:30); "They will call every fruit there (i.e., into the Garden) in safety" (44:55).

Now consider the following ayahs: "And We have taken him in Our mercy" (21:75); "and We have made them all good" (21:72).

Note how Allah attributes these actions to Himself, not to the people involved. Also note the fact that according to divine declarations, the reward is always given in place of action and effort. Keeping all this in mind, you will realize that "personal kindness" is a special honor that cannot be earned as a reward for good deeds or by one's own will.

It is probably to this reality that the ayah refers: "They have there what they desire and with Us it is more" (50:35).

Perhaps the first clause (They have what they want in it) refers to the reward of their deeds, and the second (and with us is even more) concerns what will be given to them not in lieu of action, but only by the Divine Mercy. We shall elaborate it, Allah willing, in the exegesis of this ayah.

Now, look at the life of Ibrahim (ace). He was a prophet, a messenger of God, one of the prophets Ulu'l Azm and an Imam; many of the prophets and messengers who came after him were his followers; and he was one of the good ones, as the words of Allah make clear: "And We have made all of them good" (21:72).

This ayah also shows that he was made, in this very world, one of the good ones. Consider also the fact that many prophets of lesser rank have been made, in this very world, among the good ones. So why does he pray to Allah to join him to the good ones?

It is clear from this prayer that there was a group of "good people" who had preceded him, and now he was praying to Allah to join them. Allah granted him his prayer 'in the Hereafter', as mentioned in the Quran in three places - one of which is the ayah under discussion:

"and most certainly We have chosen him in this world, and in the Hereafter, he is most certainly among the good ones (2:130)."

The other two ayahs are:

"...and We have given him his reward in this world, and in the Hereafter, he is most certainly among the good ones (29:27)."

"And We have given him good in this world, and in the Hereafter, he will certainly be among the good ones (16:122)."

If you meditate on the above details, you will know that "goodness" has many ranks, one above the other. Therefore, you should not be surprised if you are told that Ibrahim (as) had asked to be joined to Muhammad (s) and his purified offspring (as) and that Allah granted him his prayer in the Hereafter, not in this world.

Ibrahim (as) had prayed to Allah to help him with the good ones, while Muhammad (pbuh) unambiguously claims this honor for himself:

"Surely my guardian is Allah, Who has revealed the Book, and He takes the affairs of the good ones into His hands" (7:196).

It is obvious that Muhammad(s) claims the wilayah for himself. In other words, the Prophet (pbuh), according to his claim mentioned in the ayah, had already obtained "goodness"; and Ibrahim (a.s.) was praying to be joined with a group of "good ones" who had already received this rank, and that group was Muhammad (s) and his offspring. (44)

The Renovating Mission of Serigne Saliou

The whole life of our sheikh was based on his educational work, which was aimed at perfecting the being and actions of the disciples, with the aim of renewing society.

The saints follow in the footsteps of the Prophets who are the best examples for humanity; Serigne Saliou, as his name (Salah) will indicate, will be their heir.

He was following in the footsteps of his illustrious father and had dedicated his life to his mission. This mission consisted in reforming society and training scholars and sages who will perpetuate the work of Khadimou

---

[44] al-Tabataba'i, Muhammad Husayn Tafsir al Mizan vol 2p100, version anglaise Publisher(s): World Organization for Islamic Services [W.O.F.I.S.]

Rassoul.

Moreover, his father had announced to his wife that his son would be a reviver of the Way. In several verses of his writings, one will find indications in this direction:

> *"Put in my hand and my house the benefactor (salah) and establish him by the faithful guide.*
>
> *Grant me true science and beneficial work (salah) that will complete my hopes."*

In another verse:

> *He has granted me true science and beneficial work (Salah) that fills me with hope.*

In another verse:

> *"Life grants me the blessings and graces me with a slave servant benefactor (salah)."*

Serigne Saliou took his mission to heart and complied scrupulously with his father's recommendations. To this end, he devoted himself to charitable works and the education of his disciples to perfect them spiritually through "Iman", "Islam" and "Ihsan."

He declared in a sermon:

> *"As for the recommendations that I give to my mouride brothers, they are related to these words of Khadimou Rassoul:*
>
> *My writings initiate spiritual education (tarbiyya) and lead to the Lord, the one who seeks spiritual elevation (tarqiyya).*
>
> *In my writings, Allah conceals the secrets of La ilaha illa Allah.*
>
> *I have integrated what is not in books. So never be deficient in my*

service.

I call to you by these words in order to revive the Mouride Way and remind you of the epic of Khadimou Rassoul. He, in the last period of his life, ordered those who presented their children to him to provide them with the best teaching and the best education, while making them fit for honest and useful work."

This is what I call for in my Khelcom schools, even if I don't pretend to have the level. I still want to benefit from the baraka of this work initiated by Khadimou Rassoul.

I remind all mourides of this and call on them to benefit from it."

Glory be to Allah who has guided us to this. (Sura al A'raf 43)

He also told the disciples that the way in which he was initiating, was a vivification of his father's way.

Serigne Moustapha Diaw reported from Serigne Saliou: "Each of the sons of Serigne Touba had his mission and his function; this is what justifies the foundation of so many villages and schools to train disciples and children."

He also reported from the Sheikh: "I do not make you work for pecuniary gain or to exploit you, but rather for the sake of your bliss in this world and the hereafter. I want all those who accompany me or serve me to find their reward on the Day of Judgment."

Serigne Abo Gueye reported these words of Serigne Saliou: "My method and also that of the sons of Serigne Touba is the education of mourides based on agricultural work and service, combining the Shar'ia and the Haqiqa, as well as spending in the Way of Allah, satisfaction through the baraka of Sheikhul Khadim and rectitude in behavior."

The sheikh will also say: "Additions and extrapolations have invaded the Way which is like the ocean that contains everything. Now, everything that the sheikh had allowed cannot be harmful to the mouride. You must never denigrate others; but if you see a behavior different from the one by which you are educated, avoid it.

Khadimou Rassoul ordered me to educate the mourides and showed me the correct way to do so. I will follow it in principles and details.

You are too close to me; you cannot estimate me at my true value, but all the sons of Serigne Touba know me and estimate me at my true value.

In fact, there are many methods in the Way, but I will only lead you to Serigne Touba by the fastest of them.

Glory be to Allah; your chain is not long between you and Serigne Touba, there is only my humble person."

Serigne Saliou as Sheikh Tarbiyya

This educating function is that of the perfect ones like the Prophets and some awliyas, as well as the true ones who are the doctors of souls. Serigne Saliou was exemplary in this function to which he devoted his life.

Serigne Matar Kebe reported these words of Serigne Saliou: "All the sons of Serigne Touba are perfect and are suitable for teaching (ta'lim), spiritual education (tarbiyya), elevation (tarqiyya), as well as reform (islah)."

Serigne Saliou also said to his disciples: "Do not think that I receive my information from third parties; for if I was not in a position to know your slightest acts and thoughts, how could I have been your guide?

In the same way that you know the smallest corners of the fields you cultivate, I know the smallest perfections and imperfections of your souls; if I were not obliged to veil the intimate secrets, I would have revealed to you what each of you thinks and does daily."

Serigne Saliou was very pedagogical; he had a particular methodology to explain all the principles and subtleties of Tasawwuf with edifying examples and simple illustrations.

To do this, he used everyday objects such as coffee or millet, the hut, and other objects, as will be explained later in studying his methods.

He was thus able to explain to the disciples very difficult notions that required for the recipients a solid intellectual preparation and theological or philosophical training. His spiritual dimension meant that his words of wisdom conveyed the lights that enlightened the minds of the disciples.

Criteria for the Function of Sheikh

The function of the sheikh has indeed become rather unclear and many attribute it to themselves for free. However, Khadimou Rassoul explained the conditions and implications in his letters and advice.

Sheikh Tarbiyya requires three criteria:

- ➤ To know souls and their apparent and intimate states; what can perfect them and what can corrupt them, while being able to heal them through science and experience, with competence in the principles of religion and its applications.
- ➤ To know the existence or Being (wujud) as well as the multiple states of Being, legal laws, and natural laws through texts and experience, as well as through intuition and contemplation, to distinguish metaphysical realities from physical realities and to act accordingly.

> To master the governance of these realities, to give everything, its right in all fairness, without passion or temptation. This is only possible with a pure heart full of humility and self-sacrifice, a right orientation towards the divine approval which is the fruit of a spiritual education by a true Sheikh.

Abu Ali Thaqafi said: "A man can gather all the sciences and frequent sufis; one can only take from him the way if he has been educated by a Sheikh."

Junaid said: "Our science is taken from the Qur'an and the Sunnah; whoever has not learned the hadiths, has not studied with jurists and has not been educated by a Sheikh, may corrupt those who follow him."

Ibn Ata Allah says in the Hikam: "Do not accompany the one whose spiritual state does not awaken yours, nor the one whose words do not reveal Allah to you."

We are going to explain the passages quoted starting with the **first condition:** To know souls and their apparent and intimate states, what can perfect them and what can corrupt them, etc.

There are indications in the words of Serigne Saliou who said about his own case: "apart from intuition, unveiling and holiness, my long experience in spiritual education and human relationships through multiple generations have given me a knowledge of the human psychology of different mentalities, as well as the inclinations of souls.

Concerning the **second condition:** To know the Existence or Being (wujud) as well as the multiple states of Being and the legal laws as well as the natural laws, etc., our sheikh has shown himself to be exceptional and we will give further explanations on this point.

Concerning the **third condition:** Master the governance of these realities to give everything its right in all equity, etc.

The sheikh guided his followers according to the dispositions of each one, to shorten their way to Allah.

He did not allow those who make tarbiyya to engage in lucrative work so that their spiritual will (himma) would be concentrated in Allah. Even lawful and honest lucrative work could divert the disciple from his purpose while he is still in the tarbiyya.

It is for this reason that Serigne Saliou, who knows well the inclinations of souls, saved his disciples from the traps by occupying them with non-lucrative work.

Moreover, he rotated disciples from one school to another so that they would not develop routine habits, weaving friendships and complicities that could distract them from their goals.

Often, the disciples were surprised by these incessant displacements which were intended to allow them to detach themselves from everything important to them to concentrate only on the quest for the divine.

Serigne Saliou Sheikh Tarqiyya

Khadimou Rassoul said in his letter to Demba Bass Sall, that a Sheikh Tarqiyya has three criteria:

1. His eyesight enhances the efforts. Some sufis said that seeing Mohamad ibn Wasi' gave them energy for a week.

2. His word elevates the spiritual state, Abdessalam Ibn Machich said: "Do not accompany the one who prefers his person to yours, he is selfish; nor the one who prefers you to his person because it is not constant; rather frequent the one whose contemplation makes you think

of Allah and who reminds you of Him when you do not see Him. His remembrance is light for the heart and his contemplation is a key to the mysteries.

3. Its attendance energizes the lights of perfection.

Serigne Saliou was a Sheikh Tarqiyya and his work is proof of this. Sheikh Abdul Ahad Diakhaté told: "Serigne Saliou, transferring me from Khaban's school to Touba where he wanted me to teach the Quran to the children, told me: "Khadimou Rassoul gave me as an inheritance the secrets of this verse";

"O Lord, You have introduced me to semantics, and through me, You are raising up Your followers, the masters of the Quran."

Besides, many of his disciples reported his words when he said: "Khadimou Rassoul has made all his sons capable of initiating and realizing; they can all make the disciple what the tanner makes of the skin, but, the secret of the spiritual flow (madad) is of the exclusive power of the Sheikh.

Serigne Matar Kébé reported these words but said that Serigne Saliou had said: "Khadimou Rassoul characterized me by this secret of the spiritual flow." [45]

The great disciples and especially the sons of Khadimou Rassoul testified to his aptitudes and specificities; so much so that his older brother, Serigne Fallou Mbacké said: "if I could be younger, I would have put myself under the direction of Serigne Saliou."

---

[45] There is no doubt that Serigne Saliou indicates by these remarks that he is the heir of Khadimou Rassoul in the exoteric (zahir) and the esoteric (batin). Similar statements were made by Serigne Fallou Mbacke and indicated the completeness of Khadimou Rassoul's legacy by pointing out the prerogatives of the spiritual flow (madad). There is no contradiction between the two narratives as they deal with different but complementary stations.

Serigne Abdoul Ahad used to say to his son Serigne Hamza Abdoul Ahad: "it is not possible to get younger; if it were possible, I would have put myself under the direction of Serigne Saliou. That is why I chose him as sheikh for you. I want for you all the good possible; if all the good was in my possession, I would have given it to you immediately."

Serigne Sheikh Lagane, son of Serigne Abdoul Ahad told us that Serigne Saliou, sending him one day to his father, said to him: "if you want to give something to someone when you are unable to do so, you send it where he can get it with the approval of Allah.

Then he added: "Do you know the meaning of Allah's approval?"

I said, "No!"

He goes on to say: "that's what never runs out." That which you possess perishes, while that which is with Allah is imperishable." He said, "Patients will be rewarded according to their best work.

All things are perishable in this world, but the pleasure of Allah is imperishable. And if one gets it, it is for all eternity; and if one sees someone complaining about his fate, know that he is not destined for pleasure, for Allah has connected his pleasure with that of his servant, "Allah has pleased them and they are pleased (with what comes from their Lord). (Bayyina 8)

Serigne Moustapha Diaw told us that the Khalife Serigne Abdul Ahad had told him: "Allah has granted you the privilege of accompanying Serigne Saliou because those to whom Allah wills good accompany him. They are destined for success tawfikh).

He will add: "Do you know what success (tawfikh) means?" In front of his silence, he says: "it means: looking for one's necessary and complementary needs where they are. The opposite of success is failure; it means looking for one's needs where they are not found.

Serigne Abdul Khadre, on him the approval of Allah, said to all: "You must visit Serigne Saliou often in order to amplify your will (irada), to elevate your determination (himma), to strengthen your faith, and also to perfect your spiritual state.

Those who have lived with Serigne Saliou understand the precision of the words of Serigne Abdoul Khadre who synthesized the characteristics of his brother.

Serigne Shuaibou had sent many disciples to the *Daaras of* Serigne Saliou saying to them: "I am sending you to a sheikh with whom I share the same concerns regarding the teaching and education of the mourides. But, Allah has granted him privileges that are not found elsewhere, and also rare skills to perfect the disciples.

I want all the good for you; and if you stay with me, you will achieve the status of imam in religion. With Serigne Saliou, however, you will obtain the same favors and more, to become guides for others."

Serigne Abdoul Ahad, son of Serigne Modou, son of Serigne Abdoul Khadre told me that his father had taken him to Serigne Abdoul Ahad and asked him to take him with him so that he could have Allah's approval. Serigne Abdoul Ahad replied, "I will send him to a place where he will get that." And he sent me to Serigne Saliou when I was still a child.

The Principles of Spiritual Education: His Pedagogical Philosophy

After explaining the conditions necessary to be a spiritual educator and a true sheikh who cures diseases of the heart, we explained how Serigne Saliou was able to combine all these qualities and conditions.

Now we are going to study his educational philosophy explaining the intellectual, spiritual, and metaphysical dimensions, to draw from them the essential elements that constitute the main foundation of his educational philosophy.

The educational process must be based on a specific philosophical perception or vision of existence, life, and man, whether material or ideal, it is necessary to explain the educational philosophy of the mystics of Islam and their general vision of the human being and how to prepare, configure and promote him so that he is worthy of bearing the deposit of the divine caliphate on earth and assume this responsibility and also transmit its secrets.

The Sufi Vision of Existence and the Human Being

The sufis view the human from a special perspective, that of the universal man who is God's slave and his lieutenant on earth: "and when your Lord says to the angels, 'I will put a lieutenant on earth'. They replied, "You will put there he who will corrupt it and shed blood, while we praise and sanctify you" (al Baqara 30).

Sheikh Dawud ibn Mahmoud Al Qaysari says in *Matla'l Kosus al Kalim*: "The station of the universal man (Insan Kamil) implies uniting all the divine and cosmic degrees from the intellects and the universal and particular souls, as well as the cosmic degrees of existence up to the degree of the cloud (ama') which is homologated to the degree of divinity while differentiating the Lordship from the vassalage. This is how the lieutenancy is affirmed. He is the being who unites all the realities of existence. [46]

---

[46] Al Qaysari Dawud ibn Mahmoud, The book *Matla'l Kosus al Kalim*, p. 53, Beirut Lebanese edition.

Al Qaysari says about the uniqueness of its universal synthesis: "By understanding this, you will know that informal and existential realities are manifestations of human reality which is a manifestation of the name of Allah. Spirits are also modalities of the supreme human spirit, whether cosmic, elemental, or animal. Their forms are those of this reality and its consequences. For this reason, the spiritual elite speaks of the macrocosmic reality designed for the appearance of human reality and its activities. Only this peculiarity of the human being can manifest the divine secrets and thus disposes him to the divine lieutenancy." [47]

The Different Modalities of Human Perfection

In the sufi perspective, the Prophet Muhammad (sallallahu alayhi wa sallam) is the universal man par excellence, while every other person is a drop in the ocean of his indefinite perfections. Allah has testified: "Truly, you are of such moral perfection." (Sura al Qalam 4). Our Sheikh Khadimou Rassoul specified by designating the station of his singularity:

"Muhammad is singular and transcends all duality.

He surpasses all and his gifts enrich."

Sheikh Al Akbar Sidi Muhyiddin Ibn Arabi al Hatimi (May Allah sanctify his soul) says in his book *Al Insan al Kamil, in* dealing with the station of the seal of holiness:" Know that the function of the universal man (al Insan al Kamil) in the world is like the function of the speaking soul (nafs natiqa) in the human. He is the perfect that nothing can surpass, he is the Prophet Muhammad (sallallahu alayhi wa sallam), the universal man and the master of humans on the Day of Judgment." [48]

---

[47] Al Qaysari Dawud ibn Mahmoud, *idem*, p. 141.
[48] Mahmoud Mahmoud Al-Ghurab, The book ***Al Insan al Kamil*** from the words of Sheikh Al-Akbar Sidi Mohiuddin Ibn Arabi Al-Hatami.

For this reason, no human being can compete with him in the Muhammadian perfection and cannot know his realities of majesty, beauty, and perfection. Sheikh Al Akbar also says: "The station of the perfect ones that are below his station, are like the faculties in humans. They are the prophets (salvation and peace be upon them). As for the station of those below, it is like the senses for the human. The others are rather human forms and are like the animal instincts in the human." [49]

However, every human being has the possibility to develop or realize one or more of his perfections and virtues and for this purpose, Allah guides us in the Quran: "You have in the Prophet of Allah the best example for those who aspire to Allah and the ultimate day and mention Allah constantly." (Sura al Ahzab 21)

One can only rise to perfection by being characterized by its noble characteristics. One can only do it in accordance with one's abilities and potentialities and what Allah has predisposed him to from eternity: "And for all are degrees [i.e., positions resulting] according to his deeds. And your Lord is not unaware of what they do." (Sura al An'am 132).

"They are in varying degrees with Allah and Allah observes what they do." (Sura Ali U'Imran 163).

Spiritual education, with its methods of purification and detachment as well as perfection, is the only way to acquire moral and spiritual virtues and perfections.

What is spiritual education and what is its usefulness and purpose?

These are the main questions we will answer in the next chapters.

---

[49] *Idem.*

The Linguistic and Conventional Meaning of Tarbiyya

Education (Tarbiyya) is the development and realization of the individual from an inferior state to a progressively superior state. Ragheb Ispahani in his book *the terminology of the Quran* says: "Tarbiyya is the development of the thing from one state to another until its completion."[49]

Dr. Mohammed Abdullah Draz says in his book: *Kalimat Fi Mabadi'l Akhlaq:* "The word 'tarbiyya' is etymologically 'raba' which means surplus and increase. It consists in taking care of a thing so that it grows, increases, and multiplies tenfold in order to reach maturity and perfection, in relation to its potential. The perfect education is the one that takes into account all the potentialities and faculties of the human being:

- Development of his body and the maintenance of his health, this is the role of physical education
- Linguistic development is in the field of literary education
- Cognitive work that ensures healthy understanding and correct positions are in the field of intellectual education
- Scientific work, which provides access to verifiable data, belongs to scientific education
- Professional apprenticeship, which allows one to live lawfully while working honestly, is in the field of professional education
- Awakening of the senses to the beauty of creation falls within the domain of aesthetic and artistic education.
- Societal consciousness, which allows respecting the laws and rules of human society, belongs to social and national education.
- Consciousness of belonging to the human species, which

encourages the development of fraternal feelings towards all humans, belongs to human education.

- Continuous orientation towards good actions to develop good habits and noble character is supported by ethical education.

- And finally, the push to spiritual heights in the fields of religious and spiritual education." [50]

The Meaning of Education Among Philosophers

Conventional tarbiyya is the development of the physical, psychic, and cognitive functions so that they harmonize in order to be perfected through exercises.

Its purpose is to develop the individual so that he or she possesses the talents and expertise as well as the knowledge and skills necessary to have a pleasant and happy life. It is a complex operation that must deal with all human aspects: intellect and physical but also moral.

Plato defines it as: "To give the body and mind all the beauty possible and all the perfection possible." [51]

For Aristotle (322-384 AC): "The purpose of education is to enable the individual to be able to do all that is beneficial and necessary in times of peace or war. To do all noble and good work that leads to happiness. [52]

For Muslim philosophers, it is a question of "actualizing the potentialities of the individual and thus bringing them from virtuality to existence" as explained in the letters of Ikhwan al Safa. [53]

Imam Ghazali in his letter to the disciple explained the linguistic meaning

---

[50] Draz, Mohammed Abdallah, *Kalimat Fi Mabadi'l Akhlaq,* p 39.
[51] Center of belief researches, Education and Teaching According to Nahj al Balagha. Arabic version
[52] *Idem.*
[53] Ikhwan al-Safa, Rasa'il Ikhwan al-Safa', vol. 1, p. 262.

of tarbiyya by referring to "the action of the cultivator who clears the earth so that beautiful plants grow." [54] Serigne Saliou similarly explained the tarbiyya.

The ethical philosopher Ibn Miskawiya defines it as: "To educate the characters and to raise the child to raise him in the scale of human perfection according to the guidelines of the Islamic Shar'ia and its global philosophical vision." [55]

Hegel argues that the purpose of education is to encourage work and a collective spirit.

The American philosopher John Dweye advocates that education is a continuous operation that maintains and renews skills so that they are increasingly effective and useful to society. [56]

The Spiritual Education of the Sufis

It is made up of methods that allow the aspirant to develop his potentialities or to make him able to actualize the virtual perfections in their essence from eternity. Imam Baydhawi says in his wonderful Quranic commentary: "The Lord (Rabb) implies the educational sense (tarbiyya), which means bringing the thing to its perfection gradually." [57]

According to Sheikh Ismael Haqi al Barusi, "The Lord (rabbi) transcendent is the one who educates souls by graces and hearts by mercy. He also educates the souls of the worshippers by the religious laws and the hearts of the aspirants by the rules of the Tariqa, just as he educates the minds of

---

[54] Al Ghazali, Letter to the Disciple, p. 6, Dar Al-Minhaj Edition, Lebanon 2014.
[55] Ibn Miskawiya, *Tahdhib al akhlaq*, p. 29.
[56] Center of Belief Researches, Education and Teaching According to Nahj al Balagha. Arabic version
[57] Al Baydawi, Tafsyr Albydawy ('Anwar Altnzyl W'asrar Alt'awyl) vol. 1, p. ,137Dar Al Kotob Al Ilmiyah ed. see also Al Alousi, tafsyr al'alwsy, vol. 1, p. 77.

the lovers by the lights of the haqiqa." [58]

We can now conclude from all this that the concept of spiritual education among the sufis is based on a complete and comprehensive sufi vision of human existence and nature, it aims to actualize what is virtual in souls, and gradually bring them to perfection.

In the human, there is an image of the physical reality and a mind that comes from the metaphysical angelic supersensitive reality. It is by this secret that the human can receive the flow of the divine lights and thanks to a spiritual education he can rise from the angelic world (malakut) to the archetypal world (jabarut) and to the glorious world (adhamut) which is the secret of the invisible. Thus, he contemplates by the divine light obtained by his conformity the realities of beauty (jamal) and majesty (jalal) and thus he positions himself in the lieutenancy of the True (Haqq) having the knowledge of the manifest (shahada) and the non-manifest (ghayb).

Souls naturally have a tendency towards perfection and want to escape from darkness to light, and with the help of a true master, they always want to ascend from the bodily world to the heart, then to the spirit, then to the secret, and even more secret and more secret, in order to realize the divine word: "O soul at peace, return to your Lord who approves all pleasures and join my servants, then enter into my paradise. (Sura al Balad 27-30)

Spiritual education is referred to in the Quran as purification (tazkiyya): "Allah has favored the believers by sending a prophet among them, who recites the verses and purifies them while teaching them the book and wisdom while they were in obvious error. (Sura al 'Imran 164).

---

[58] Ismael, Haqi, *Tafsir Ruh al Bayan* vol. 1, p. 88, 89.

Allah has gratified those who seek to know Him, entrusting them to guides; it is the Tarbiyya Sheikhs who show them the way and teach them the signs and verses that lift the veils and show the gate. They purge them of the imperfections that can hinder esoteric knowledge and detach them from the carnal bonds so that they can enjoy the closeness and intimacy of their Lord. They teach them the truths of the sacred book and the wisdom of the Shar'ia and the different stages of the spiritual path. Thus, they train them in both Shar'ia and Haqiqa when they could not previously distinguish between the two.

This community of sages and knowers has always existed because the earth is never without such personalities who lead to Allah; and those who think otherwise limit divine graces and omnipotence and try to close the gates of mercy before the believers whom Allah preserves us from being among such deniers." [59]

Commenting on the verse above, Sidi Ibn Ajiba says in (Al Bahr Al Madid): "Yuzakihim means: he purifies them from the stain of sins and imperfections that hinder knowledge. He also purifies them from sensual defilements, so that they can contemplate God, and be close and intimate with God." [60]

According to Seyyid Hussein Tabatabai in his commentary al Mizan: "tazkiyya means an increase of good that has the meaning of "baraka." This purification implies that it accustoms them to noble virtues and good deeds. In this way, they perfect their humanity and succeed in this life and the afterlife." [61]

---

[59] Ibn Ajiba, *Al bahr Al madid,* vol. 1, p. 396, edition Dar al Kotob al Ilmiyah Beirut Lebanon.
[60] Ibn Ajiba, *idem.*
[61] Al Tabatabai, Seyyid Hussein, Tafsir al Mizan, vol. 19, p. 265, Teachers of the Hawza edition of Qom Iran.

The Aims of Spiritual Education

The principle of spiritual education is the preparation of the human being to carry the divine deposit by purifying the soul of its vices and imperfections while developing virtues and qualities. Sidi Abdelaziz Dabbagh in Al Ibriz clearly explained these purposes by saying:

"The purpose of spiritual education is to purify our being (al-dhat) and to cleanse it of its vanities so that it becomes capable of bearing the secret. This can only be done by illuminating the darkness of the body, cutting ourselves off from material attachments, and moving away from lies. Sometimes, because of the purity of the fundamental nature, Allah disposes us to do this without intermediaries. Such was the situation of the three noble generations who were the best of the generations.

Members of these generations were committed to the truth and sought it. If they slept, they slept in the truth. If they were awake, they were awake in the truth. And if they were moving, their movement was in truth. Thus, the person who has been enlightened by Allah, who has seen his heart and found it sincere in his commitment to Him and his apostle, seeks only that which is pleasing to the Lord and the Prophet (sallallahu alayhi wa sallam).

For this reason, there was much good in such people and the light of truth shone in their bodies, and religious science (ilm) emanated from their words to the point of giving them independent legal authority in interpretation (ijtihad). What they were rewarded with cannot be described.

Therefore, spiritual education was not necessary for such generations.

The Sheikh, on meeting his disciple, who was to be the possessor of his secret and the heir of his light, breathed his breath into him. And by this alone, the disciple receives enlightenment because of the purity of his being, the clarity of his mind, and also because of the determination (Himma) of the disciple to behave according to the rules of propriety (adab).

But sometimes the separation of the darkness from the bodies occurs through the sheikh that causes it. And it is after the noble generations when intentions have been corrupted and inner convictions have become blurred. Spirits are then engaged in worldly affairs, seeking to attain the satisfaction of desires and the enjoyment of pleasures.

The Sheikh, endowed with deep vision, when he meets his disciple and heir, recognizes and preserves him. He sees that the reason of the disciple is still entangled and that his limbs are subject to the imperatives of the carnal soul. Thus, if he finds the novice in this state, he orders him to undertake a spiritual retreat (khalwa), a remembrance of God (zikr), and also to reduce his food.

In spiritual retreat, he is separated from worldly values and considers himself among the number of the dead. By constantly remembering God, false speech disappears and language games no longer make sense. By decreasing food, the vapors in the blood reduce the superfluous, and the spirit concentrates in Allah and His Messenger. If the novice then achieves this cleanliness and purity, his body is able to carry the secret. And this is what the Sheikhs aim at in their training and by imposing a spiritual retreat." [62]

---

[62] Sidy Ahmad ibn Mubarak, *The Ibriz* book, p. 350, al Maktaba al Hilmiyya edition, Beirut, Lebanon.

The Principles of Spiritual Education in Sheikhul Khadim

Sheikh Muhammad Bashir dealt with this subject in "Minan al Baqi al Qadim" where he explained the principles as well as the methods and purpose of spiritual education. According to him, when our sheikh was surprised by a higher imperative, that of educating his companions by the spiritual will (himma), he devoted himself to the task and guided the disciples towards the paths of initiation and spiritual realization on impeccable religious bases because he was endowed with a true physiognomy (firasa sadiqa) from which the Prophet (peace and salvation be upon him) said: fear the physiognomy of the believer, he sees by the light of Allah.

Khadimou Rassoul's method was based on total detachment in order to consecrate oneself to Allah by directing one's spiritual will in all sincerity towards divine pleasure. This way was borrowed at the behest of the Prophet Muhammad (peace be upon him) who exhorted him: "Educate your companions by spiritual will (himma) and not only by didactic teaching."

Sidi Ahmad ibn Ajiba said in his commentary "Al Bahr al Madid": Allah wanted for each era a particular education that corresponds to the reality of the time. In the same way, Allah wanted for each people legislation and worship according to their wisdom. Whoever guides the aspirants to a single method for all by referring to the methods of the ancients completely ignores the spiritual path, for if there is only one method for all Allah would not have sent different prophets with different followers/groups. Every prophet and saint came from Allah with miracles or wonders appropriate to their time and environment. In some times, hatred and jealousy predominate and Allah sends a chosen one to spread harmony and love; in other times, magnificence and ostentation predominate and Allah sends a chosen one to teach humility and self-denial. In other times it is love in this world and wealth that prevails. Allah sends a chosen one to teach detachment and asceticism. This is how we can understand the different methods adapted to the times and places of the time.

The meaning of education (tarbiyya) by the spiritual state (hal) and the will (himma) is to educate the believers in the prophetic way by guiding them to Allah through the precisions of contemplation and vision.

Sidi Ibn Ajiba says: "The definition of will (himma) is the knowledge of Allah through the precisions of contemplation and vision. The definition of the spiritual state (hal) is the awakening of the heart during the vision of the sheikh who recalls the Lord." The Prophet (pbuh) said: "The best among you is the one whose vision is a divine reminder."

Sidi Abdelaziz Dabbagh [63] says in "Kitab al Ibriz" concerning the education of the disciple by the will (himma) of his Sheikh: "The himma of the Perfect Sheikh (Kamil) is the light of his faith in Allah by which he raises his disciple from one state to another. If the disciple's love for his sheikh is aroused by the love of Allah, the sheikh may assist his disciple whether he is in his presence or away from him, even if he has been dead for thousands of years. That is why the saints of all ages are connected with the light of the faith of the Prophet Muhammad, peace and salvation upon him, who assists them and educates and uplifts them because their sincere love comes

---

[63] Abd al-Aziz ibn Mas'ud al-Dabbagh al-Idrisi al-Hasani was a Gnostic from the city of Fez born in 1679 (1090 AH). His family came to Fez in the early 1500s from the town of Salé in northwest Morocco. His teachings were recorded in a long book dedicated to him by his disciple Ahmad ibn al-Mubarak al-Lamati al-Sijilmasi (d. 1743 / 1156 AH) called al-Dhahab al-Ibriz min kalam Sayyidi al-Ghawth Abd al- ' Aziz al-Dabbagh (pure gold according to the words of Sayyidi Abd al-Aziz al-Dabbagh).

from the light of faith in Allah.

But if the disciple's love is personal, he will only benefit from his sheikh in his presence and when he is far from his person, he will not benefit from it.

The proof of personal love is that the attachment is conditioned by an earthly or celestial benefit either to obtain gains or to protect oneself from dangers. As for the love of faith, it is the exclusive quest for the Face of Allah without any condition of gain or prevention and if the disciple finds a deficiency in the absence of his Sheikh, it comes from him and not from his Sheikh."

Sidi Ahmad Ibn Ajiba treated the subject with great competence in his Quranic commentary "al Bahr al Madid ", he says: "As religious laws are different according to distinct communities, the methods of spiritual education are different according to people and times ." Allah says: "to each group, a law and a cult have been given" (Sura al Ma'ida 48). Ultimately, it depends on the will and the spiritual state by which the education was done in the early days of Islam. The proximity of the sheikh and the companionship were sufficient for purification and true Gnosis from the period of the companions and their disciples until the third century of the Hegira because the hearts were still in the proximity of the prophetic light.

Later, when hearts became darker, education through rites had become common and particular clothing distinguished some, such as the wearing of patchwork or the wearing of the rosary around the neck and other instruments that characterize those who stand out in this world. Exercises to tame and uplift the soul became essential as well as purification of the heart and the use of litanies (wird), so that Tasawwuf became an education by will and spiritual state as well as a system of etiquette.

This was so until the 9th century of the Hegira when some suitors who had neither the will nor the spiritual state, put forward conveniences until Sheikh Al Hadhrami announced that spiritual education by conveniences was over and only education by will and spiritual states remained, one should refer to the Qur'an and the Sunnah and not deviate from them.

Al Hadhrami wanted above all to restore order to the sufi way by cutting off the road to those who had made Tasawwuf of mere convenience. He guided the sufis of his time as any true master must do in accordance with the realities of his time.

Sheikh Muhammad Bashir, in dealing with the methods of Khadimou Rassoul, said: "He led the disciples in the way by weaning them from the delights of this world, by diverting them from power and having and by occupying them by honest and beneficial work in all sincerity in intentions and acts but especially by respecting the purposes of the law and wisdom in all work."

Khadimou Rassoul's Goals of Spiritual Education

Sheikh Muhammad Lamine Diop explained the aims of spiritual education according to the questions and answers:

- **Question:** What was the Sheikh calling for and what were the orientations in his path?
- **Answer:** The Sheikh called for sincerity which is the spirit of all work and he directed to the knowledge of Allah who ensures the junction (wusul) whose meaning is that the servant becomes a pure slave of Allah in his acts and intentions as well as in his words and his inner

and outer states.

Sheikh Muhammad Bashir explains this in "Minan al Baqi al Qadim":

"The Sheikh taught the intricacies of wisdom in order to unveil to everyone the evils of the soul while explaining the truths of religion. Then he initiated the disciples until they adorned themselves with virtues through the perfection of morals and the purification of hearts. Then he realizes them by the illumination of the intellects by uniting the faculties through total concentration in Allah. All this begins with sincere repentance and working with determination until souls are molded by faith and acquire the ideal characteristics.

Finally, the Sheikh directs each person in the course and tasks most appropriate to his case, because he knows best what is best for everyone. However, he was measured and wise in all dispositions and ensured the respect of the Shar'ia as well as the haqiqa. For this reason, the baraka was attached to his works and countless people benefited from his contribution, some of whom became, in turn, great spiritual masters, each according to his capacities and potentialities."

The Methods of Spiritual Education of Sheikhul Khadim

Sheikh Muhammad Lamine Diop explained these different methods in "Irwa al Nadim": "The Sheikhs of Tarbiyya make the disciples work hard, they direct them towards learning and teaching as well as towards zikr and service (khidma) and towards hadiya and love. They make them discover the pernicious illnesses of the soul so that they can correct themselves. Then they lead them to the junction with Allah's permission and assistance. But in truth the methods of education (tarbiyya) are innumerable."

When the Sheikh appealed and engaged in spiritual education, he had his disciples borrow all kinds of techniques and methods from asceticism with emphasis on hunger which is a foundation of spiritual education, [64] then toil such as fieldwork, and frequent zikr consisting of repetition of the formula: "There is no God but God" as well as fikr and religious songs which are prayers and eulogies on the Prophet Muhammad (peace and salvation upon him), maintaining ritual cleanliness and isolation by keeping them away from urban centers and especially keeping them away from women.

This path was beneficial for both men and women, for those who followed him had committed themselves body and soul to his mission and gave their sweat as well as their money in self-denial for the Face of Allah who said: "Allah bought from the believers their souls and their wealth to reward them with paradise." (Quran 9:112).

Although the methods of spiritual education are numerous in the Sheikh's path, they can nevertheless be concentrated in three principles: beneficial knowledge (ilm nafi'), good deeds (amal salih), and agreed rules of decorum (adab mardhi'), as the Sheikh explains in these verses:

"He who asks for the junction with the Majestic must preserve himself through the Sunnah of the one sent.

He must accompany an authentic master who does not deviate from the path on the exoteric as well as on the esoteric level.

It guides through knowledge and worship and educates through the abandonment of profane acts.

---

[64] Hunger and fasting are part of the fundamentals of spiritual education in the path of Khadimou Rassoul who did not allow those who walked with him through spiritual exercises (riyada) to eat more than a handful of millet and a sip of water a day. Serigne Mbacké Bousso reported this information, as did Sokhna Fat Dia Mbacké (Fatima al Kubra) the eldest daughter of Khadimou Rassoul, as well as Serigne Fallou Mbacké and others.

Your beauty is knowledge and spiritual path and good dispositions, persevere on this, you will be far from vanities." [65]

In other verses, he says:

"Know that knowledge and actions, as well as the rules of decorum, will bring you to perfection. [66]

Know also that knowledge and action are the means to obtain happiness tomorrow.

Dedicate yourself to this and to the purification of every imperfection and heal the ills of your soul. [67]

Knowledge and action are two jewels that make you gain happiness in this world and beyond." [68]

Varieties of Methods According to Different Abilities

Khadimou Rassoul had various methods in the education of his disciples because the dispositions and aptitudes of each were different. Sheikh Muhammad Bashir divided the mourides into two groups: one was initiated by bookish knowledge and the other by divine service (khidma) and spiritual will. I will bring back a text from *Minan al Baqi* which explains this:

"His followers were, in part, visitors seeking blessings and guidance through good counsel and in part those who made a pact of allegiance to work in the way; he counseled them by recalling the divine and prophetic teachings while instilling in them virtues and detachment. He initiated them

---

[65] Bamba Sheikh Ahmadou, The Locks of Hell "Maghaliqu Niran."
[66] Bamba Sheikh Ahmadou, *Illumination of the Heart* "Mounawwiru-Cudur"
[67] Bamba Sheikh Ahmadou, the *Itineraries of Paradise* "Massalik al Jinan."
[68] Bamba Sheikh Ahmadou, *Idem*.

to the wirds contained in the Qur'an and the Sunnah or to one of the Tariqas he was licensed to teach.

This category of disciples would leave and then return to benefit again from his blessings and guidance, they were initiated by orality (qal).

The author of the Tara'if [69] stated that the tarbiyya is done by orality (qal) or by exemplarity (hal). The Prophet (pbuh) said: "Speak with people at the level of their understanding" [70] and in another Hadith: "Treat everyone according to the respect due to his rank." [71]

Thus, each disciple must be oriented toward his field of excellence so that he can develop his potential. Our Sheikh on him the approval of Allah directed each one according to his abilities with wisdom and good examples while drawing his attention to the hidden vices of the soul, the traps of passions, temptations, and satan. He prescribed piety and good morals like a physician of souls to perfect those who are inclined towards spiritual realization.

The other part was composed of the disciples who entrusted themselves to him body and soul and gave up all their own initiative to serve him and carry out his orders to obtain heavenly bliss. He educated them by subtleties and example so that divine benevolence would amplify their spiritual will.

This category contemplated the divine will in the acts and words of their Sheikh and needed no arguments or confirmation because their intuitiveness dispensed them from it. The author of Tara'if explained this

---

[69] This is Sidi Mohammad the Khalife of Sidi Mukhtar al Kunti.
[70] Hadith reported by Daylami. Muslim reported in the introduction to his Sahih a hadith that is consistent with the Prophet (pbuh): Ibn Mas'ud said that the Prophet (pbuh) said: "When you speak out of the understanding of those you are speaking to, you may create misfortune for some."
[71] Sahih Muslim.

form of tarbiyya: Like the snail that raises its young by smell.

Our Sheikh (may Allah be pleased with him) educated his followers by weaning them from earthly delights and pleasures while purifying their intentions and engaging them in good deeds. He warned them against the pitfalls of power and wealth and inculcated in them the purposes of Shar'ia and wisdom in every act of life because he knew the shortcomings of his people and the realities of his generation.

As the common people did not have the aptitudes required for religious instruction because of widespread illiteracy and the decadent morals of the time, the common members were given obligations and recommendations, while at the same time they were given manual work to combat laziness, because idleness is the source of corruption, especially when it is fostered by the pride and haughtiness that characterizes their compatriots.

Once the disciples became accustomed to obeying and working in common without distinction of caste or social rank, he inculcated in them egalitarianism and altruism while making them understand that excellence is manifested in the virtues and perfections that result from the liberation from vices and corruption." [72]

Serigne Saliou's Method in Spiritual Education

Serigne Saliou did not invent a new method in spiritual education but revived the methods of his illustrious father, which gave marvelous results as he trained generations of true mourides and pious scholars, and sincere ascetics.

---

[72] Mbacké Serigne Mouhammed Bachir, *Minan Al Baqi,* pp. 38, 39, 40, Dar al muqattam edition, Egypt 2017.

These methods can be summarized in three main axes: beneficial knowledge, useful work, and agreed rules of decorum.

Serigne Sylla reported according to Khadimou Rassoul: "Everything can be summed up in three axes: beneficial knowledge, useful work, and the rules of decorum. Useful work is produced by submission and obedience to your Lord. Agreed rules of decency are the result of the education of a genuine guide who leads the disciple to Allah and brings him to His nearness." [73]

The Three Principles of Spiritual Education

Serigne Saliou constantly insisted on these three mysteries that had to be brought together for success because by neglecting one or the other, there was the risk of missing the spiritual path. Personally, we remember when he visited us in Ndiouroul after having ordered us to settle there after Niarou. He brought everyone together and explained to us with clarity and illustrative force the secrets of spiritual education. Among the examples he gave, we remember: "In our path, it is necessary for the aspirant to gather three things which are knowledge, work, and the rules of decorum. Then he illustrated by saying: the aspirant, during his initiation, is like someone who wants to prepare coffee. If he has enough coffee but no water, he will never be able to drink coffee. On the other hand, if he has water but no coffee, it will be the same. And if he has both but no sugar it will be bitter. He necessarily needs all three: coffee, water, and sugar in the right proportions to enjoy a good cup of coffee. The aspirant who wants to reach the perfection to which he can aspire must bring together knowledge, work, and the rules of decorum. One must be assiduous in the quest for

---

[73] Syll Serigne Mouhammed, *Jawami' al Kalim.*

knowledge, serious in the agricultural work, and vigilant as [well as] scrupulous in the purification of the soul."

Then, he insisted on an important fact which is discipline and conformity in full submission to the authority of guardianship. In Islamic terminology, this is obedience to what we like or dislike. He also said: "The way was originally known as the way of conformity; it necessarily requires obedience and conformity."

He illustrated this with the train and the cars and said, "the head end of the train that contains the engine can drive a large number of cars but if one of the cars becomes unconnected it stops. And if the head is running without driving cars, it makes no sense. Thus, discipline and compliance are needed to ensure that the cars are properly reattached and that the train arrives at its destination performing its function effectively. This is the case for aspirants with their guide or his substitute."

He also recalled that Serigne Muhammad Lamine Diop Dagana when handing over his son Habibou, said: "O my son, do as your Sheikh commands and do not worry about anything else. If he orders you to graze the flocks, you take care of them, and if he orders you to learn sciences, you take care of nothing else, and if he directs you towards the education of your soul, apply yourself and put all your will into it. If you do so, you will achieve perfection and success in this life and the hereafter."

Then Serigne Saliou commented: "Serigne Muhammad Lamine Diop did not start by knowing this, even though he knew how important it was, but he started with grazing and then he mentioned the other methods because he wanted to let his son know that the most important thing was obedience to orders and willingness to apply them without hesitation or questioning because in this lies success and happiness. Don't do anything without permission because permission is a condition for success." [74]

Then, Serigne Saliou explained the harmony between knowledge and action so that one does not unbalance the other. He said: "If it were not for the country work the Serere Animists would have been ahead of you by their ardor. They are more competent in this field. It is necessary to bring together knowledge and work in all measure and moderation."

Finally, he gave a lot of advice on good manners in the *daaras and the* importance of mercy and benevolence towards the children on whom one must take care of education as well as health and hygiene.

The Fundamental Axes of Spiritual Education of Serigne Saliou

We will analyze the content of Serigne Saliou's speech and its implications, especially the fundamental axes: beneficial knowledge, useful work, and the rules of decorum. Al-Raghib al-Isfahani [75] in his book: *Al Dhari'a Ila Makarim Al Shar'ia* (the means for the benefits of the Shar'ia) explained that the greatest projects of mankind were three: "the colonization of the earth (imara), the worship of God (ibada) and the lieutenancy (khilafa).

- the colonization of the earth: "And He raised you up from the earth and gave it to you." (Sura Hud 61). Thus Allah makes the earth subject to the needs of mankind.

- Worship of God: "I created the jinn and the human only so that they could worship me." (al Dhari'at 56). For this, we must obey Allah in

---

[74] Bamba, Sheikh Ahmadou, Al Majmu'a al Cughra, p. 222.
[75] Abul-Qasim al-Husayn bin Mufaddal bin Muhammad, better known as Raghib Isfahani (Persian: Abu al-Qasim Husayn Ibn Muhammad al-Ragheb al-Isfahani), was an eleventh-century Muslim scholar in Qur'anic exegesis and Arabic language.

His commandments and prohibitions.

- the lieutenancy: "He gives you the lieutenancy on earth to see what you do." (al A'raf 129).

One must follow the divine imperative to the extent of human possibilities while practicing the best policy in accordance with Shar'ia values. These values are wisdom, justice, beneficence, and virtue. The purpose is to attain bliss here below and in the hereafter and to enjoy the proximity of the divine in paradise.

Everything is only as valuable for its purpose as the horse in battle and the sword in combat. But if the purpose is not judicious, the thing in question loses its value. If the horse is not used against the enemy, it will be used to carry loads or to move around, and eventually, it will be used as food when needed. The sword if not used in combat, it will be used to slice food or wood. Thus, man if he does not serve for the lieutenancy or worship or colonization of the earth, he will be like a beast of burden or less. For this reason, Allah says: "Some of them are like beasts of burden or of lesser condition." (al Furqan 44) [76]

One: Beneficial Knowledge

The first axis, the most fundamental, are knowledge and learning because it is the noblest for spiritual realization and elevation. Indeed, this axis has enabled humanity to progress in all aspects of life on earth.

However, Khadimou Rassoul while inciting the disciples to knowledge and learning insisted on beneficial and useful knowledge. Sheikh Muhammad Bashir, when giving details about this in "Minan al Baqi", said: "The

---

[76] Al-Raghib al-Isfahani, *Al Dhari'a Ila Makarim Al Shari'a*.

knowledge Khadimou Rassoul speaks of is the beneficial knowledge from the Quran and the Sunnah." [77]

Scholars have stated that beneficial knowledge is that which enables the servant to know his Lord, to draw near to Him until he gets close to Him, and to live His Omnipresence, His Omniscience, and to worship Him as if he were seeing Him. The one who does not acquire knowledge in this way may find himself in the condition denounced by the Prophet Muhammad (peace and salvation be upon him) where knowledge becomes an argument against its holder because it has not been useful since the heart remained hardened and the lustful soul was attracted by the vanities of this low world. Khadimou Rassoul explained this in "Massalik al Jinan":

Beneficial knowledge is that which is learned and taught for the Face of Allah, not that which is learned for glory, controversy, or reputation.

Neither is it the one that serves to covet the goods of this world or to obtain an eminent office.

Especially not one that serves as an artifice to conquer hearts and souls; be aware of what I am saying!

All those who have applied themselves in the quest for knowledge, for the reasons I have cited

Those who have not repented before old age or death and have not tried to right their wrongs or make up for what they have omitted in their youth, will have nothing but wrongs, blame and punishment on the Day of Judgment and Questioning.

Their knowledge will be an argument against them. What a peril!

---

[77] Mbacké Serigne Bachirou, *Minan al Baqi al Qadim*.

Beneficial knowledge is, unequivocally, that which arouses in the knower (Arif) a reverential fear of the Creator, as well as humility, asceticism, courtesy, spiritual poverty, and modesty.

The Knower ("Arif") is one who has purified his heart and tamed his soul by forbidding what Allah has forbidden.

He who is not so, can in no way pretend to escape the infernal punishment announced by our Lord.

Sincerity in Motivation

The useful knowledge in the thought of Khadimou Rassoul is that which is acquired for the Face of Allah and which is used to obtain divine pleasure. This knowledge must be purely dedicated to the Lord and useful for the believers in its theories as well as in its applications. Otherwise, it may be harmful if these conditions are not met.

In *Massalik al Jinan* the Sheikh says:

Not all sciences are beneficial and not all scholars ("Ulema") are at the same level of dignity.

Some sciences corrupt the heart, arouse pride and turn away from the Lord.

Some scholars will be rewarded tomorrow only with blame and torment.

In the poetry of our Sheikh Hilali, on him be the divine approval, true knowledge is that which arouses the fear of the Lord.

He who is devoid of reverential fear ("taqwa") is certainly a deplorable ignoramus.

I affirm that the knowledge sought for fame is not beneficial.

Those seeking fame or polemics risk falling into ostentation.

Any knowledge sought for personal purposes is harmful, such as that used to issue opinions of jurisprudence ("fatwa") or to sit as a judge (Cadi) at the risk of committing iniquities.

It is the same for the knowledge acquired in order to impose itself on its contemporaries.

Scientists who spend their lives in leisure and vanity will have regrets tomorrow.

As for the knowledge that fills the heart with bitterness, fatuity, and jealousy, or that leads to discord, antagonism and adversity, it is even more detrimental to believers.

For it hinders the lights of faith and encourages pride and rivalry. It provokes hatred and hostility, even war.

The same is true of knowledge that leads to polemics and plots or that serves as a ploy to obtain the honors and vanities of this world.

The Usefulness of Knowledge is in its Practical Results

While the intent is important in the pursuit of knowledge, outcomes are also important and knowledge can also be classified as beneficial, futile, or harmful based on its purpose.

Khadim Rassoul says in *Massalik*:

Beneficial knowledge is that which reveals to man his imperfections. It inculcates patience, clemency, sincerity, modesty, generosity, and truthfulness.

It also introduces him to solitude, meditation, intellectual reflection, and the nobility of the heart.

It arouses in him reverential fear and abandonment to the divine will, just as it incites him to invocation and asceticism.

True knowledge must also drive away all forms of greed and must turn the heart away from anyone other than the Lord.

He suppresses jealousy and ostentation as well as pride and fatuity, to draw Muslims to the Lord and to give them good counsel.

Knowledge that does not lead to wisdom and good guidance leads to unhappiness and perdition.

Anyone who helps someone acquire knowledge for dishonest purposes will have participated in any resulting wrongdoing.

Such as the case of the one who sells arms to a brigand.

Knowledge cannot be reduced to erudition. It is light and discernment. Seek the face of the Majestic Lord in your quest, O my boy!

You will be rewarded with paradise.

He who does not fear the Lord of the Worlds cannot, under any circumstances, be a scholar even if he masters all disciplines.

The Importance of the Educational System in Mouridism

It is obvious that the knowledge advocated by the Sheikh is one of the most beneficial means for the spiritual upliftment of the mourides since it enriches the intellect in order to make humans fit for their function as Allah's khalif on earth. Worship of Allah requires knowledge. This is why the educational system is important in Mouridism, especially the one established by Serigne Saliou Mbacké because it is open to children and adults.

The children first learn and memorize the Quran with a teacher who then teaches them religious sciences and usually, he also serves as an imam.

There was always a teacher in the school who supervised the work of the other teachers, whose number varied between 12 and 24 depending on the configuration of the school and the number of students.

Serigne Saliou took care of the students and teachers as well as all the staff of the many schools while supervising the work. Moreover, one day he came to Ndiouroul, he was accompanied by a young student who had just mastered the Quran, as the person in charge of teaching, he summoned me and ordered me to insert him into the staff as an auxiliary teacher under the supervision of another master to do his apprenticeship with an expert before becoming a teacher in his turn. He explained that the teacher must do practicums with other teachers who have the skill and expertise before he in turn can teach the students.

Difficulties and Trials in Building Schools

Serigne Hamza ibn Serigne Abdoulahad informed us that Serigne Saliou had told him: "at the beginning of this mission I was beginning to lose hope given the difficulties encountered on a daily basis. I often put hope in a student and then I was disillusioned when the student left the school without an understandable reason. Then the parents' complaints were constant until my hopes began to fade to the point where I thought I would stop this venture. When by the greatest chance I was rummaging through the belongings left by my father I found a piece of paper where he had written: *For the Face of Allah, I must establish teachers who will train disciples who have the abilities and potentialities to work for Allah.* It was then that I revived my will and made a firm resolution to continue my work without worrying about difficulties because I took these words as a sign and a message from Khadimou Rassoul.

He often showed this leaf to the teachers of his schools to strengthen their will and arm them with patience in order to persevere in the path traced by Khadimou Rassoul who faced terrible trials and recalled that he made a pact with Allah to teach for His blessed face.

He also said, "If you follow someone's tracks and you know that when you pass by a specific place that person was injured by thorns and at the same place you get injured by thorns, you will know that you are on the right path."

The Recommendation of the Qasidas Reading

In addition to learning the Quran through memorization and commentary, Serigne Saliou was also concerned with Khadimou Rassoul's Qasidas which are prayers over the Prophet Muhammad (peace and salvation over him) and eulogies full of blessings and which help to obtain the closeness to Allah as their author stipulates:

My writings send the worshipper to his Lord without a spiritual retreat.

Allah the Transcendent is the bestower.

My writings guide the aspirant who seeks spiritual education.

As well as he who yearns to be joined to his Lord

My writings surpass the Sheikhs of the Tarbiyya

As well as all the goods and also the Sheikhs of the tarqiyya

Through my writings, Allah distills the secrets of La ilaha illa Allah.

Serigne Saliou wanted to educate the disciples in the pure way of Khadimou Rassoul and insisted on the role of remembrance (zikr) and prophetic eulogies (amdah nabawiya). He recalled the words of his father who said:

My Qasidas and my children come from the treasures of the other world; I brought them out of the treasury of generosity so that they may help humans to perfect themselves. On the Day of Judgment, I will return them to the treasures from which I took them.

For this reason, the Qasidas were very important in the education provided by Serigne Saliou who had put in all his schools' teachers who teach children the Qasidas in addition to teaching the Quranic sciences. For this, he had collected about fifty Qasidas gathered in a volume published by Khalife Serigne Abdoul Ahad who had installed a printing press in the library of Touba "Daaray Kamil" in front of the mosque of Touba.

Serigne Saliou ordered all disciples to memorize these Qasidas, or at least what they could memorize.

The Qasidas Choirs (Korels)

Whole generations of Qasidas singers came from the schools of Serigne Saliou who insisted that the rhythms and melodies should be the same as those advocated by Khadim Rassoul. To this end, he often brought great Qasida singers to demonstrate in schools so that students could imitate the rhythms and melodies. Sometimes there were Serigne Yousso Ndao and Serigne Mbay Dakar or El Haj Cissé who came to sing in the *daaras*.

Serigne Saliou ordered Serigne Moustapha Qasida Mbacké to record Serigne Massamba Mbacké's choirs so that the students could imitate them in the *daaras*. Recordings of Sheikh Muhammad Bashir's choirs were also taken to practice on their melody during the day and recited in the evening in front of Serigne Saliou who was very attentive to rhythm and pronunciation and gave advice and guidance to each member he knew personally.

Serigne Saliou wanted the Qasidas sung by the choirs to be the same as those sung before Khadimou Rassoul. To achieve this, he had operated a collection and each time a choir was formed he ordered Serigne Abdou Guèye Mouride Sadikh to buy these Qasidas from them.

When Serigne Saliou became the Khalife-General of the Mourides, he ordered his disciples to recite certain protective Qasidas, including "Hisnoul Abrar", "Wa Kaana Haqqan" and "Wa Laqad Karrammna"; so that they would be a protection for the country and the people against evils and calamities. He ordered Serigne Saliou Sy to go around the *Daaras* to echo his "ndiguel" order.

When the Gulf War broke out, he ordered to recite "Farrij Bijahil Moustafa an Ommatihi" in order to help Muslims to overcome this ordeal.

He forbade certain Qasidas or collections of Khadimou Rassoul such as "Diwanoul Folk al Mash'oun" or "Asma' Ahl Badr" because he said that they are part of Khadimou Rassoul's treasures and children should not touch the affairs of grown-ups, for fear that they might find things that are beyond their understanding.

For this he had once sent Serigne Abdou Gueye and Serigne Abdoul Ahad Diakhaté to tell certain talibés to replace the recitation of the Folk by the recitation of the "Diwan of the Qassaids Quraniya."

The Teaching of Religious Sciences

Children were to learn the Qur'an and Qasidas in order to memorize the Book of Allah from childhood and then prayers and eulogies about the Prophet Muhammad (peace and salvation be upon him). Only after that, they began to learn the religious sciences - tawhid, fiqh, tasawwuf, ilm kalam, mantaq, usul as well as the various disciplines of the Arabic language (grammar, lexicography, conjugation, rhetoric, prosody, and others).

The Methodology of the Schools of Serigne Saliou

The cycle begins by learning the writings of Khadimou Rassoul in tawhid, fiqh, and tasawwuf. First Tazawwud al Sighar then al Jawhar al Nafis and Nahj Qadha al Haj. Then it is Tazawwud al Chubban, Maghaliq al Niran, then Mounawwar al Soudour, Massalik al Jinan and Mawahib al Quddus are taught at the end of the cycle because the subject is difficult and the concepts very specialized.

Later, the student begins to study the basic books taught in religious schools in Senegal and Mauritania (*Mukhtasar Al Akhdari, Matn Ibn Achir, achmawiya, risalat ibn abi zaydashal il masalik and his commentary Misbah al salik , aqrab al masalik of Dardir, Mukhtasar Khalil*). Then some students will become passionate about *Usul al-Fiqh*.

For Arabic language sciences, students start with grammar in *Saadat al tolaab of* Sheikhul Khadim, before moving on to *al ajroumia*. In conjugation, they learn *nuzhat al dharif* from the Mauritanian scholar ijaija komlili, then *lamiat al afa'l* . They resume grammar lessons later, learning *Alfiat ibn Malik* and *al ihmirar from* the great Mauritanian scholar Mokhtar ibn Bouna.

In lexicography, students learn qasida *al jad bil jad* and *wasia,* then *saramti hibalaki ba'da wasliki zaynabi,* then *Lamiat al arab wal ajm* and *chamaqmaqia* and others. In poetry, they are taught *burda* and *hamzia from* Bousairi and *dalia* from Yousi and the poets of the jahiliya. In rhetoric, they learn *Maqamat al Hariri.*

In prosodic techniques, they are taught *Mubayin al ichkal of* the Madiakhaté kala cadi and, in linguistics, *Tabsirat al adhan* and *Oqoud al juman.*

Once this course is completed, the student has a perfect command of the Arabic language and its disciplines and knows the secrets of the Shar'ia to the point of being able to teach students in turn in these different disciplines.

Two: Work (A'mal) and Service (Khidma)

Beneficial work is very important in Serigne Saliou's pedagogical philosophy because humans must populate the earth and civilize it. Otherwise, he would be like the beasts. This is why work and divine service are necessary for spiritual pedagogy.

In the Qur'an, work and its derivatives are mentioned three hundred and seventy-one times and all commentators and linguists have explained it as the conscious action produced by humans for a purpose.

The Meanings of the Works in the Quran

In addition to its linguistic meaning which is conscious work, the notion of work appears in the Quran in three ways:

1. The creation of Allah and His works as in the verse: do they not see that we have created for them by the work of our hand's cattle and that they have possession of them?
2. Religious work for the Face of Allah and to obtain the rewards of the hereafter. In the Quran: {And who speaks better words than one who calls to Allah and does good deeds and proclaims I am a Muslim}. [Quran 41:33]

    And also: {O Messengers! Eat of what is lawful and pleasing and do good deeds, for I am aware of all that you do}! [Quran 23:51]

3. Economic work to enjoy a good life as this verse says: (Let them feed on its fruits and what their hands produce, should they not be grateful).

According to the Quranic usage of this concept, it can be said that it encompasses worship, divine service, and lawful work as well as other sufi meanings and notions that Khadimou Rassoul emphasized and revived in his path of Mouridullahi.

We cannot develop all these points in this short passage, but we will underline that Serigne Saliou wanted to inculcate his disciples with the *daaras* all these elements by making sure that they realized them.

The Results of the Spiritual Education of Serigne Saliou

Serigne Saliou's methods have succeeded in achieving two important objectives of the sufi thought of Mouridism:

1) To prepare the true hard-working and productive mouride who will know how to rehabilitate abandoned lands to make them productive because it is part of the human mission to populate the land and bring out its benefits. Thus, the mouride learns the techniques of agriculture and useful trades during his first years of initiation so that he can work and produce and thus provide for his needs and those of his family once he leaves the *daara*.

2) To educate the mouride on ethical values and high aspirations by dedicating oneself to the service of Allah and by devoting oneself to the service of Muslims with abnegation and mercy as Khadimou Rassoul teaches us in this verse of (**Matlaboul as Shifa**):

"Consecrate us, Lord, to the service of the Muslims always and in all mercy."

This is how Serigne Saliou educated his disciples with this notion that made them hard workers by day and devotees by night. They were examples of abnegation and devotion and played an eminent role in the economy of the country, especially in agriculture.

Indeed, the aspirants learned agricultural techniques and various trades in addition to religious education in order to be able to provide for themselves and their families when they finish their education. But, above all, they were imbued with values and virtues in order to be beneficial to society.

All his life, Serigne Saliou put the fruit of his fields in the Khalifat's coffers to serve the noble projects of Khadimou Rassoul which are of public utility and he taught the aspirants the abnegation and devotion that will ensure them the baraka.

He succeeds in instilling this spirit of firm will (irada sadiqa) and high aspiration (himma 'aliya) in the disciples by making them love work, volunteerism, giving of themselves and the best of one's possessions solely for the Face of Allah.

Three: The Rules of Propriety and the Nobility of the Soul

These are the characteristics that enable human beings to ensure the Khalifat on earth to the extent of their potentialities because they must ensure justice and benevolence while practicing a wise policy of forbidding evil and ordering good. The essence of the Tasawwuf is to adorn oneself with the rules of decorum and divine characteristics, as Ibn Arabi explains: "The wisdom that keeps all beings in existence is divine, then Allah created man and made him carry this deposit that allows him to manage creation, which made him his Khalifa. For this, the human being must be worthy of this privilege in order to be a sufi sage, otherwise, he would be an arrogant ignoramus. Wisdom being the opposite of ignorance, Tasawwuf would be the characterization by the divine names and attributes so that one can realize them in oneself before being unable to manage the creation. Whoever is aware of these realities and manages to manage the names and attributes will be infallible and all his actions and initiatives will be efficient. May Allah favor us to be among the sufis who work for him and honor his rights."

The Reality of the Rules of Decorum (Adab)

These are the characteristics of the well-educated man who sets a good example and directs towards good while preventing evil. For men of ethics, it is the sum of virtues (makarimoul akhlaq).

Bukhari in his book (al adab al mufrad) explains: "The rules of propriety (adab) would be the fact of mastering one's soul to bend to the noble virtues in acts and words approved by Islamic law and sound reason. Etymologically, the word (adab) comes from the banquet to which the chosen guests are invited."

The Importance of the Rules of Decorum in Mouridism

Khadimou Rassoul gives great importance to the rules of decorum in the spiritual path. In this regard, he says, "The baraka is a dwelling place where all the goods of this world and the hereafter are gathered together, while the door of entry is the rules of decorum (adab): 'enter houses through the gates.'" (Sura al Baqara 189).

Serigne Sylla reported in *Jawami' al Kalim* the following words of Khadimou Rassoul: "the ways to reach Allah are as numerous as human souls but the most pleasing to Allah is that of the approved (adab); thus the Tasawwuf is mainly the (adab)."

Khadimou Rassoul explained the importance of (Adab) for a mouride: (Adab) embellishes any enterprise and its absence alters any enterprise.

In *Massalik al Jinan*, he says:

"Know that Allah favors us with His grace and light in this life and the Hereafter, that the spiritual man cannot have a better grace than consistency in the rules of decorum (adab).

For the servant, it is the best way to approach his Lord, but also to reach paradise.

All those who hope to commune with the Lord without complying with the rules of propriety are not intelligent and are even unconscious.

It has been mentioned that it is one-third of our religion, hence their attested eminence."

Categories for Rules of Decorum in Mouridism

In his book *Nahj Qadha'al Haj*, Khadimou Rassoul explains in detail the (adab) for the mourides. In *Jawami' al Kalim* Serigne Sylla reported from the Sheikh: the (adab) are of two orders (those with Allah and those with humans).

- Those with Allah are obeying His commandments and refraining from His prohibitions, giving Him thanks for His blessings, and being patient in times of trial.
- Those with humans are three: honor the venerable, avoid simulators and leave others in their care.

In *Massalik al Jinan* the Sheikh divided the (adab) into exoteric adab (zahir) and esoteric adab (batin):

According to the Deymani, there are two categories: exoteric propriety (adab zahir) which concerns the relationship with humanity;

And the esoteric propriety (adab batin) which concerns the relationship with the divinity.

The esoteric must be in perfect symbiosis with the exoteric.

In the esoteric (adab), one must be vigilant with Allah:

He who commits infractions in the rules of esoteric propriety (adab batin) is banished from divine closeness and remains veiled.

The expulsion from the divine enclosure and the veil are worse than any trial and more serious than any punishment.

Some offenses are bold, namely, opposing his decrees by saying, "If Allah does this" or "I wish He would do this" or "Maybe He will do that" or "If He had done that."

As also the fact of opposing his choices, or one of his servants who fulfill a function, such as honorable Sheikhs who should rather be loved for the Face of God.

One should not put one's own choices and projections on what the Lord has decided as a priority, for that is very dangerous.

Neither should one covet greedily covet the largesse of one's neighbor, nor complain to creatures, nor fear anyone.

Do not hope or fear anything else besides your Lord Transcendent.

Adab with Yourself

One can enumerate in the exoteric: courtesy and noble character, as well as modesty because to be modest is the sign of elevated consciousness.

As well as using the right hand and formulating the "Basmala" in any business is very important.

Likewise, proper attitudes during meals, as well as tooth picking are among the attested exhortations; they should not be neglected. The same applies to shaking hands in greetings.

To recite the Quran consistently, to spread generosity and promote peace, and also to visit the sick, and respond correctly to greetings are all recommendations; be inspired by my versification.

You must take a vow of mercy to him who sneezes in your presence and put your hand over your mouth when you have to yawn; this is how the spiritual man acts.

One must not enter a dwelling without permission, O my brothers!

Adab with the Creatures

And you must know how to forgive those who have deprived you of your rights, just as you must learn to give even to those who have humiliated you.

Don't hesitate to reconnect with those who have separated from you.

We must be aware that blood ties are sacred, O my brothers!

O disciple, be kind to your parents even if they are unbelievers.

Educate your offspring in the best possible way, while being kind to children and respectful to the elderly.

Above all, consider your neighbor as yourself, and behave in a straightforward manner.

A wise man mentioned in a will addressed to his virtuous son:

"Seek to acquire the noble characters (Makaram el Akhlaq), while purifying your deeds from all hypocrisy: the "adab", then the "adab" and then the "adab." In fact, you should be pious to your mother and father, and to your uncle, aunt, older brother, and the elderly, for the elderly are worthy of all respect; all those who are eminent, honor them, and those who are less distinguished than you, treat them with mercy.

The Importance of (Adab) in Serigne Saliou's Pedagogy

Serigne Saliou attached great importance to the (adab) because it was the gateway to divine closeness. He often recounted anecdotes about Khadimou Rassoul: One day the Sheikh ordered a disciple to bring him such and such a person and the disciple quickly got up and scattered the sand over those present.

Khadimou Rassoul challenged him to teach him good manners when getting up and the disciple flatly apologized. Then he left and quickly returned with the man who was of a certain age and seemed so out of breath that he could not speak.

Khadimou Rassoul addressed the disciple to tell him that this was not the way to behave with old people but rather to walk behind them at their own pace. The disciple apologized again, but the Sheikh said, "Sincere repentance is not something that is repeated over and over again."

Serigne Hamza Abdoulahad related to me in this sense: at the beginning when I accompanied Serigne Saliou I had such veneration for him because of his majesty and I hardly dared to speak to him. One day he sneezed and I did not tell him the ritual formula: May Allah have mercy on you. He turned to a little boy who was with us in the *daara* and said to him: Among the rules of decorum is customary to say the ritual formula when someone sneezes in front of you.

I understood that he subtly wanted to educate me by the prophetic rules of propriety. May Allah reward him amply, he was of such a soul elevation.

The Aims of Spiritual Education

After the exposition of the pedagogical methods of Serigne Saliou's teaching, we will explain the aims of spiritual education which are the junction with Allah and the obtaining of His approval.

The mouride only wants the pleasure of the Merciful Lord in everything he does.

He who desires nothing but the pleasure of his Lord.

Will obtain the junction with Him and moreover all the goods

Serigne Saliou often explained to the disciples that the purpose of their spiritual education (tarbiyya) was the junction with Allah and the attainment of His pleasure in this life and in the Hereafter as stipulated in the Quran:

Their Lord announces to them mercy from Him and pleasure as well as paradises where they will have bliss for all eternity. Allah has immense rewards. (al Tawba 21-22).

When the mouride reaches the stage of perfection through education and purification, he becomes able to carry the deposit and the secrets of bondage as explained by Khadimou Rassoul in *Jawamai'l Kalim*: Wisdom is like rain and the heart of the mouride is like earth while the heart of the renegade is like stone.

The chests of free men are the graves of secrets. The free man does not worship the phenomenal world (dunya), the carnal soul (nafs), passion (hawa), and Satan (shaytan). The chest of such a man becomes a tomb for the lights and secrets, as well as for the blessings and goods of this world and the hereafter.

On the Approval of Allah, Serigne Saliou said: *"It is a light that Allah projects in the heart of the mouride. This light will be perceived by the relatives and it will persist as long as the mouride remains in the states that allowed him to reach this privilege. If he neglects his states, this light will disappear. Like plants that need water to grow, the mouride needs spiritual states to progress."*

Serigne Saliou explained the signs by which the mouride acknowledges the Approval of Allah: *"It is the fact of noting the respect and reverence of the family and relatives. Even sinners feel confused before him and show him respect. All will ask him for prayers and seek his blessings."*

However, when a mouride leaves the *daara* without having obtained approval, he will only find mockery and disrespect from his family and relatives.

Serigne Saliou also says: *"The quickest way to obtain the Approval of Allah is through knowledge (ilm) and practice (a'mal) and the rules of propriety (adab)."*

He often gave illustrations using the hut or the coffee shop. If someone wants to build a hut, he has to put together the pillars, the roof, and the walls. Similarly, for the tarbiyya, the pillars are knowledge, the roof is the practice and the partitions are the rules of decorum.

Sometimes he would illustrate with coffee by explaining that its preparation required three things: coffee powder, sugar, and water; otherwise, its preparation would not be successful. Coffee powder is like knowledge, sugar is like practice, while the rules of propriety are like water.

Khadimou Rassoul said in *Jawamai'l Kalim*:

"The baraka that makes the mourides obtain the benefits makes them forget the sorrows of the khidma."

He commented on this line by deconstructing the word baraka:

Ba: (bay'oul foudhoul) means the abstention from futility exoterically (zahir) by controlling one's organs to avoid the forbidden and the blameworthy. Esoterically (batin) by controlling one's thoughts in order to avoid thinking about the forbidden and the blameworthy.

Ra: (raf'oul himma) elevation of aspiration towards the Transcendent Lord without sharing with anything.

Ka: (kasb'oul khoyour) acquisition of benefits through intention and action as well as words.

Ta: (tawba nasouh) sincere repentance for all we know of our defects and imperfections and all that we ignore
Knowing that if we fulfill all the obligations and recommendations, it will be only a small part of Allah's rights over us: "They have not esteemed Allah in His true measure."

Ha: (hadiya) it is through him that comes the guidance (hidaya) that leads to the paradise promised to the pious.

We deduce that baraka is not obtained for free or by trickery but by paying the price. The mouride, by working for his Sheikh and following his instructions, will obtain the price of the khidma's punishments:

"Their Lord announces mercy to them from him and a pleasure as well as paradises where they will have a perennial bliss for all eternity. Allah has immense rewards." (al Tawba 21-22)

Discipline in Schools

Serigne Saliou was very strict about discipline and ensured order, obedience to authority as well as a healthy environment, and good understanding and respect for one's fellow man by giving priority to community interest over personal interest. He advised against imitating non-Muslims, avoiding injustice, and being a good neighbor. All these points will be analyzed in order to benefit from this beneficial teaching.

The Importance of Discipline

The discipline of the schools was very rigorous and Serigne Saliou personally saw to its smooth running. Sometimes he was uncompromising, especially when it risked spoiling the established order. Serigne Bass Abdoulkarim told us: "Some students from Khelcom were expelled because of their behavior and I went to see Serigne Saliou to try to reintegrate them because other students liked them a lot and I was afraid that it would affect their morale.

Serigne Saliou says to me: It is not serious if it affects the morale of some, it is less serious than their return which could cause damage to the discipline and pedagogy of the school because these students are negligent in the quest for knowledge and their attitude can influence others."

Obedience to Authority

In the discipline of the schools and villages of Serigne Saliou, there were always people in charge who kept order and who were called *Diawregns [of the] daara*. Each one had under his orders ten persons in charge who watched over some of the disciples.

Serigne Hamza Mbacké tells us these words of Serigne Saliou: "authority did not mean any superiority or spiritual elevation because it is only the disciplinary order for the good running of the community. Every group needs a leader so that there can be a discipline like the wagons that must necessarily be coupled to the locomotive that will carry the whole train to its final destination. Wagons without locomotives cannot run and a locomotive without wagons would be absurd, so a leader must always ensure the good condition of those under his responsibility and to walk together, with the rhythms that can bring them all together until the arrival at the right destination."

The Importance of a Healthy Environment

Serigne Hamza Abdoul Ahad reported from Serigne Saliou that the sufi companionship implied rigor and discipline: "whoever accompanies us will benefit from our company if he accompanies us and studies. If he works and does not study, he will also benefit from our companionship. As for the one who does not want to accompany me, does not study, and does not work, he will not be able to benefit from us because spiritual realization can only be achieved through companionship and perseverance.

The Importance of Exemplarity

Serigne Saliou often repeated that it was necessary to avoid following the example of the miscreants and libertines because it extinguishes the light of the mouride who walks on the spiritual path. He warned against the handicaps and obstacles that dissipate the light of realization obtained by the mourides in spiritual exercises such as prayers, fasting, reading the Quran, litanies, zikr, Qasaids, khidma, the search for knowledge, etc.

He said that resembling the settlers in lifestyle, clothing, and language hinders the enlightenment of the spirituality acquired in its realization.

Allah said: "O you who believe, do not take my enemies and yours as allies whom you love, for they have denigrated the truth that has been revealed to you, and have expelled you and the Prophet (pbuh). If you believe in your Lord when you went out to fight in my way to gain my approval, how can you show them affection! I know what you declare and what you conceal. Whoever does this among you will go astray from the right path. (Sura 60:1)

Allah also says: "A community that believes in Allah and the Last Day does not sympathize with those who defy Allah and His Prophet even if they are their fathers or their children or their brothers or their clan. Faith has been engraved in their hearts and they have been affirmed by a spirit of their Lord who will bring them to Paradise where rivers flow so that they may reside there forever. He has accepted them and they are content with Him. They are the followers of Allah; indeed, it is the followers of Allah who will be pleased." (Sura 58:22)

The enlightenment that comes from reciting the Qur'an and the Qasidas of Khadimou Rassoul cannot coexist with the enemies of Allah and their customs. Therefore, whoever seeks to sympathize with them or resemble them will lose the privileges obtained during his initiation and realization. The benefits of spiritual education are not pecuniary or merely pedagogical, for in all the *daaras of the* country such benefits can be obtained, but it is rather the pleasure of Allah which is the quest of the mouride and this is translated by the lights of the baraka which results from the khidma. For this reason, it is imperative not to mix with the enemies of Allah and to frequent the saints who love and serve Allah, for the opposite would be like one who finds pure milk and mixes it with blood or excrement. Can a holy man drink such milk even though some assure him that it is permitted?

Serigne Saliou advised his disciples not to try to resemble the colonists even in their clothing and to avoid European dress. He based this on the fact that Ahl Badr's angels recognized Khadimou Rassoul's persecutors by their outfits and did not want his followers to be deprived of the flow of angels.

He reported the words of Khadimou Rassoul who said: "He who resembles a people can be taken for one of them and he who does not want to be a suspect should not resemble the suspects."

The Importance of Mercy and Caring for Children

Serigne Saliou was merciful and benevolent towards the children and insisted on educating them with kindness and not with rigor like Khadimou Rassoul:

The way of the adab is to be merciful to children.

And especially towards parents and also to honor the elderly.

Make your neighbor as yourself for the face of the transcendent Lord

The Lord gives good news to the orphans through me and makes them forget their parents through me.

You have perfected my being forever guided by me my family without pain or sorrow.

Thus Serigne Saliou could not stand the abuse of children and whoever did so was immediately dismissed or taken away from school.

The Importance of the Public Interest

Serigne Saliou ordered the disciples to also look after the public interest and thus fulfill individual obligations (fard ayn) and community obligations (fard kifaya); he said: the mouride must not only be concerned with his own person to perfect it but he must also be concerned with his environment. Even the madmen when they walk in the streets and find dirt or obstacles for the passers-by, they keep them out of the way. Therefore, it is imperative for everyone to take care of the public welfare.

He reported an anecdote from Khadimou Rassoul who asked a Mauritanian scientist if there were cats in Mauritania. The Mauritanian answered: "Yes there are but they are only interested in their needs."

The Importance of Avoiding Injustice

Serigne Saliou warned his disciples against all forms of injustice, especially towards neighbors. He said that many of the evils he suffered were due to the wrongs done by the disciples toward others. He often gave illustrations or anecdotes to clarify his thoughts and teach his disciples certain rules of decorum. He said that Khadimou Rassoul said that the hadiya [received] from Serigne Madoumbé Mbacké were the most useful for him. But, once Serigne Maboumbé brought a lot of Hadiya as usual, except that there were suspicious things he did not know about.

Khadimou Rassoul recited a Quranic ayah: "And those who forgive their neighbor, for Allah loves the benefactors." Then, he searched in the hadiya and took out some money that he gave to Serigne Madoumbé ordering him to return it to its owner.

A Few Words of Wisdom

Serigne Chouhaybou Abou Medien Guèye reported a lot of advice given by Serigne Saliou to the disciples but we will content ourselves with a few to allow the readers to benefit from them.

The Sheikh often said: the mouride must necessarily have a strong will and a high aspiration. Whoever wants to accompany me in my mission must adorn himself with patience and resolution by detaching himself from this lowly world and its temptations. He must accept the frugality of the life of the *Daaras* and leave only to attend to specific needs because the fact of being absent without real necessity is very harmful for the teachers as well as for the students who are learning religious sciences and also for those who are in the Khidma.

This rule must be scrupulously respected because by abstaining from this healthy environment one risks being contaminated by the evils of the profane society and getting caught in the traps of this phenomenal world. Only the one who achieves such detachment for the Face of Allah will be able to benefit from his commitment to the work of Khadimou Rassoul and will see the benefits of the Khidma as he will see all his needs effortlessly met.

Indeed, it is the trivialities of life that push people to go to others either to settle needs or for family or friendly visits that are of social order, but they are recurring needs. And even if the mouride says that there are duties to be obeyed and that there are divine and prophetic recommendations for family and friendly visits, know that the rewards are tiny compared to the rewards obtained in perseverance in the Khidma for the Face of Allah. By absenteeism, the mouride may spoil the work on himself that he undertakes in the Khidma, or at least he blocks or delays its realization which is a necessity for him while these reasons for absence are secondary.

The wise man does not leave the necessary for the accessory and especially when one seeks the Face of Allah and His approval one should not worry about the appreciation of people whose criteria of value are more of the customary order than spiritual.

Besides, you can never satisfy everyone, nor achieve everything you want even if you spend your life chasing after it; above all, you have to satisfy the person you work for. He also mentioned this line:

"No one has ever been able to satisfy all their needs in this life and no one has been able to realize all their ambitions."

The Need for Companionship

Serigne Saliou often recalled the need for companionship between the guide and the disciple during the period of spiritual education. Khadimou Rassoul said: Tarbiyya by companionship (suhba) requires a continuous presence between the guide and the disciple because educating an absent one would be an impossibility. Then, he related the following anecdote: a disciple came to see Khadimou Rassoul to do the tarbiyya so that he could purify himself of his defects and acquire virtues.

Khadimou Rassoul said to him: "this requires a companionship with a Sheikh Tarbiyya but personally, I no longer have that time; but go to one of my disciples whom I have educated and you will obtain what you are looking for, go to Balla Fally Dieng."

Moreover, before occupying the Khalifat Serigne Saliou was constant in the *daaras* because he personally watched over the tarbiyya of the disciples and only left for specific needs. He sometimes went to Touba to visit family or relatives or to Mbour and Thies or Dakar or other cities, but above all, he traveled in his numerous *daaras*.

The Rules of Propriety of the Companionship Between the Sheikh and the Disciple

Serigne Saliou explained: "Companionship is not a question of duration, but rather of quality because companionship can only be beneficial when certain rules are respected. Just as a long life full of sins cannot be beneficial in the afterlife. A long companionship, as well as a long life, will only be beneficial according to its quality. If a man lives a thousand years in sin, he will find in the hereafter only the benefits of the times when he did well; likewise, he who makes tarbiyya will enjoy only the benefits of the times when he followed the rules and bent to convenience. So, whether the companionship lasts a year or ten or forty, the most important thing is in the quality and not in the quantity."

He also warned the disciples against bad manners and unpleasantness as well as insolence towards a Sheikh Tarbiyya as this is a terrible handicap for the disciple. He said: The most unfortunate of the disciples is the one whom the Sheikh avoids correcting so as not to provoke unpleasant reactions from him.

Even when he wants to send someone for needs, he avoids it as much as possible unless he can't find someone else for the task. And even if he has to, he thinks long and hard about it. May Allah preserve you from being among such a disciple.

The Difference Between the Student (Talibé) and the Aspirant (Mouride)

Serigne Saliou explained the difference between the Talibé and the mouride by saying that there are many similarities except that the Talibé does not depart from his habits and characteristics so if you want to help him and make him benefit from your contribution you must take into account his specificities and his nature.

On the other hand, the mouride has to give up his characteristics and his habits because he must not possess anything or let himself be possessed by anything, he is like a dead body in the hands of the washer, he turns him over as he wishes. He gave the example of the carpet and the turban when they are spread out; the carpet becomes flat and discovers all its patterns while the turban rolls up in any way you want and can be used for the head or as a belt or for other uses.

The Secrets of the Baraka and the Spiritual Flow (Madad)

Serigne Saliou always advised the disciples to stay in the *daaras* and avoid wandering around. On this subject, he used to say: "Don't think that the spiritual flow (madad) reaches you everywhere and at all times; it is rather a divine exhalation that reaches from time to time those who do tarbiyya in the *daaras*. When this happens and the recipient is not present, he must blame only himself."

He often explained that the baraka and the spiritual flow were not his responsibility because if it had been, he would have given it to everyone as soon as they presented themselves and would not need to keep it for months or years. It is the responsibility of Khadim Rassoul for whom he only works by preparing the recipients. When Khadimou Rassoul finds a clean container suitable for serving, he pours out his flow and fills it with baraka and benefits commensurate with the recipient's abilities and possibilities in accordance with what was recorded from eternity and preserved in the guarded tablet (Lawh Mahfouz): "Allah erases and confirms what He wills;

He has possession of the archetype of the book."

He also recalled the anecdote of Serigne Modou Moustapha and Serigne Fallou when he recommended them to be concerned about the tarbiyya of the mourides. They left perplexed because they did not know how to realize the disciples by the spiritual flow (madad) and by the baraka after the period of purification (tasfiyya) of vices and imperfections. They went back to ask him about this and his answer was decisive: your duty is to prepare the recipients so that they can receive the enlightenment, as for the flow, the baraka, and the benefits, I will personally take care of it and I will put in each clean container what only Allah knows about flow, baraka, and benefits.

Serigne Sylla reported that Khadimou Rassoul said: "My flow is constantly increasing with every sunrise through the secret of the verse: and was taught by us a growing flow with every sunrise through the secret of the ayah: 'And he taught you what you did not know.' (Nisa 114) But those who are not attached to me continue to be distanced at every sunrise by the secret of the ayah: 'But the majority of men do not know.'" (Ara'f 187)

Tarbiyya and the Mouride

Among Serigne Saliou's maxims of wisdom: he who has seeds can do with what he wants, either he keeps them or sells them or lends them, but when the rainy season comes and the seeds are sown, he has no choice but to wait for the harvest because if he hurries for the harvest, he will lose the capital and the profit and will have neither the fruits nor the seeds. On the other hand, if he waits until the end, he will have everything: fruits, seeds, leaves, and derivatives.

Serigne Abou Medien Guèye says that Serigne Saliou reunited him with Serigne Mahmoud Bousso and tells them: "The mouride during their tarbiyya is like a garden where there is everything, even garbage, and weeds. He must know that all the disciplines of the tarbiyya such as knowledge, work, and rules of decorum are like the various works to maintain the garden such as cleaning, watering, pruning, sowing, harvesting, and others. For this, the mouride, must demonstrate perseverance in all the works, will get the blessings and lights of all the tarbiyya. Thus, he homologated the work of the Sheikh Tarbiyya to the work of the gardener."

Mercy Towards Children

Serigne Saliou often recommended that teachers treat children with kindness and subtlety without ever using violence. He said: "The Quranic teacher is like the fighter in the way of Allah as long as he does not violate the children because if he does, he will be like a coward running away from the fight. However, this flight is a major sin according to the ayah: "O you who believe, if you meet the unbelievers in battle, you must not flee, for he who does so without strategic need or to join his own troops will suffer the wrath of God and have hell as his dwelling place." (al Anfa'l 15-16).

Serigne Shuaibou Guèye reported from Serigne Saliou these words: "Whoever wants to educate children must be gentle and affectionate so that they love and obey him in his presence or absence because by using violence they will obey in his presence and disobey in his absence and especially this will generate hatred and resentment that will manifest itself when the children grow up and no longer allow themselves to be violent and even risk being turned away from the tarbiyya."

Tips for a Successful Tarbiyya

When disciples had to move to another *daara*, Serigne Saliou said, "There is no difference between this *daara* and the other one, I recommend that you do not do acts that require punishment, because that will force you to be moved again. However, I am sending you to this *daara* because your parents and relatives live nearby and it would be easier for them to visit you. Concentrate on your studies and Khidma as well as on ethics and the rules of propriety and be obedient to your educators (teachers) and do not remove yourself without a reason because the baraka will visit you in the *daara* and if you are absent, your share will escape you.

Beware of Satan, he can in a second destroy all the work of day and night; be persevering in the works and do not allow yourself to be distracted but above all avoid prohibitions.

Also, avoid ball games and other games, avoid dating women and the lifestyle of non-Muslims and unbelieving settlers because these are things, I am uncompromising about. Those who cannot conform can take their belongings and join their own. As for the illnesses of the soul, they can be cured by companionship and tarbiyya as one washes the dirt out of clothes, provided one remains constantly in the *daara*. If you follow my advice and wait until I finish my work you will get a baraka that will make you forget all the pain and fatigue of the khidma. And that will make everything you undertake easier for you by the grace of Allah. It is then that you will become aware of my advice."

Tips for Patience

Serigne Saliou said: "Each disciple must take his share of the trials experienced by the first disciples of Khadimou Rassoul in Khoumag Mauritania."

He also said: "It is possible for me to make the life of the *daaras* easy but it is customary among the mourides to take the example of the great mouride figures in Khoumag.

In my childhood, I lived in the same conditions as my brothers because Khadimou Rassoul had ordered that we be treated like all the mourides and he sent us nothing except a jar of clarified butter which was already a surprise for us. At the same time, some Sheikhs and disciples were living in very good conditions while we had difficulty filling our stomachs except that we were convinced that our Sheikh wanted the best for us."

He sometimes recounted the difficult experiences of the tarbiyya period: "I remember a period of Ramadan when we found little to cut the fast and we suffered unbearable hunger while Khadimou Rassoul was aware of our situation and even I think he had ordered our uncle Serigne Hamza Diakhaté to let us live these states like the pious ancients.

However, during the same period, goods were pouring in from everywhere to Khadimou Rassoul in Diourbel and to all the mourides so that the houses were constantly full of visitors who were accommodated and fed copiously. During this time, we were ordered to clean the *daaras* and do all kinds of work until Khadimou Rassoul's departure.

These are times for which I give thanks to Allah and I am only doing with you what my Sheikhs were doing with us and it is only for your sake I am not deceiving you and I am perceptive in this immaculate way: *Say this is my way I call to my Lord in all evidence, I and those who follow me. Glory be to Allah, I am not among those who join together.*

Reasons for Mouride Emancipation

In the 1970s, Serigne Saliou had invested some of his disciples and at the same time he gave clarifications on the reasons for the emancipation of the mouride:

- he does not comply with the rules or does not want to continue his tarbiyya and stays only by constraint. The Sheikh must then release him with subtlety without putting him in an indelicate position.
- he wants to leave on his own and stop the tarbiyya to go home.
- he finishes his spiritual journey which will be crowned by the approval of his Sheikh who congratulates him and perhaps invests him as his representative in the locality where he will settle.

His Affection for His Disciples

According to Serigne Moustapha Diaw, Serigne Saliou said: "Each one of us has in the family his mission, which is to found schools and villages in order to create the environment of the tarbiyya for the mourides. Now, when I listen to someone who criticizes the disciples who make the tarbiyya, I have a lot of pain because we, sons of Khadimou Rassoul, each have our own methods and each of us knows what best suits the abilities of our disciples.

Personally, I take disciples and keep them away from the temptations in this low world and the daily concerns of the common people by satisfying all their needs so that they can be concerned about living their religion and perfecting their souls, and I stay with them all this time in the most difficult conditions. But when a person comes from the city to criticize them and implicitly tells me that what I do doesn't produce any results, when that person can't stay for an hour or less in those same conditions, it bothers me. Sometimes a person stays for only a few minutes and allows himself to criticize or vilify my disciples and the work for which I have sacrificed my entire life; this hurts me painfully."

Some Personalities Educated in the *Daaras*

Some mouride elites distinguished themselves by their piety and science as well as by their nobility of soul, among them scholars (alim), jurisconsults (faqih) while others became great merchants or businessmen or respected notables in the country. Some have become authorities in the mouride way either by their science or their ethics. Others were talented poets and others were authors in different Islamic sciences such as fiqh, tasawwuf, grammar, lexicography, usul al-fiqh, astronomy, and others. Serigne Saliou Touré had composed collections of poetry, as well as Serigne Habibou Diop, Serigne Elhaj Lo, Serigne Khadim Toure son of Serigne Abdelwahid Touré, Serigne Khalil Absa Mbacké, Serigne Sheikh Lo, Serigne Khadim Guèye, Serigne Galasse Diattara and others.

Some have even written treatises on logic and philosophy, and we have composed several books in different disciplines. At a very young age, we had versified a treatise on the principles of law (usul fiqh) which became a school classic that I taught in the *daaras*. Serigne Khalil Absa Mbacké had done the same for the sciences of hadith (ilm mustalah al hadith).

It is impossible to enumerate the disciples of Serigne Saliou because they can be counted in thousands or rather tens of thousands since he formed several generations, and we apologize to all those who are not mentioned in the book and who amply deserve to appear in it, but a special book is needed for the subject which will certainly be published. We believe that Serigne Saliou Touré and Serigne Saliou Sy deserve a special mention, however.

Saliou Touré Sign

He is part of a family known for its science and piety which has a reputation for teaching the Quran and the various Islamic sciences. His father Serigne Modou Coumba Touré of Mbackol was one of the great disciples of Khadimou Rassoul and he was a close friend of Serigne Ababacar Diakhaté the son of Cadi Madiakhaté Kala on whom he wrote poems and texts.

His mother, the pious Sokhna Anta Khouma, was a member of the family of the great Waliyou Mame Ghana Birane Khouma of Cayor who had left Timbuktu with his family and disciples to settle in Cayor. During his journey, from Mali to Senegal, he produced many wonders and spread Islam on his way to the point that people told his story.

Serigne Saliou Touré accompanied Serigne Saliou since his childhood because it was the latter who baptized him and gave him his name Saliou. He first learned the Quran from his father in Keur Madiob in Mbackol. But when he arrived at Sura Qaf, his father entrusted him to his namesake Serigne Saliou Mbacké whom he will never leave.

Serigne Saliou Mbacké entrusted him, in turn, to Serigne Mor Mbaye Cissé who taught him the Quran that Serigne Saliou Touré mastered through memorization, psalmody, and writing. Then he entrusted him to the illustrious scholars of Diourbel such as Serigne Muhammad Dème and Serigne Lamine Diop Dagana with whom he studied Islamic sciences (fiqh, Arabic language, and literature). He had as school companions the great scholars of Mouridism, including Serigne Muntakha Bassirou Mbacké, the current Khalif, as well as Serigne Moustapha Lo and Serigne Ahmed Dame Touré who composed in Wolof the viaticum of the Muslim in the fiqh.

Serigne Saliou Touré became one of the great scholars of the country and composed works in particular on fiqh, including a study on the legality of kissing the hand according to the arguments of the Quran, the Sunnah, and the statements of the Sahabas and Tabi'ins.

He became the authority of the mourides in Thies, while continuing his research in different disciplines and he had an impressive library that contained prestigious works in tawhid, fiqh, and tasawwuf but also encyclopedias and history books.

He also had an incredible gift for poetry and he composed collections in several fields including eulogies and wisdom. However, he devoted himself to his parents' mission of teaching the Quran and Islamic sciences, and he founded a school in Thies next to the mosque where he officiated for the prayers of the helper. This school had 250 students and every year at least 10 students memorize the Quran.

He also insisted on the sufi tarbiyya for his children and his relatives whom he sent to the *daaras of* Serigne Saliou Mbacké so that they could acquire noble virtues in addition to knowledge. On their return, he kept them with him so that they, in turn, could teach Islamic sciences. His school became the most famous in the region of Thies.

The Sufi Spiritual Dimension of Serigne Saliou Touré

In addition to the exoteric sciences that he mastered Serigne Saliou Touré was an expert (arif), a sincere mouride (sadikh), and a loving sufi who had annihilated himself in Khadimou Rassoul. He had remained in the service of

Serigne Saliou long after finishing his studies in Diourbel. He had served in Gott where he supervised the Quranic teaching; then he moved from one *daara* to another according to the directives of his Sheikh who had total confidence in him.

He is known to have performed certain wonders (karamat) and unveilings (kushufat/kashifu) during his service in the *daaras and* he saw the Prophet Muhammad (peace and salvation upon him) and also Khadimou Rassoul. He served Serigne Saliou Mbacké faithfully until the latter's departure in 2007 and he was among those who washed the body and buried him. This was an immense honor in this life and the afterlife.

Serigne Saliou Touré held the position of imam in the mosque of Thies on the orders of Serigne Abdoul Ahad Mbacké in 1984. During this magisterium, he managed to reunite the mourides and increase their rank in this central region which brought together all ethnic groups of Senegal. His house was a shelter for the needy as well as for widows and orphans and travelers. The most prestigious personalities of Senegal and Mauritania, passing through Thies, did not fail to visit him.

For more than forty years, Serigne Saliou Touré lived like this until old age and illness handicapped him (we ask Allah to take care of him and reward him).

Serigne Saliou Sy

Serigne Saliou Sy was raised by his father Serigne Malick Bassine Sy of Saloum, a great disciple of Khadimou Rassoul. Serigne Saliou nicknamed him the Benefactor Sheikh (al Sheikh al salah) and every time he passed by Saloum he went to visit him.

Serigne Saliou Sy learned the Quran with his brother Serigne Fallou Sy and he wrote a very nice Quran that he gave to his father's khalif, Serigne Modou Faty Sy. The latter offered it to Serigne Saliou Mbacké with two thoroughbred horses in 1959 when Serigne Saliou left Saloum through the forest of Khelcom which he had coveted since that time.

Serigne Saliou Mbacké took care of the education of Serigne Saliou Sy whom he sent to Diourbel to learn religious sciences at Serigne Mohamad Dème. He spent all his time learning but during the winter he joined Serigne Saliou in the fields to serve. Finally, after brilliantly completing his studies, he joined his Sheikh to serve him faithfully and complete his spiritual realization so that he had become the perfect model of the mouride by his virtues and noble character.

He was a sincere mouride and a sufi who had been extinguished (died) in the love of Allah and the Prophet Muhammad (peace and salvation on him) as well as the love of Khadimou Rassoul and Serigne Saliou who had total confidence in him and entrusted him with many *Daaras* including Khaban, Ndiouroul, Ndokha, and others.

He was pious and noble of heart so he reflected the virtues taught by Serigne Saliou. His delicacy towards children and his pedagogy gave convincing results so that all those who were under his direction inherited from him some of his characteristics. He was patient and endured difficulties without complaining while being sensitive to the point of crying at the slightest opportunity.

One day he was leading the prayer and at the end, he saw that Serigne Saliou Mbacké was praying behind him, which put him in such a state that he lost consciousness. Serigne Saliou loved him very much and gave him as his wife his daughter Sokhna Amina, of whom he had one daughter.

From the time he had put himself under the guidance of his Sheikh, he served him faithfully until his death on March 4, 2004, may Allah accept him in His wide paradise.

CONCLUSION

I take refuge in Allah by the name of Allah and my success is only by Allah.

I thank Allah for all glorification and pray for the most distinguished of worshippers, his family and virtuous companions, and all those who have followed their example among the pure and saints who have enlightened the community. And may Allah accept his servant Sheikh al-Khadim and all aspiring leaders with resolve.

I can see with great pride and happiness the impressive efforts of our honorable brother on the life of the great master, the axis of the mourides, and the guide of the benefactors: the fifth Khalif Serigne Saliou Mbacké (on him the approval of Allah as well as on his predecessors).

In truth, this work is of paramount importance because it deals with certain multidimensional aspects of his life on which we must meditate, especially since his varied achievements are obvious to the happiness of all.

I congratulate current and future generations for publishing this exciting and informative book that will be a model for any similar work. It is a meticulous work that has fulfilled the conditions of research, as well as the most rigorous academic criteria, in addition to his clear and lyrical style.

It should be noted that the personal relationship between the author of the book and Serigne Saliou Mbacké was not an obstacle to the intellectual objectivity that presides over all scientific work, despite the fact that the subject matter arouses a great deal of affectivity and empathy, the sheikh being not only a spiritual guide but also a beloved relative of the author of the book.

Indeed, the latter had the immense honor of being educated by his grandfather Serigne Saliou and was thus able to witness many of his actions and gestures, which allowed him to draw directly his inspiration from the holy man of knowledge and advice. But far from being satisfied with this, he pushed his investigations with all those who could inform him about particular aspects, words, or acts that could be mentioned while specifying his sources and verifying their reliability.

The extraordinary abilities that the author has shown in different fields of knowledge, which are Islamic sciences and the history of civilizations as well as the knowledge of sufis, have enabled him to gather the necessary elements for the success of this kind of work.

All these factors will prove important for the objectivity and seriousness of the subject being treated, but also for any study that is intended to be circumspect.

The work is full of benefit for the whole community which, by the concrete example of the men of God who have attained the highest spiritual dimensions, can learn from self-sacrifice, asceticism, generosity, and sincerity in the relationship with Allah. Such men are the masters whose concern is the dissemination of knowledge, as well as spiritual education, by personifying Islamic virtues and values in their own person.

Finally, we congratulate our beloved brother for this wonderful work and hope that it will be a promising taste for other books, given its immense potential that predisposes it to research and publication.

Serigne Sheikh Mbacké Walo

BIBLIOGRAPHICAL REFERENCES

Note: The majority, if not almost all of the bibliography is in Arabic and is not available in French. We had to put the titles in phonetics to facilitate the researchers' task.

MOURIDE SPRINGS

The works of Sheikh Ahmadou Bamba in the Khadim Rassoul Library, Touba Senegal

1. *Al Jawhar al Nafis*. 1. Touba Senegal: Rawud El-Rayhin, 2016.
2. *Asma' ahl badr*. Khadim Rassoul Library, Touba Senegal, n.d.
3. *Bismi-Ilaahi Ikfinil Akdara Ya Allahu*. Khadim Rassoul Library, Touba Senegal, n.d.
4. Advice to his son Serigne Fallou Mbacké. Khadim Rassoul Library, Touba Senegal, n.d.
5. *Diwan: al Amdah al Nabawiya*. n.d.
6. *Diwan: al Fouyoudhat al Rabbaniya Fil Dhikr*. s.d.
7. *Diwan: al Fouyoudhat al Rabbaniya Fil Dhikr Wal Chukr Wal Tahadduth Bil Ni'am*. s.d.
8. *Diwan: al Fulk al Mach'oun*. n.d.
9. *Diwan: al Fouyoudhat al Rabbaniyafil Qasaid al Mutarraza bil Ayyam wal Chouhour wal A'wam*. n.d.
10. *Diwan: al Qasaids al Muqayyada bil A'yat al Qor'ani*. s.d.
11. *Diwan: Mafatih al Jinan*. Khadim Rassoul Library, Touba Senegal, n.d.
12. *Farrij Bijahi*. Khadim Rassoul Library, Touba Senegal, n.d.
13. *Hisnoul Abrar*. Khadim Rassoul Library, Touba Senegal, n.d.
14. *Huqqal Buka*. Khadim Rassoul Library, Touba Senegal, n.d.
15. *Innallaha Achtara*. Khadim Rassoul Library, Touba Senegal, n.d.
16. *Jalibatoul Maraghib*. Khadim Rassoul Library, Touba Senegal, n.d.
17. The collection "Al Fuyudat al Rabbaniyya fi Dhkr ." Touba: collected by Serigne Modou Diagne, s.d.
18. The collection "Al Fuyudat al Rabbaniyya fil Ayyam." Touba Senegal: Bibliothèque Sheikhoul khadim, s.d.
19. The collection "Al Majmu'a." Touba Senegal: Khadim Rassoul Library, Touba Senegal, n.d.
20. The collection "Al Muqayyada Bi Ghayril Al Ayat Al Quraniya." 1: Khadim Rassoul Library, Touba Senegal, n.d.

21. The collection "Des Sciences Religieuses." Khadim Rassoul Library, Touba Senegal, n.d.
22. The collection "Fulk al Machhun." 1. Khadim Rassoul Library, Touba Senegal, n.d.
23. The collection "Silkoul Jawahir." Touba Senegal: Bibliothèque Sheikhoul Khadim, s.d.
24. The collection "Silkoul Jawahir." Khadim Rassoul Library, Touba Senegal, n.d.
25. The *Al Quraaniya* collection. 1. Khadim Rassoul Library, Touba Senegal, n.d.
26. Letter to Serigne Demba Basine Sall. Khadim Rassoul Library, Touba Senegal, n.d.
27. *Maghaliq al Niran* "The Locks of Hell." Khadim Rassoul Library, Touba Senegal, n.d.
28. *Massalik al Jinan* "The Itineraries of Paradise." 1. ed. Rawud El-Rayhin, 2015.
29. *Matlaboul Chifa*. Khadim Rassoul Library, Touba Senegal, n.d.
30. *Matlaboul Fawzeyni*. Khadim Rassoul Library, Touba Senegal, n.d.
31. *Mawahib al Qoddous*. Touba Senegal: Ed. Rawud El-Rayhin, 2015.
32. *Mawahiboun Nafih*. Khadim Rassoul Library, Touba Senegal, n.d.
33. *Min wa Caya Sheikh al khadim*. Rawud El-Rayhin, Touba Senegal, 2018, n.d.
34. *Moulayyin Al Soudour*. Khadim Rassoul Library, Touba Senegal, n.d.
35. *Mounawuru Welding*. Khadim Rassoul Library, Touba Senegal, n.d.
36. *Mounawwir Al Soudour*. Khadim Rassoul Library, Touba Senegal, n.d.
37. *Mounawwiru-Çudur*. Khadim Rassoul Library, Touba Senegal, n.d.
38. *Nourou Daarayni*. Khadim Rassoul Library, Touba Senegal, n.d.
39. Poem in Acrotic of the Letters of "Yawma Al Ahad Safar." Khadim Rassoul Library, Touba Senegal, n.d.
40. *Qasida: Asirou Ma'al Abrar*. s.d.
41. *Qasida: Bismil Ilahi Ikfinil Akdar* . s.d.
42. *Qasida: Ta'iya*. s.d.
43. *Qasida: Ya Dhal Bucharat Bil Ayat Wal Souwari*. n.d.
44. *Qasida: Ya Rabbi Bil Moustapha Al Mukhtar Min Moudhar*. n.d.
45. *Qasida in Acrostic Letters of Yawm Al Ahad Safar*. n.d.
46. Qasida in acrotic of the letters of "Yawma Al Ahad Safar." Khadim Rassoul Library, Touba Senegal, n.d.
47. *Qasida Yawm Al Ahad*. Khadim Rassoul Library, Touba Senegal, n.d.

48. *Saadat al Tolaab*, Bibliothèque Khadim Rassoul, Touba Senegal, n.d.
49. *Sahadatou Toullab*. Khadim Rassoul Library, Touba Senegal, n.d.
50. *Tazawud Al Cighar*. Khadim Rassoul Library, Touba Senegal, n.d.
51. *Tazawwud Al Chubban*. Khadim Rassoul Library, Touba Senegal, n.d.
52. *Wa Kaana Haqqane*. Khadim Rassoul Library, Touba Senegal, n.d.
53. The Works of The Great Mouride Figures
54. BOUSSO, Serigne Fallou. Cf. Document of the Conference "Sheikh al Khadim and the Koran." Rawdu Rayahin 2016, n.d.
55. BOUSSO, Serigne Mbacké. Collection of Writings by S.M. Bousso "Min Kitabat Sheikh M. Bousso." MARROC, n.d.
56. BOUSSO, Serigne Modou. The Biography of Serigne Mbacké Bousso. n.d.
57. From authors, group. Sheikh Mohammad Mustapha the perfect example in Arabic. n.d.
58. DEM, Serigne Mouhammad. Letter to Serigne Modou Khabbane Mbacké manuscript. Serigne Mor Mbaye Cissé library, n.d.
59. Diakhaté, Mouhammad Adam. *The Life of the Fifth Khalifa of the Mourides Arabic version*. Manuscript, n.d.
60. The Family Tree of the Diakhate Family. Handwritten, n.d.
61. DIOP, Serigne Mouhammadou Lamine Dagana. Irwa' An Nadim "L'Abreuvement du Commensal dans la Douce Source d'Amour du Serviteur." ed Tunisia.
62. Mauritanians, poets. *The Collection of Poems by Mauritanian scholars*. book in Arabic, Bibliotheque Khadim Rassoul, Touba Senegal, no date s.d.
63. Mbacke, Serigne Bachirou. *Minan Al Baqi Al Qadim* "The Benefits Of Eternal", Edition Dar al muqattam, Egypt 2017. n.d.
64. Mbacke, Serigne Khalil. *Serigne Saliou the Sun of His Time*. Touba Senegal, San Date s.d.
65. MISKA, Dr. Mohammad ibn Ahmad. *The Prodigies of Sheikh A. Bamba* "Karamat Sheikh Ahmadou Bamba." Khadim Center for Studies 2017, n.d.
66. SYLL, Serigne Mouhamed. *Jawami' Al Kalim*. Khadim Center for Studies 2017, n.d.

GENERAL SOURCES

1. Al Koran . n.d.
2. Abderrazak. *Al Musannaf*. Publisher: Dar Al-Taaseel , 2015, n.d.
3. Abou Daoud. *Al Sunan*. Dar Al-Resala Editorial 2009, n.d.
4. Ahmad, Ibn Hanbal. *Musnad.* Al-Resala Publishing 2009, n.d.
5. Al-Akhdari, Abu Zaid Abdul Rahman bin Muhammad. *Mukhtasar al-Akhdari.* n.d.
6. Al-Alousi. *(Rwha Alm'aany Fy Tfsyr Alqraan Al'azym Walsb'almthany).* Beirut - Lebanon: Dar al Kotob al Ilmiyah, 2014.
7. Al-Asfahani. *Mufradat al quran.* Dar al Kotob al Ilmiyya, Beiruth , n.d.
8. Al-Asfahani, Al Raghib. *Aldhari'a Ila Makarim Al Chari'a.* Dar al Kotob al Ilmiyya, Beiruth 1980, n.d.
9. Al-asfahani, Al Raghib. *Mufradat al Quran "the Terminology of the Qur'an."* Dar al Qalam, n.d.
10. Al-Awfi, Nafis Al-Din Abu Al-Hazm Makki Bin Auf Bin Abi Taher Ismail Bin Makki. *Al-Awfia, Treatise on Muslim Law.* Manuscripts of the Islamic University of Medina, n.d.
11. Al-bartali, Al Talib Mouhamad. *Fathu al Chakur Fi Mahrifat A'yan al Tukrur.* Markaz Najibawayhi, Cairo egybt 2010, n.d.
12. Al-Baydawi. *('Anwar Altnzyl w'Asrar Alt'awyl).* Beirut - Lebanon: Dar al Kotob al Ilmiyah, 2019.
13. Al-Bayhaqi. *Sunan al Bayhaqi* . Dar al Kotob Al'ilmiyya, 2003, n.d.
14. Al-beckri. *Al Massalik Wal Mamalik.* [1st] edit Dar al Kotob al Ilmiyya Beiruth 2003, n.d.
15. *Al Massalik Wal Mamalik.* 1st edit Dar al Kotob al Ilmiyya Beiruth 2003, n.d.
16. Al-Boukhari. *Al Adab al Mufrad.* s.d.
17. *Sahih al Boukhari.* n.d.
18. Al-Cha'rani. *Tabaqaat Alkubra.* Egypt. Dar El Fikr, Cairo, 1955, n.d.
19. Al-Ghazali, Abu Hamid. *Letter to the Disciple (Ayyuha 'l-Walad) Sabbagh, Toufic (tr.) English translation.* Beirut: International Commission for the Translation of Masterpieces, 1959. n.d.
20. Al-Ghazali, Abu Hamid Muhammad. *Ihyaa Uloum Din "Relaunching the Sciences of Religion."* Dar Al-Ghad Al-Arabi 1987, n.d.
21. Al-Ghurabi, Mahmoud Mahmoud. *Al Insan al Kamil Min Kalam Sheikh Al-Akbar.* PDF version on the net, n.d.

22. Al-Harawi, Khawâdjâ Abdallâh al-Ansârîl. *Manazil al sairin.* Dar Nachiroun 2012, n.d.
23. Al-Hariri, Alqasim ibn Ali. *Al Maqamaat.* Dar al Kotob al Ilmiyya, lebanon beirut 2010, n.d.
24. Al-Hassani, Al-Hassan bin Sheikh Suleiman. *History of Bani Al-Saleh, the honorable Kombi Al-Saleh, the kings of Ghana and Mali of Sudan.* Dar Yusuf bin Tashfin / Imam Malik Library / 1st edition 2009, n.d.
25. Al-Jilani, Sheikh Abdul Qadir. *Al-ghonya.* Dar al kotob al ilmiyya, undated Lebanese Beirut, n.d.
26. Al-jili, abdul karim. *Al Insan al Kamil.* Dar al Kotob al Ilmiyya, lebanon beirut 2016, n.d.
27. Al-Jundi, Khalil Ibn Ishaq. *Mukhtasar Khalil.* DAR, n.d.
28. Al-Jurjani. *Al-Tahrifat.* Dar al kotob al ilmiyya, lebanon beirut 1983 , n.d.
29. AL-KACHANI, Abel razzaq. *Moe'jam Istilahat al Sufiyya.* Dar al manar, egypt 1992, n.d.
30. AL-NAHWI, Khalil. *Bilad Chinguit al Manara Wal Ribat.* Edition , n.d.
31. Al-Nisa'i. Sunan Al-Nasa'i Al-Kubra. Al-Resala Publishers 2001, n.d.
32. Al-Qaysary, Dawood bin Mahmoud. *Matlah al Khucus Commentary on fusus al Hikam, studied by Ayatollah Hassanzadeh, Amoly.* Publications du Liban, n.d.
33. Al-Qayrawānī, Ibn-Abī Zayd. *Risalah.* n.d.
34. Al-Qushairi, Abdul Karim bin. *The Treaty on Sufism. Directed by Maarouf Zreik, Ali Abdul Hamid Balta Ji.* Dar Al-Jeel Beirut 1990, n.d.
35. Al-Rumi, Jalal al Din. *Qasida nay.* n.d.
36. AL-SANOUSI, adou abdallh yousouf. *Umm al Barahin with Commentary.* edd Istikhama 1351 h, n.d.
37. Al-Shaarani, Abdul-Wahab. *Tabaqaat "The Biography of the Saints."* Dar Al-Fikr Edition, 1998, n.d.
38. Al-Soyuti, Jalal al Din. *Mo'jam Maqalid al 'Ulum,.* Maktabat al Adab, Cairo Egypt 2004, n.d.
39. Al-Tabarani. *Al-Mu'jam Al-Awsat.* Publisher: Dar Al-Harameen undated, n.d.
40. Al-Tabatabai, Ayatollah Mohammad Hossein Tabâtabâï,. *Tafsir al Mizan "An Exegesis of the Holy Quran."* Publications of the teachers' group in the Hawza of Qom, 1402 AH., n.d.
41. Al-Tirmidhi. Sunan Al-Tirmidhi. Publisher: Dar Al-Gharb Al-Islami, 1996, n.d.

42. BA, Dr. Omar Salih. *Al Thaqafa Al'arabiyya al Islamiyya Fi Garbi Afriqiya.* Dar al Minhaj 2007, n.d.
43. CHALABI, Ahmad. *The Encyclopedia of the History of Islam, v. Arabic.* Dar, n.d.
44. DRAZ, Dr. Mohammed Abdallah. *Kalimat Fi Mabadi'l Akhlaq.* Dar , n.d.
45. Ibn Ajiba, Abu Al-Abbas Ahmed bin Muhammad. *Iyqaz al Himam "Awakening Determination" Edited by Dr. Sheikh Asim Ibrahim Al-Kayyali.* Dar al Kutub al Ilmiya Beirut 2016, n.d.
46. *Rasael "The Letters of Ibn Ajiba."* Dar al Kotub al Ilmiyya 2006, n.d.
47. Ibn Asim, Muhammad Abu Bakr Ibn Asim. *Tuhfat al hukkaam.* Dar al Afaq al-Arabiyya 2011.s.d.
48. IBN Bouna, Al-Mukhtar Al-Jakani. *Al Ihmirar.* edition: Muhammad Mahfouz bin Ahmed Mauritania, 1424 AH 2003 EC, n.d.
49. Ibn Rajab, Abd al-Rahman bin Shihab al-Din. *Collector of Science and Wisdom to explain Fifty Hadiths Of The Mosques of the word. Director: Tariq bin Awad Allah bin Muhammad Abu Muaz. Ed.* n.d.
50. Ibn-Arabi. *Al Futuhat Al Makkiyya.* Dar al Kotob al Ilmiyya, Beirut, Lebanon 2006, n.d.
51. *Al Kawkab al Durri Fi Manaqib Dhi Noun al Misri.* Dar al Kutub al Ilmiyya, Beiruth 2005, n.d.
52. *Al Mokhtar Min Rasail Ibn Arabi.* Dar al Kotob, Beiruth 2005, n.d.
53. *Mawaqi' al Nujum.* Dar al Kotob, Beiruth 2007, n.d.
54. *Rasail ibn Arabi.* Dar Sader, 1997, 558 AH 638, n.d.
55. *Tanazzul al Amlak.* Dar al Kotob al Ilmiyya, Beirut 2008, n.d.
56. Ibn-Battouta. *Tuhfat al nudhar.* Dar Yahya Al-Alem, Beirut, Lebanon, 1987, n.d.
57. Ibn-Bouna, Al-Mukhtar Al-Jakani. *Al Ihmirar.* Edition: Muhammad Mahfouz bin Ahmed Mauritania, 2003 n.d.
58. Ibn-Miskawayh, Abu Ali Ahmed bin Muhammad bin Yaqoub Miskawayh. *Tahdhib al Akhlaq.* Publisher: Maktaba al Thaqafa al Diniyya, Undated, n.d.
59. Ibn-Mubarak, Ahmed bin Muhammad bin Ali al-Malti. *Al-Ebriz Min Kalam Sidi Abdel-Aziz.* Al Maktaba al Ilmiyya, Beirut Lebanon Undated, n.d.
60. IBRACHI. *Usus al Tarbiyya .* n.d.
61. Ikhwan-al Safa. *Rasael Ikhwan al Safa.* s.d.
62. Ismael, Haqi al barusi. *Tafsir Ruh al Bayan .* dar , s.d.
63. MEGHA, Dr. Abd al-Rahman Muhammad. *The Jurisprudence Movement and its Men in Western Sudan: From the 8th to the 13th Century* AH BOOK *in Arabic* / Casablanca: Publications of the Ministry of Awqaf and Islamic Affairs, 2011.

64. SANNEH, Lamin. *The Jakhanke Muslim Clerics: A Religious and Historical Study of Islam in Senegambia.* Lanham, MD: University Press of America. 1989, s.d.
65. SYLLA, Abdoulkadre. *Muslims in Senegal Contemporary realities and future prospects in Arabic.* Edition Ri'asat Al-Mahakim Al-Shariyyah Wal-Shu'un al Diniyyah, (Presidium of the Sharia Courts and Religious Affairs) Doha Qatar,1406H n.d.
66. Thierno, KA. *School of Pir Saniokhor: Arab-Islamic History, Teaching and Culture in Senegal from the 18th to the 20th century.* (Dakar: GIA) 2002, n.d.
67. Other sources
68. Eric S. Ross. *Sufi City: Urban Design and Archetypes in Touba,* Cambridge University Press 2006, s.d.
69. FAGE, John Donnelly. *Introduction to the History of West Africa.* Cambridge University Press 1955, s.d.
70. Hunke, Sigrid: *"Allah's sun over the Occident - Our Arab heritage",...* Frankfurt a.M.; Hamburg: Fischer Library, 1965, s.d.

INTERVIEWS

1. Diakhaté, Serigne Omar
2. Diakhaté, Serigne Tayyib
3. Diakhaté, Serigne Abdoul Ahad Diakhaté
4. Diakhaté, Serigne Saliou
5. Ould Al Emir, Dr. Sidi Ahmad
6. Ould Ishaq, Sheikh Hamid
7. Diaw, Serigne Moustapha
8. Diop, Serigne Abibou, son of S Mouhamed L Dagana
9. Fahmy Sheikh Abdallah,
10. Guèye, Serigne Abo
11. Kébé, Serigne Abdou Khadre
12. Kébé, Serigne Mokhtar
13. Mbacké Serigne Sheikh Lagane
14. Mbacké, Serigne Abdousamad Chouayb
15. Mbacké, Serigne Mboussobé
16. Mbacké, Serigne Hamzatou Abdou Lahad
17. Mbacké, Serigne Moustapha Abou Khadre
18. Mbacké, Serigne Khalil Moustapha Absa
19. Mbacké, Serigne Bachirou Khelcom
20. Mbacké, Serigne Khadim Moustapha Absa
21. Mbacké, Serigne Moustapha Abdou Khadre
22. Mbacké, Serigne Moustapha Saliou
23. Mbacké, Serigne Mourtada Saliou
24. Mbacké, Serigne Fallou Chouhayb
25. Mbacké, Sokhna Asta Walo Saliou
26. Mbacké, Serigne Sheikh Walo
27. Mbacké, Serigne Abdou Lahad Baghdad
28. Sourang, Dr. Moustapha

Sallalâhu Allah Muhammadin

Made in the USA
Middletown, DE
17 April 2022